Look To This Day For It Is Life

The Story of All Tribes Christian Camp
St. Joseph Island, Ontario

Look To This Day For It Is Life

The Story of All Tribes Christian Camp
St. Joseph Island, Ontario

Also known as
Indiana Wesleyan University's Canadian Campus

by

Millie Jacobs Troyer

Premiere Publishing
Indianapolis

Look To This Day For It Is Life
Millie Jacobs Troyer

Publisher: Premiere Publishing Co., LLC
Nathan Birky, Publisher
Editor: Bobbie Sease
Graphic Designer: Gary Phillips

Direct correspondence, permission and purchase requests to:

Millie Jacobs Troyer
P. O. Box 147
Richards Landing, Ontario, Canada
P0R 1J0

Scripture Quotations:

Unless otherwise noted, Scripture quotations are from the Holy Bible, King James Version (KJV).

Illustrations are by Karen and Robin Reilly.

Troyer, Millie Jacobs
Look To This Day For It Is Life
ISBN 0-9664049-2-0

Premiere Publishing Co., LLC
P. O. Box 50821
Indianapolis, Indiana 46250-0821

Printed in the United States of America
Evangel Press, Nappanee, Indiana

To Dick
who loved me and shared my dream

and to

the thousands of campers
who taught me so much

It was Dick's desire
that all proceeds from this book would go to
All Tribes Christian Camp

Table of Contents

Forward

When Millie Jacobs Troyer's life journey nears its end, don't expect her to have a long list of things she wishes she had done. Millie, through drive and determination, has pretty much done everything she ever wanted to do.

Millie's multifaceted life is full of meaning and purpose. She has given much of her life for the glory of her beloved Indiana Wesleyan University and all of her life for the glory of the Lord.

If there had not been a Millie Jacobs Troyer in Indiana Wesleyan's history, the University would have had to create one! Millie and her late and beloved husband Dick were Indiana Wesleyan's unofficial cheerleaders for all sorts of causes – ranging from student scholarships to the subject of this book, All Tribes Christian Camp.

This book is as much about Millie's can-do spirit and her uncanny ability to find support for all manner of projects, as it is about All Tribes Camp itself. Once Millie decided that Indiana Wesleyan should have a Canadian campus, there was no stopping her.

She and Dick raised the money and mobilized a virtual army of volunteers for what continues to be, and will always be, a work in progress. All Tribes Camp already has become an important part of the spiritual and academic life of Indiana Wesleyan, and its influence promises to grow for future generations to experience.

The All Tribes name is reminiscent of Millie's Native American ancestry. When viewed in its entirety, Millie's life has been quite a mission with one theme: "To the glory of God!"

Dr. Howard T. Noggle
Special Assistant to the President
Indiana Wesleyan University

Preface

In 1999 after I had shared the story of All Tribes Christian Camp with "Morning Break," a discussion group of Island ladies, Elsie Hadden Mole said, "Millie, this story should be put in writing." She echoed the words of other friends over the years who have urged me to do the same. I gave Elsie the same answer I'd given them: "I am still living the chapters. The story isn't finished yet." The truth was, and is, that writing for me is hard work. I would rather chop wood or dig ditches than sit down and write anything beyond letters to my family or friends. I tend to write the same way that I talk—offhand and breezy. How could I ever write a book? I am not a scholar, nor am I a writer.

When the subject came up a few months later, Elsie offered to assist me in putting this "book" together. I shared the idea with Dick and he was all for it, but he thought the book should include my autobiography, as well as the story of the camp. He offered to help us and as an added incentive suggested that all proceeds from the book go to the camp.

We left for our trip in the fall of 1999 and I began writing "on the road." Dashing down my thoughts on a yellow legal pad, I would then read them to Dick as he drove. He was an appreciative audience, but I soon learned that the real work was to follow. The long-ago words of my former professor, Dr. Mary Dodd, seemed to echo in the RV: "Nothing beautiful is written. It is rewritten." I was too wordy. The grammar had to be corrected. The sentence structure and paragraphs had to be rearranged. The facts had to be verified. Many times, I all but gave up in despair. However, Dick encouraged me to persevere and in the process we had fun. Still, I had many reservations about putting my life on paper. It made me feel vulnerable—actually, downright naked! Who would really be interested in reading about my life and a Christian camp on an island in Ontario?

When Dick died on December 8, 1999, I knew I could never complete the task. A trip to Africa and Madagascar, followed by a full camping season kept me busy the next several months.

The next fall, I started to think seriously about the unfinished task. With help and encouragement I began picking up the threads again. Soon I found myself writing the chapters in my head. Then suddenly it was as if a dam burst. I completed the bulk of the later chapters in December 2000.

Although I miss Dick's companionship and encouragement, writing has been wonderful therapy for me. During what might have been a very difficult time in my life, I have kept my mind off loss and grief by recalling so many of the pleasant times we shared together. As All Tribes Christian Camp prepares to "pass the torch" in 2002 to a new couple, this is a good time to reflect on how the camp fulfilled not only my lifelong dream, but helped countless others in their walk with Christ.

So here is my story. I trust you will be challenged to give of your best to Him and to others.

Millie Jacobs Troyer '48
St. Joseph Island
September, 2001

Note: The number after an individual's name indicates the year of graduation from Marion College/Indiana Wesleyan Univeristy.

Acknowledgments

God sent several good-hearted souls along to make *Look To This Day* possible. I wish to express my deepest thanks to the following:

Dick, my best friend and sweetheart, for his quiet, steady encouragement and for keeping me on track.

Elsie Hadden Mole, who suggested I write the book and, after deciphering my horrible scribbling, produced the first typewritten drafts. We then together went over several more drafts before submitting the manuscript.

Ruth Gilbertson (Mrs. Don), who gave freely of her time and the use of Gilbertson Enterprises' office equipment for reams of copying and endless faxes.

Karen Reilly Murray and her son Robin, who gave their time and talent for the delightful sketches—not for me, but for the Lord.

Howard Noggle, my friend in the faith, for his kind and gracious forward to this book.

Dr. James Barnes, Bishop Donald Bastian, Pastor Tom Gurnick, and author Cindy Crawford for their kind endorsements.

Pauline Troyer, my sister-in-law, who re-sketched the camp map (originally drawn by Tracey Stevens).

Nathan Birky ('80), publisher of Triangle Publishing, for his ready acceptance of this challenge to print *Look to This Day*, something that certainly does not qualify as a textbook!

Gary Phillips, for his skillful design and layout of the book.

Bobbie Sease, editor, for her professional touch in polishing the manuscript.

Again, I must pay tribute to all you campers, counselors, and fellow followers of our Christ who have permitted me to be a part of your lives. I am indeed richer for knowing you.

Finally, I am deeply indebted to God for His promises, especially Psalm 37:4, "Delight yourself in the Lord and He will give you the desires of your heart" (NIV). He has done that and much, much more!

Introduction

"I am camp. Come with me and I will do you good."

Anonymous

The kids in my neighborhood and I grew up with our feet in the nearby creeks, ponds, and lakes. We camped in empty lots, fields, and the Bass Farm's woods. It was glorious. We felt free as birds. We became brown as berries during summer and our tough bare feet rejected our shoes come fall and school time.

Then one summer when I was in junior high school, I stepped into a YWCA camp near Winona Lake. It was the perfect blend of structure and freedom. Allowed to choose from a wide variety of activities, we found ourselves in a camp-sized, outdoors classroom. Our instructors were qualified and fun to be with. I did not feel restricted or imprisoned as I did in school.

Millie at Y Camp, 1938

My first time away from home, I learned much from the campers and staff. The group prevailed over the individual and there was much give and take in the dorms, the dining hall, on the playing fields, and at the waterfront. Our sports teams worked together for a common goal, but we were also taught that we did not have to win. I learned that getting along with others is the basis for healthy living. I discovered that camp is indeed a natural environment for social and spiritual living and sharing. At camp, everything involved the interaction of individuals.

Being at camp for an extended period of time was a painless way of cutting the apron strings to my mother. We were close, and being the youngest of three girls, I just might have been a bit spoiled. The high school senior who was my tennis counselor that summer made me feel extremely important. She unknowingly passed on to me her love of camping, an appreciation for other campers, and a great devotion to the out-of-doors. At night in my bunk I dreamed of becoming just like her.

Somewhere along the line I discovered that being a camp counselor was more than fun and games. It involved a great deal of commitment, responsibility, and hard work. A nameless counselor said it well:

> *Somewhere between adolescence and adulthood there occurs in human development an age which is physically and psychologically impossible. It is that unfathomable stage known as the camp counselor, a creature undefined by psychologists, misunderstood by camp directors, worshipped by campers, either admired or doubted by parents, and unheard of by the rest of society.*
>
> *A camp counselor is a rare combination of doctor, lawyer, and Indian chief. She is a competent psychologist with her sophomore textbook as proof. She is an underpaid babysitter with neither TV or fridge. She is a strict disciplinarian with a twinkle in her eye, a minister of all faiths with a question of her own. She is a referee, coach, teacher and adviser. She is an example of womanhood in worn-out tennis shoes, a sweatshirt two sizes too large and a hat two sizes too small. She is a humorist in a crisis, a doctor in an emergency, a song leader and an entertainer. She is an idol with her head in a cloud of woodsmoke and her feet in the mud. She is a comforter in a leaky tent on a cold night and a pal who has just loaned someone her last pair of dry socks.*

She is a teacher of the out-of-doors, knee-deep in poison ivy.

A counselor is handy for patching up broken friendships, bloody noses and torn jeans. She is good at locating lost bathing suits, fixing paths and running from bats. She is a friendly guide in the middle of a cold, dark, wet night on the windy path to the cabin or overnight site. Who but she can cure homesickness, air out a wet bed, play sixteen board games in succession, carry two packs, cook on a hike and sing forty-eight camp songs every night?

A counselor is expected to repair ten years of damage to Mary in ten days, make Susie into a woman, rehabilitate Jeannie, allow June to be an individual, and help Patty adjust to the group. She is entrusted with the most prized possession of twelve adults much older than she. She is expected to teach them to live in the out-of-doors — even though she spends nine months of the year in Sault Ste. Marie, Ottawa or Toronto. She is expected to teach indigenous activities when she can't even spell the word, and to guide the youngsters in social adjustment when she hasn't even reached the legal age, and to ensure the health and safety of each one when she herself has a sunburned nose, a Band-Aid on her thumb and a blister on her heel.

To that observer I say a hearty amen! And I must confess that the job of camp director is even more demanding than a camp counselor, but equally satisfying. Someone has said that a camp director must be part plumber and part poet. I know that to be a fact. To me one's camp philosophy should be such that will give happiness and opportunity for a good measure of mental, physical and spiritual growth to every camper under her care.

In my enthusiasm for the out-of-doors camp, I have been called everything from "Nature Girl" to "Nature Nut." However, I do not hold a sentimental "beauty of nature" attitude toward a world unspoiled by man. After all we seem to be doing our best to destroy what He has given us. I believe that in getting to know God through nature, we get to know ourselves. This does not mean that I worship nature and that my love of the out-of-doors ever takes the place of worshipping in a church. We need the fellowship of believers: "Not forsaking the assembling of ourselves together" (Hebrews 10:25). I fully agree with the one who said, "You say you can worship God just as well out on the golf course, when what you are really doing is worshipping on God's course."

To me camping has become a way of life. It is as old as civilization for, of course, that is where man first learned to survive. Nonetheless, good camping is a skill, and you do have to learn it. (It helps to love it.) No one automatically becomes a really top-notch camper, and yet camping is not a difficult, mysterious "something" to master. There is no deep hidden talent required.

To really enjoy camping and the out-of-doors I think one must experience the sights, sounds, and smells. Writing this introduction has naturally evoked endless memories from the many camps in which I have had a part. It has been my good fortune to be involved in camps with the YWCA, YMCA, Boy Scouts, Cub Scouts, Girl Scouts, Girl Guides, CGIT, Wesleyan, Free Methodist, and United Churches, Wheaton College in Illinois, Bluffton College in Ohio, and Indiana Wesleyan University. These camps have spread out for nearly seventy of my years, and yet the enjoyment and love I have received from the campers could keep me going another seventy years. (On the other side of the coin, my most challenging experience as a camper took place at Honey Rock Camp in Wisconsin. More on that in Chapter 15.)

A pivotal time in my camping "career" came at Camp Pauwating, the YMCA camp. I felt strongly that we needed to meet more than just the recreational needs of the campers. My boss, R. J. Smith, granted me permission to incorporate spiritual aspects into the program. After all, I reasoned with him, the Y motto was "spirit, mind, and body."

The campers helped to build an outdoor chapel where we had

daily Bible studies and vespers. The following letter from one of those campers, a foster child in an unhappy home, confirmed my wisdom in including a spiritual program at Pauwating:

> Dear Millie,
>
> You have made a difference in the lives of many children. You have held out the lifeline. I know because I was one of those children. You cared about me when I was young. Your loving care and the joy of camp life kept me from taking some wrong turns. When my days were the darkest and I had no one to turn to—then I would remember your smile and the camp songs we sang and the sermons you gave us every day in the chapel we built.
>
> I will always remember even though many years have passed. Those memories linger in my mind. Thanks, you did make a difference.
>
> I love you lots,
> Rose
> Vancouver, B.C.

My love for camping and campers seems to come naturally to me. I cannot explain it, but kids bring out the best in me. Someone once told me, "Camping is your life." I replied a little defensively, "That is a pretty strong statement." My husband Dick interjected, "Don't tell me that it isn't true. I know that better than anyone else!"

Over the past fifty years, people have asked me if campers have changed. For the most part, I can honestly say they have not. I bump into very few youngsters with a "been there, done that" attitude. Camp is a common leveler. Remove children from their dependency upon the TV, computers, other superficial competition, and overly protective parents, and they can be kids who have fun in

God's backyard. A plaque on my office wall holds more than a grain of truth: "The secret of dealing successfully with a child is not to be its parent."

One person taught me more about the joys of camping and living than anyone I know: Penny McGregor (Mrs. J. R.). I met Penny at a CGIT conference in Toronto. No one ever gave more to the cause than she did, although Mr. Mac, her husband, gave just as much to the boys and young men. The McGregors were a childless couple who poured out their lives for the young people in the Ottawa area. She and I became soul mates early in our acquaintance. I was deeply impressed by her enthusiasm, spirit, vision, energy, and her love for Camp Kalalla. She was a walking encyclopedia on camping, with a song or a poem for every occasion. (I learned most of my camp songs at CGIT camps. Too bad I didn't also learn to carry a tune.) Penny enriched our programs with her creative ideas, poems, and songs. Her version of the "Lion Hunt" was priceless. She also had an endless supply of sayings. One day as we were climbing Mt. Everest (Camp Kalalla's version), everyone was huffing and puffing except for Penny and me. She chuckled and said, "A woman may fool a few people with a new hair-do or some make-up, but she won't fool a hill!" Adjectives fail me when I think of Penny and I bless her memory. The untitled poem at the end of this book was her favorite.

As I have been reflecting on this book in recent days, I realize the Lord has given me many great years. I readily agree they have been wonderful ones. And, yes, camping has played a great role in my life. At the risk of repetition, I am most grateful to Him and to all of the parents who have entrusted me with the care of their most prized possessions—their children. And I do thank the thousands of campers who have enriched my life.

It all goes back to that junior high girl dreaming in her bunk of being "just like" the senior girl who made such an impact on her. That unnamed girl was the spark that ultimately resulted in All Tribes Christian Camp.

Who can measure all the good
Born within a tangled wood?
There a child in dreams can see
Just the person she wants to be,
And in silent hours can plan
Her conception of a woman
Here beneath the friendly leaves.

(With apologies to Edgar Guest)
Millie Jacobs Troyer
St. Joseph Island, Ontario

Salutation of the Dawn

Look to this day for it is life,
The very life of life.
In its brief course lie all the
Verities and realities of our existence
The bliss of growth
The glory of action
The splendor of beauty.
For yesterday is but a dream
And tomorrow is only a vision.
But today well lived makes
Every yesterday a dream of happiness
And every tomorrow a vision of hope.
Look well therefore to this day
For such is the salutation of the dawn.

from the Sanskrit

Chapter One

A Firecracker of a Girl

"Before I formed you in the womb I knew you."
Jeremiah 1:5

I came into this world on May 14, 1924 in what was then the northwest corner of Fort Wayne, Indiana. Because I followed two sisters and one brother (Betty Ann, Ruth Marie, and Jack), my father, John W. Jacobs, had his heart set on another boy to "even things up." My mother, Pearl Irene Shores Jacobs, was so sure I would be a boy that she did not even have a girl's name picked out. When her third daughter arrived, the kindly Dr. Huffman turned to my mother and asked, "What are you going to name her?"

"We'll have to think about that," she replied.

He quipped, "I think Liza Jane would suit her."

My parents settled on Mildred Jane. That was shortened to Janer when the expected son later came on the scene. Charles Robert "Chick" could not pronounce Mildred. Several years later I boarded with an elderly couple who liked Millie better. Over the years I have heard Millicent, Milla, Millie Jane, Mern, and even Jake, but Mildred Jane most often got my full attention—especially when my father called me by that name. This generally meant a few well-chosen words or a spanking would follow. Even though he did not believe in the Bible, he did live by one Bible-based proverb: "Spare the rod and spoil the child."

Mildred Jane "Millie" Jacobs

My father was a hardworking family man who owned and operated a trucking business before the Great Depression. Needing additional space for his trucks, he acquired half a city block and a home at 1823 Steup Street. He then erected a huge barn, which served as a repair shop and storage area. My last real "licking" at his hands took place behind that barn.

Over the years a mound of old tires had accumulated there. Some of the trucks were equipped with hard rubber tires, but the ones in the pile were mostly ordinary air tires with tubes. Frequently my father would say that one of these days we would have a real bonfire out there. His "one of these days" went on for months until Chick, the neighborhood gang, and I decided "it was time." We were not smart enough to realize the huge billows of black smoke would be seen from the other side of the barn. As Dad rounded the corner, our comrades disappeared like a vapor. Chick and I not only were caught red-handed, but went to our rooms "red-bottomed."

However, Dad's love for his family and his zest for life were infectious. Our huge yard was ideal for special holidays. During Easter he would color a bushel of eggs and then hide them. Along with the real eggs were jellybeans, chocolate and hard-covered marshmallow eggs. When Dad gave the signal, our sidekicks and we dashed about like bunnies on a mission. He enjoyed watching us as much as we enjoyed scampering around the yard. Needless to say, many of us did not have an appetite for the ham and sweet tater dinner later in the day. It took us years to learn why Mother's tea towels were mottled with color at that time of year.

Explosive Fun

The Fourth of July meant a picnic and a riot of color all day long and late into the evening. Dad supplied us with cherry bombs that exploded upon impacting a hard surface, smoke worms that wiggled through the grass and sand, and wee tiny crackers all bound together with one fuse that pop-popped all over the place. The thick three-inchers blew tin cans high in the air. A mixture of carbide and water made acetylene gas and would hurtle larger missiles into space. But our favorites were the inch-and-a-half Zebra firecrackers, which would put the fear of God in unsuspecting friend or foe. If held too long, the Zebras left us with stinging fingers and salty tears. By nightfall we were ready for the real show. Dad had an arsenal of rockets that exploded with sound and color in the night sky. Pinwheels whirred like crazy on nearby utility poles and we danced with glee, waving sparklers and acting as if there were no tomorrow.

Because of many later episodes with firecrackers, this would be a good time to include an apology to friends for my use and misuse of those "crackers." I would like especially to mention the many Camp Wakonda campers on Lake McCarroll behind Echo Bay,

Ontario, who were rudely awakened early in the morning. Nor should I fail to mention Mary Graham, the camp cook, and Nellie McLeod, the camp business manager at that time (both now deceased), who somehow survived when several crackers went off in the old cook stove just as they were taking a roast out of the oven. Lorna McKinney owes me one. She salvaged a few unspent crackers and set them off under my chair in the dining hall. Poor Nellie spent the rest of the evening meal weeping in the outhouse and threatened to have customs inspect my baggage the next time I crossed the international border to come to camp.

Of course, I shouldn't leave out the 12 p.m. and 1 a.m. explosions on the third floor of old Teter Hall at Marion College (now known as Indiana Wesleyan University in Marion, Indiana). In my defense, this was simply a way to settle a score with some dorm mates who had "papered" my room and hidden my suitcases prior to a scheduled early morning departure for camp. The late Clifton Letherer ('46), the school treasurer, would have expelled me from the school, but he had moderated by the time I returned to campus in the fall.

And there was the time I threw a box of old Christmas decorations into my fireplace on West Wayne Street in Fort Wayne. I didn't realize a box of Zebras was also packed in that box. The other tenants in the building realized it soon enough. For some reason my black cocker spaniel, Lady Regina, never quite enjoyed napping in front of a crackling fire again. At Camp Kalalla in Quebec, June Sully Bennett poured a few drops of hot tea on the hand I held over the cup, indicating to her I didn't want any of the strong brew. Of course in retaliation I had to set off firecrackers under the floor of the McGregor Lodge where she was eating lunch. Visitors to my cabin on the Island were often abruptly torn from sleep by such unexpected noises. Grandson Danny all but jumped out of his skin and the cache (tree house) early one morning. The list could go on and on but I hereby vow to never again inflict such punishment on friends or foe . . . maybe.

Free As Birds

My love for the out-of-doors and for camping goes back to my earliest childhood. Our neighborhood was full of vacant lots, ideal for children's shacks, tents, tree houses, and underground caves. We scrounged materials from the neighbors, or begged scraps from builders working on new houses. The fields were for ball games and wrestling or boxing matches. Under the corner streetlights we played hide and seek, kick the can, and other games. We never felt unsafe on the streets. We were not robbed of our childhood freedom—as too many children today are—by the violence on television. TV had not yet come into use.

However, we produced our own "violence" from time to time. Often we were left in the dark when someone decided to shoot out the streetlight with a slingshot. Those same street corners had old wooden culverts for drainage. Rabbits regularly took refuge in the culverts and we often added meat to our tables by ferreting them out after we saw their tracks in the snow. One of us would hold a gunnysack over one end of the culvert while the other used a long pole to chase the poor hare out.

My father taught me to use a .22-caliber rifle at an early age. We enjoyed many rabbit, squirrel, and pheasant hunting expeditions together. We kids also became sharpshooters with slingshots, using small stones, tiny green apples, ball bearings, and marbles for ammunition. We often bagged squirrels, rabbits, pigeons, and English sparrows. The latter were only wee morsels when fried, but we thought them great fare.

We lived a mere block from the Nickel Plate Railroad. Just over the tracks, the huge Bass Dairy Farm sat across the highway from the present site of the University of St. Francis. The farm offered acres and acres of field corn and a large woods with a creek. We had tree houses, Tarzan swings, and campsites galore. The creek cooled us in the hot and humid days of summer and also provided us with fish, turtles, and clams for our cookouts. We feasted on roasted corn until very late in the season, challenging our molars when the cobs became overripe, hard, and red. The cornrows were fantastic for hide-and-seek and follow-the-leader. We made maze trails through the stalks, doubtless damaging more than a little as we tromped through them.

The railroad tracks and boxcars on a nearby siding also occupied hours of our time. A "Hobo Camp" often included colorful characters bedding down for the night after they had begged a meal from marked homes. Some cooked Hobo stew in tin cans. We loved their wild stories about riding the rails from east to west. After they taught us how to pry open a boxcar, we had a neat place to hang out on rainy days. The hobos were experts at jumping onto moving trains and shared their know-how with us. This was precarious business, but we felt free as birds as we stood on top of a car with the wind streaming through our hair and shirts. The challenge of it all was to jump off before the train gathered too much speed. Skinned knees, scraped hands, and torn overalls were often difficult to explain to our concerned mothers.

The hobos had a system of marking the homes where they could count on a handout. Mother was a generous soul and frequently made them sandwiches or soup. We always had a huge garden and the family put up jars and jars of goodies for the winter. The shelves in the cold room of the basement were filled with them and with sacks and sacks of carrots, potatoes, and cabbages. Before the last frost, we picked green tomatoes, wrapped them in newspapers, and packed them away so that we had ripe tomatoes right up until Christmas time. I can still taste the pinches of kraut we snitched from the huge crocks my father stored in a back shed. Except for homemade root beer, soft drinks were unknown to us. However, an old neighbor made up several barrels of cider each fall. We became quite adept at siphoning off long sips of his brew using straws from the straw pile he kept for bedding down his horses.

The Old and the New

We made lots of ice cream in the summer in old, hand-cranked freezers. In winter we had our share of "ice cream" on the way to school. Milk came in heavy, glass quart bottles with narrow necks.

If left out on the porch too long after it was delivered, the cream would freeze and push two or three inches out of the bottle. We broke off the cream, replaced the cap, and went on our way licking cream from our lips and sticky fingers.

Along with milk, ice was also delivered to our doors. Residents would place a card in the window indicating the amount of ice needed: 25, 50, 75, or 100 pounds. As the iceman scored the huge blocks of ice with his pick, the chips flew every which way. He often kindly tossed us a chip or two. If we wrapped them in newspaper, they lasted a long time and quenched our thirst on hot days. The old iceboxes were not too efficient. Ours kept my mother and sisters busy carrying out, emptying, and replacing the huge dishpan of water from the melting ice underneath the box.

I well remember the first refrigerator I ever saw. It came to the home of our neighbors, the Bauers. Mother and the other women were very envious. The white General Electric monitor-top model had a noisy compressor above the storage unit. We soon learned that if we gathered close together in front of this amazing box and opened the door, it would cool us off. We could even suck on wee cubes of ice it manufactured. It was marvelous, amazing, delightful, and refreshing until Mr. Bauer or George thundered up the back steps, threw open the screen door, and yelled, "Will you blankety-blank kids get out of here? And STAY out!" We scattered to every corner of the neighborhood, only to return on the next hot day after a game of ball or tug of war.

We often heard the sounds of creaking wagon wheels and horses' hooves on our streets. Wally Payton, a trash man with a long, stringy beard made his rounds with a rickety, old wagon and a skinny nag he called his horse. He was one of the early recyclers. What he could not use or sell he sold for scrap iron, rags, or whatever else. That old man gave the neighbor kids a penny for every wart he touched. Maybe it was the dirt on his finger, but the warts seemed to disappear after that. The boys used to pick up toads when they could find them, hoping to get more warts to "sell." Pennies were worth something in the 30's.

We earned nickels and dimes by doing errands and helping our

Dad and his mules

neighbors. We also picked up corn for the farmers late in the fall after the pickers were through. We were sure our fingers and hands were going to drop off as a result of the cold.

Radios had been invented, of course, but at first we only had a crystal radio. In order to hear it, we had to pass around a set of headphones. Imagine our delight when a nice brown box arrived in our home, complete with three dials and a wire that plugged into the wall. At last we could hear broadcasts and programs as a family—such entertaining characters as Amos and Andy, Gracie Allen and George Burns, to name a few. However, I best remember huddling around the radio to hear Joe Lewis, Jack Dempsey and other boxers slug it out. We took in every move and honed our pugilistic skills while listening to and picturing every move they made. Early radio enriched our minds because we had to imagine what we were seeing.

A special treat was a long hike to the old Wells Street Theater. We each clutched a thin dime in our hands, enough for the price of the movie but not enough for popcorn. So we always popped ours at home before we left and carried it with us. We sat on the edge of our seats as the MGM lion roared from the silver screen announcing the next chapter in the Tom Mix or Lone Ranger series. We roared with laughter at the antics of Our Gang. What lovable characters they were. We learned much from them and copied some of their tricks. Shirley Temple fascinated us with her "Big Rock Candy Mountain" song, her beauty, and her seemingly rich lifestyle. She wowed the boys, that's for sure. Although I agreed that she was pretty, I wrote her off as a sissy.

Cars were uncommon in those days and the end of the line for the nearest streetcar was several blocks away from our home. So a trip to the store or "uptown" was most often by foot. When we had a dime or token to spare, we took the streetcar, paying our fare under the watchful eye of the conductor. If he was trying to make up time, the trolley car swayed back and forth until we feared we were going right off the tracks. Once we made it to the downtown stores, more coins were required if we happened to need the washroom. At that time the stalls in washrooms were always locked, and it took a coin to open one. We could circumvent that by having the smallest one among us crawl under the stall and open the door from the inside. Nobody had to pay a cent! That was nothing short of cheating, and over the years I have been trying to settle those old debts. Rarely do I use a public restroom now without thinking about the generosity of today's business people. They provide us with free toilets, paper, water, and towels. In gratitude, I pick up the waste paper and wipe off the counters and sinks. (My husband Dick used to say that when I saw the sign "Clean Rest Rooms" I took it literally!)

Mother

On shopping trips with mother in downtown Fort Wayne, I wondered why the elevator operators in the department stores and the people who cleared the tables in the restaurants were always black. It bothered me and I did not like the way they were treated by some people. I recall defending them and wanted to do something about their plight. Why, oh why, did color make such a difference concerning the jobs people had or how they were treated?

When our family finally got a car, we drove to see my grandmother in Arcola, Indiana every Sunday afternoon. During almost every trip we hit a chicken or two as the flock scattered on the dusty roads at our approach. Even more rare was a trip that didn't have Dad repairing a tire. It was not easy to pull off the tire and patch the inner tube.

City water had not been extended to our part of the town. Iron pumps with huge handles stood like sentinels all around us. One of our chores was to keep the drinking pail in the kitchen filled. We also had to pump the water for mother every Monday for wash days. We were usually rewarded later in the day by being allowed to make tents with sheets spread over several chairs. Every Monday also meant that we would have cornbread and navy soup beans for supper. They simmered on the back of the stove all afternoon.

The old pump and wash tubs, of course, were perfect for water fights. We filled lots of containers and drew a line for sides. Some of these containers were old tin cans. When tossed at the enemy, they not only soaked them, but also caused cuts and gashes that usually necessitated first aid. And who can ever forget the experience of accepting a dare and then leaving a piece of your tongue on a frozen pump handle?

As Christmas approached we often hiked downtown to see and hear the sights and sounds of the holiday season. In the late afternoon, we were intrigued with the huge candle that appeared on our one and only skyscraper, the Lincoln Tower. The cumulative effect of individual electric candles in the building's windows was a lovely sight in the heart of downtown Fort Wayne. The metal outline of a huge deer seemed to leap into midair at the John Deere Implement Store. We were bug-eyed over the glittering displays in the Woolworth's and Kresge's 5 and 10 stores. We only looked, however. We did not buy our gifts then—we always handmade our Christmas gifts to exchange with one another.

Christmas, like Easter and the Fourth of July, brought the boy out in my father. We would awaken early Christmas morning with first the scent and then the sight of a huge gaily decorated balsam tree that reached to the ceiling. The whole house was decorated to the hilt. The cookies and milk we had left for Santa had disappeared. The right package matched the right child, and we felt special and loved beyond measure. Who can ever forget the smell of Tinker Toys when the box was opened? One Christmas I received the much-desired tricycle I had requested from Santa. However, that tricycle also had a little doll sitting daintily on the seat. In a rage I threw the doll across the room and climbed on the trike. I was promptly removed and paddled by my father. I think at this point my mother realized she had a real tomboy on her hands.

Going for the Jugular

My brother Jack was the first of my siblings to make a hospital trip. When word came to us that he had broken his arm falling from one of my father's trucks, we sobbed uncontrollably. It wasn't until he walked into the house with a plaster-of-paris cast on his arm that we calmed down. We thought he had broken his arm right off!

News that Dr. Huffman was coming to our house to give us our childhood shots sent us scrambling for safety under Mother's bed. We had heard that needles were involved. Despite our tears and cries of protest, we were pulled out feet first and given the required shots. As we grew older the injuries continued and our hospital visits increased. We played hard—many of our ball games, boxing and wrestling matches ended up in slugging matches. We went for the jugular! Some of my worst fights involved defending Chick. In response, his attackers got my fists and Chick got my hugs as I hauled him home for Mother to console.

Dad used huge, metal chutes to put coal in his customers' basements. We asked if we could have a chute that he had discarded because of a torn seam on one side. He gave us permission—if we were careful. We had discovered that these chutes made great slides when propped against the crotch of a tree. One day Kenny D. gave me a hard shove and I lost my balance. My right arm got caught on the torn metal. The cut required stitches, but only after I had chased Kenny home where he found refuge behind the door he slammed in my face. For months he took the long way around our home to go to the store for his mother. I still have the scar.

In another bloody deal, I was more concerned about my mother's reaction to a three-cornered tear in my brand-new overalls than I was with the huge gash in the upper part of my leg. I had fallen on a spike in a railroad tie. By the time I arrived home, my sock and shoe were full of blood. Somehow Mother overlooked the torn overalls in her hurry to get me to the hospital for stitches once again. Another scar is a visible reminder of that episode.

Boys in our neighborhood outnumbered girls. I felt proud to be accepted as one of the boys. However, I was annoyed that one girl in our neighborhood was giving girls in general a bad name. She tattled and ratted on everyone about everything. One day on the way to school, I decided to settle a score with her. That little session landed me in the principal's office for punching. On the way home that night, the girl and her mother met me in a pony-drawn buggy. The mother threatened me loudly and made several passes at me with her whip. Fortunately, we were near the golf course. I struck off, dodging behind and around the red haw (hawthorn) trees to throw her off course. I managed to make it home safely and without any welts.

That same family lived in a storefront building with a huge glass window. They were easy targets for soaping on Halloween. One night we soaped it "good" and waited in the dark for a reaction. Somehow I got separated from my friends. I heard a low whistle and went in that direction. In doing so, I walked right into the arms of Mr. C. His clothes reeked of tobacco smoke and his breath was foul. As he shook me hard and started to make ugly threats, he suddenly sneezed and lost his grip. I was off like a shot, spared from the punishment I deserved.

At the golf course I first experienced being "temporarily

deprived of consciousness." After school and on Saturdays we often picked up lost balls and broken clubs, then played the back nine with them. One day a friend and I were feuding over an old golf iron. He threw it hard and I did not duck in time. The force of the impact knocked me off my feet. Not only did I see stars, but the wooden handle had a nail in it that cut my left cheek. My mother was more than a little upset with my bloodied face and with my so-called friend, who kept repeating, "I'm sorry. I really didn't mean it." I recovered, of course, and the scar is scarcely visible sixty some years later.

One of the boys in our group, Phil Ragan, had to take violin lessons once a week in his home. His family had the only cement sidewalk in the area. Since it was sloped, it was ideal for roller skating or for walking metal barrels. Walking barrels was a lot like logrolling. Since walking barrels was done on cement rather than water, however, the noise was horrific. You can be sure there was a horrendous noise inside the music room as well! Often on the day of his lesson, Phil found himself on the inside trying to make music while we were on the outside making our own just to taunt him. Poor Mrs. Ragan would call over to my mother saying, "Irene, I wish you'd make those children stop that." Needless to say, I had mixed emotions when years later I stood in front of Phil's open casket and recalled our misdeeds.

Important Lessons

During the Depression, my father lost his business. Even before that, times were increasingly tight for everyone and we were told to take care of our belongings. Drinking glasses and dishes were especially scarce. If we broke something, even by accident, our usually calm father would treat it as a disaster.

In our household, if one of us got up from the table to get a drink from the water pail, several requests for refills usually followed. One day Jack was at the pail and I asked him to fill my glass. He made a motion with his hands behind Dad's back for me to toss the glass to him. Foolishly I did so. Instead of catching the glass, Jack

Dad's trucks and drivers

sidestepped it and it went crashing to the floor. Needless to say our father was more than a little upset and some dire action followed on his part. During that time I made up my mind that if I ever owned something and somebody broke it accidentally, I would not scold him. I thought then, and do now, that things are only things. As the Bible says, "Set your minds on things above, not on earthly things" (Colossians 3:2, NIV).

Spring was a special time for our outdoor activities. We turned to marble playing very early in the season. Often we scraped the snow and ice from an area of black asphalt. Our knuckles would be chapped and raw from the cold. We usually played "circles." In this game you snap the marble into a ring marked on the ground and then, by using the thumb and forefinger, knock your opponent's marble out of the ring. "Plunks" was a little easier to play and better for the fingers, too. You merely had to stand back a certain distance and score by hitting your opponent's marble. This was a good way for an adept marble player to add more trophies to his or her collection. I still have an old bag of those trophies, along with some marbles my father passed on to me. They are prized possessions.

However, some well-meaning soul took the joy out of winning for me by asking if I knew I was gambling. The possibility had never occurred to me, but I took the advice and never played for keeps again. That event shaped my philosophy about gambling and the something-for-nothing ideas promoted so freely today. I fully agree that the lottery or other games or tickets of chance are part of a fantasy world meant to deceive us and lure us away from real life. How easy it is to replace reality with a vision of a so-called better life. This fantasy world also sends the wrong message to our youth, which especially disturbs me. A simple game of marbles led to my later convictions: I will gladly make a donation to a worthy cause, but refuse to buy lottery or raffle tickets of any kind.

In my childhood, Spring was also the time to build and fly kites. The men at the lumberyard on Leesburg Road were most generous with the narrow strips cut from boards that we used for struts. Often we would beg the grocer to use a little extra string on our purchases, so we could save up for kite-flying time. Colorful paper or newspaper for the body, old rags for the tail, and a huge ball of twine made up from odd pieces of string sent our creations high into the sky.

For the most part, my childhood was a busy and happy time. However, my mind was not always focused on the next diversion. Like the high-flying kites, my thoughts soared on currents of imagination, sweeping me into a future about which I could only dream.

Chapter Two

Finding Christ and the Church

"I love Thy Kingdom, Lord, the house of Thine Abode."
Timothy Dwight

Doubtless you have noticed that the Jacobs were not a church-going family. I only recall going to church with my mother once when I was very young. At the Christmas Eve service, I was impressed with the candles glowing from the windows and being given a small red New Testament. I felt so secure and proud to walk home with my mother that cold winter evening, clinging to her hand and clutching that very special gift in my other hand. My heart was so warmed by the evening's experience, that I barely needed the blue chinchilla-like fur coat that shielded me from the frosty night air.

We had another kind of "spiritual awareness" when some of us sneaked in to hear a spiritualist in a neighbor's home. We were intrigued with the dark room and her "messages" from the dead to the adults. We had heard that she was able to make the table and other objects move. We never saw that happen, but my visits ceased after the night she had a "message" for me. I was wide-eyed and all ears until I heard her say, "One of these days they are going to pick you up in pieces along the tracks and carry you home in a bushel basket!" You can be sure that I did not go near the railroad tracks for a long time. Nor did I return for any further messages.

When my sister Betty and her close friend Winnifred Ragan came home from a meeting at a little Wesleyan Methodist church, they announced that they had accepted Christ as their Savior. We were not impressed. In fact, we made life quite miserable for them with our teasing and taunting, although the changes we observed in them raised some questions in our minds. However, we refused their many invitations to accompany them to Sunday school and church.

The 100-Acre Gang

At that point in my life our neighborhood gang was of more interest to me. Gangs are not a new phenomenon. As you have discovered, I was the tomboy in the neighborhood. Considering myself "one of the boys," I much preferred overalls to dresses. My only childhood photo is an old tintype that depicts a mad, pouting little girl. Aunt Blossom had bought me a pink dress adorned with wee, black bows. Mother made me take off my beloved overalls and get into that dress so they could take a picture of me. I was disgusted! A few years later, I was most uncomfortable wearing a frilly, organdy dress for my eighth-grade graduation. My choice was to be with the gang.

In the inner sanctum of our shacks or tree houses, we often scratched our wrists to draw blood. Signing a bloody X next to our names was a pledge of loyalty to one another. We were known as the "100-Acre Gang." Just beyond the little white church that Betty and Winnifred attended lived the "Hungry Hill Gang." Armed with slingshots, we put them on the run if they ventured into our territory! We usually came to a halt near the church, for just beyond was their territory. If a service were in progress, we made it a point to sing or yell loud enough to disturb the singer or speaker. We were not above pulling the main light switch and leaving them in the dark either.

Millie and Tonkie Bell

Old Brother Uhrick, the pastor, spent a lot of time calling on our homes. Needless to say, we gave him a wide berth if we saw him coming, and you can be sure we never returned home until he was gone.

Attitude Adjustment

Around 1936 Betty and Winnifred managed to break through to me and I found myself going with them to services from time to time. I had noticed that the young people from the church lived consistent lives at school—they were the same at school as they were at church. Watching them pray, it seemed "like Greek to me," but the Holy Spirit was faithful. In due time I found myself kneeling at an altar of prayer. I did not know any prayer beyond "Now I lay me down to sleep." But that didn't matter. With instruction I learned to pray with conviction, asking for forgiveness and accepting a new way of life.

The Sunday school teacher was a kindly old soul with a gentle voice and a twinkle in his eyes. However, what impressed me most was his cheerfulness and consistent living. Sunday after Sunday I watched as two men carried him through the door and sat him in a front pew. A victim of polio, Albert Kidwell had not walked for years. But he never complained. "Uncle" Albert Kidwell gave me insights into God's Word and created a hunger and thirst for truth that has never been satisfied. Our class, eager to hear every word, sat on the floor around him. His interest in us as individuals was something special.

A trio of older women who really knew how to pray impressed me. One of them, Blanche Neat, was a real "Mother in Israel" to me. It was my happy privilege years later to pay tribute to her on her 100th birthday. The old church had become a Fellowship Hall by then and a large group met to honor her on that memorable occasion. In my tribute, I used a story a Catholic priest in Quebec told me when he learned I was Methodist:

> *Three Methodist ministers were scheduled to play golf with a priest one day after mass. They slipped into the back of the church to wait for him. The priest spotted them standing in the shadows, so he whispered to the altar boy, "Three chairs for the Methodists." The altar boy, not quite understanding him, ignored the command, so the priest repeated a bit louder, "Three chairs for the Methodists." Immediately in a loud, clear voice the altar boy called out, "Three cheers for the Methodists!"*

We gave three cheers that day to Mrs. Neat for her 100 years of faithfulness, grace, and beauty. A new church known as Spring Street Wesleyan Church has been built across the way. Although my membership is elsewhere, I join them for worship services as often as possible. Sometimes when I look about during the service, I am struck by the fact that my involvement in that church goes back beyond any of the present members. Also while there I am reminded of the many faithful individuals who touched my life for good in that congregation. They no longer sit in those pews, for they have become a part of that great cloud of witnesses we read about in Hebrews 12:1.

Mrs. Blanche Neat, Mother in Israel

(Edna Lee Lodge, the jewel of All Tribes Christian Camp, is privileged to have four of the original pews from that little church on Fourth Street. When the Spring Street Wesleyan Church was built, the old pews were going to be disposed of, but Ed Grabill and Dick accepted them and put them into storage. At the completion of the Edna Lee Lodge in 1994, Dick surprised me and brought them north to the camp. They are very special to me, for in them I learned to pray and learned the beautiful old hymns of the church.)

Progressing in Faith

The real turning point in my spiritual life came when I started high school and walked the long, long blocks to and from school with Sis and her friends. We did not have the luxury of school buses nor did the taxpayers have the burden of that expense. May Hollopeter, Dick's first wife, was part of that group. My language at times was strong enough to make a sailor blush, but for some strange reason I felt embarrassed to talk that way in front of them.

During a church service in 1938, I accepted Christ as my Savior and Lord. I was fourteen years of age. My father knew something had happened to me because I no longer exhibited my characteristic temper. Previously, whenever I was unhappy about something, I would stomp out of the house and slam the screen door behind me. Dad would wait until I was some distance from home before calling out, "Come back here and shut that door like a lady!" (Later at Marion College, one dean of women reminded me of my father. Often I would dash down the three flights of stairs in Teter Hall, eager to get to the gym or to some activity on campus. On my return she would often say, "Millie, I do wish you would come down those steps like a lady.")

I began to feel badly if I let a curse word slip out. Foul language seemed to sour in my mouth and I learned to replace my "colorful" expressions with decent words. My inner desires and thoughts also changed. But it was a struggle. Once when some really bad words spilled out, I talked with my pastor. He said, "You can't stop the birds from flying over your head, but you can prevent them from nesting there." He also warned us to watch what books we read or pictures we gazed upon, for we would be hanging images upon the walls of our minds. Some of these images would remain to bless us, but others would haunt us forever. What sound advice that has been.

The natural progression of my faith is that as I grew in the Lord, I wanted to share the Good News with others. My minister didn't have to urge me to join in the calling program. I spent many Saturdays and weekday evenings calling on others, just as the minister and faithful church members had called on us all during my rough and tumble tomboy years. It was something I had to do. Listening to God's prompting would later lead me to Marion College and to procuring a local minister's license so that I could assist at church whenever I was needed.

It All Works Together

We marvel at the computer and the other advancements in technology, but we should be more impressed with the mind God has given us. How quickly memories—good and bad—engulf us. A recent study by biopsychologist Robert H. Jensen and his colleagues at Illinois University focuses on why emotionally charged memories endure. The study centers on the vagus nerve, which extends from the brain to most of the body's internal organs. It serves as a two-way street, relaying orders from the brain to regulate such things as the heart rate, while keeping the brain informed about what is going on in the organs. It also conducts neural messages to the brain in response to hormonal substances released from emotionally charged experiences. Of special interest is how to manage or modulate these messages to enhance the retention of pleasant memories as opposed to unpleasant ones.

Read It and Heed it

Upon becoming a Christian, I read the Bible from cover to cover over and over again. I believed every word of it and have endeavored to live by it. My philosophy towards life has been shaped by it. I recall hearing a minister's wife say, "Read it and heed it." We are bound to develop a positive attitude toward life if we take the Word seriously, or take to heart the admonitions of the writers of that Book. Even Job has much to teach us. In spite of all his problems he proclaimed, "I know that my Redeemer lives" (Job 19:25, NIV). "Count it all joy," James 1:2 tells us. And Paul urges us to "[forget] those things which are behind, and [reach] forth unto those things which are before" (Philippians 3:13). To put the best construction on everything keeps one positive rather than negative—it's a way of making sure the vagus nerve transmits pleasant memories instead of bitter ones.

Chapter Three

Dark Days

(1938-1942)

"Remember your Creator in the days of your youth."

Eccl. 12:1 NIV

During my junior high school years, Mother was diagnosed with cancer of the stomach. She suffered greatly and needed expensive pain pills. Ninety cents for each yellow capsule was a big item in those days and we had no health insurance. During that time my father worked as a road foreman with a construction company. He seemed to be away from home much of the time. His presence on weekends brightened our lives and dwelling, but during the week our home felt like a house of death. We had to be quiet so as not to disturb Mother.

You Can Make It

How we looked forward to Dad's return. He always brought home a small surprise for us, perhaps a box of Cracker Jack, containing caramel corn and a small prize—a simple but special treat. However, it was his presence we needed most. Some summers we were able to go along with him and live near his work site. The most exciting of these opportunities was renting a cottage at a lake in Michigan. Not only was Dad home every night, but we could also fish and hunt frogs. Dad made us gigs from old broom handles with sharp nails to spear the frogs. We later fried the legs.

Dad taught me to swim at a very early age. One time he was with a group of adults on a raft some distance from shore. I decided to swim out to the raft but soon found the distance and the deep water a challenge. Panic and fear seemed to prevail among his friends, but he remained calm and steady. His voice still comes back to me. "You will make it, Janer. You will make it!" And I did.

Later while teaching swimming at the "Y" or at camps, I used the same psychology on my swimmers. "You can make it!" I would call out. Some needed a little help, but I never lost a swimmer. I did have a close call at the "Y" though. Mary Smith Porter, the general manager's daughter, ran over to me and said, "I think there is someone on the bottom of the pool." I jumped in, glasses and all, and picked up a small, lifeless form. In seconds the Boy's Worker, Gus Kalcun, was beside me. Together we revived her before she was taken to the hospital. Imagine my shock to see her back for the next swim period. I was even more astonished thirty years later when she looked me up on the Island and asked, "Do you remember me?" Oh yes, I remembered her. "How could I ever forget you, Dorothy?" I told her.

By the time I was in high school, Dad had landed a job in Fort Wayne that permitted him to stay at home. Quite often he would take me with him on the evenings he checked out the condition of the concrete they had poured during the day. Bales of straw had been opened and spread over the finished concrete so it would not set too quickly. I earned my first three dollars by turning bales over and catching the black crickets that had taken refuge there from the heat. I sold them for a penny a piece to fishermen. From those earnings, I offered my first tithe of thirty cents. I was most proud to be able to put those precious coins in the collection plate at the church. I have tithed ever since. "Bring ye all the tithes into the storehouse" (Malachi 3:10).

On that same job, as the crew built a four-lane highway between Fort Wayne and Huntington, Dad scratched his finger on a tar barrel one evening while checking out the road. He failed to report it to the office the next day. That was a costly error, for the insurance did not cover his medical expenses. The scratch led to blood poisoning and a nasty, red streak running up the length of his arm. Then the bone in his upper arm became infected. His whole arm looked like a bluish stovepipe. It was horrible and frightened me considerably. I detested the sight of it. How could a mere scratch cause so much trouble and pain? Dad was hospitalized for most of nine months.

Better Days Ahead

At one point both of my parents were in the hospital at the same time. Grandmother Hill was living with us at that time. When my mother took a turn for the worse, Grandmother summoned the ambulance. The ambulance driver insisted that a family member ride along. Grandmother decided that it would be best for her to stay at the house, so I was elected to accompany Mother and was literally thrown into the vehicle. What a wild ride that turned out to be! The Shoney's ambulance crew was known to put the fear of God into patients, passengers, and passing motorists as well. Sirens blared as the wild, reckless drivers sped to the hospital. We made it safely, but even today the sound still screams in my ears.

During that time I wanted to be with my parents as much as I could, so I visited them faithfully each evening after school—even though Dad preferred us to be home at night to study and to play. I detested those narrow halls in St. Joseph Hospital. The rustle of the nuns' garments and the clicking of their heels echoed down the dark corridors, intensifying my discomfort and fear. Those were difficult days indeed.

However, Dad was always upbeat and worked hard to make our dark world brighter. "There will be better days ahead," he said, and there were. In spite of things falling down all around him, he never gave up. I still do not know where he got the money so we could attend the sectional basketball tourney at our school that year, but it was important to us and to him.

At some point during that time, I fell in love with Harley-Davidson motorcycles. The rumble of the powerful engine and the flash of chrome as one roared by were the focus of my life. I could hardly wait to grow up and ride one. Dad was dead set against those crazy machines, but he listened patiently to my ramblings.

On one of my visits, the ward of four men seemed unusually quiet. Gone were the jovial remarks and normal banter. I tiptoed in and asked what was wrong. Dad beckoned me to come close and then motioned to the patient in the bed next to his. He wanted me to carefully observe the young man who was wrapped in bandages and resembled a mummy. The next night the bandaged man was not there. He had died as a result of a horrible motorcycle accident. Although I still love color and action, my interest in the speed and noise of motorcycles suddenly waned, and we never mentioned the subject again.

As he recovered, Dad's arm became stiff at the elbow and remained that way. An open wound around the bone had to be dressed daily for the rest of his life. In spite of that, he could still shoot a gun and handle a fishing pole. However, he was never able to work again. Medical bills forced us to sell our home and move to Knapp Lake, north of Fort Wayne. Dad purchased a lake lot and friends helped us build a home. A screened-in porch on the front served as our confectionery store and bait business. We also rented out boats. We were optimistic about working together as a family to make a living. And we did.

Mother's Tears

Just prior to our move to Knapp Lake, Jack had joined the Civilian Conservation Corps. He then went into the U.S. Navy sometime before the beginning of World War II. When he came home on his first furlough, our family met him at the Greyhound Bus Station. Our big brother looked so handsome and so important in his uniform, and Chick and I were very proud of him. To celebrate, we all went across the street to Fort Wayne's first drive-in restaurant. There we had our first hamburgers with the "works" and frozen chocolate milkshakes called Frosties. When Jack described the ship he lived on, we refused to believe him. A boat longer than a football field that was made of steel and would not sink? How could that be? When Jack left, Mother cried. Chick and I could not understand why she would shed tears when her son was getting a monthly check, wore a uniform, and lived on a ship. It sounded glamorous and exciting to us.

Mother also wept each spring when we went to the cemetery to "decorate" the graves. We took huge armloads of peonies and irises on Memorial Day or, as it was often called then, "Decoration Day." We younger ones dashed about, oblivious to the significance of the day. To us it was a family outing and we saw no reason to be sad. When I returned to the cemetery years later to visit my folks' graves, I took my two young godchildren, Beth Kidd ('80) and Brad Bollinger with me. As I knelt to pull a few weeds around the headstones, Beth sensed my sadness and said, "Doggone it, Mern, we didn't even get to know them, did we?"

A Hard Transition

Moving to Knapp Lake was a great adventure for us. Dad, Chick, and I had come to this area to fish for years. We had always used a friend's cottage, but talked about someday building a log cabin. Dad never lived to see that happen, but I blessed his memory when we dedicated my log cabin in Algoma in 1968. (Algoma is a Canadian district. While similar to a county in Indiana, a district is much larger.) However, leaving the home in which we were born and the neighborhood in which we grew up was not easy. Getting ready for the move was also hard work. Betty, Chick, and I had to clean every nook and cranny. Mother would not think of leaving unless the house was spotless.

Our difficult move was redeemed by the sheer wonder of the chain of lakes we could now explore. We fished and swam, trapped small game and gigged frogs. Many a night we slept in one of our larger boats, allowing the gentle waves to rock us to sleep under a canopy of stars. We were poor, but rich in many ways. Dad taught Chick and me to use a crosscut saw and pointed us in the direction of the abundance of oak trees nearby. We cut wood around the clock, for we knew we were saving money. Not only that, it was fun. We cut wood before and after school and on weekends. We attempted to wear each other down. Finally Dad said, "If you two don't stop, the neighbors will report me for child abuse."

Dad fished summer and winter. One of Dad's ice-fishing expeditions nearly ended in disaster. He and our dog, Skippy, often went alone. In the spring the ice would begin to recede from the shore of the lakes. We got around that by placing planks as a bridge to the ice. One year he pressed his luck a bit too far and fell in. How he ever managed to climb out with the use of only one arm we will never know. I do know the feeling in the pit of my stomach when I walked into the house after school to discover wet clothes all over the place and Dad sitting in his chair grinning like a Cheshire cat.

With our large garden, we lived well. But we did not have money to spare, which meant I couldn't afford all the two- or three-cent stamps I would need to keep in touch with my friends in Fort Wayne.

Although living at the lake was good for our family, Mother's health had continued to deteriorate. I tried to be more understanding and helpful around the house. One morning before going to school, I decided to fix her breakfast tray. I sat on the bed while she ate and we had a most pleasant chat. Later in the morning, I turned in my seat at school to see our neighbor, Mr. Shaw, at the back of the classroom. Somehow I knew immediately that the morning's breakfast chat had been my last conversation with my mother.

When I arrived home, my father took me in his arms and wept. It was the one and only time I ever saw him cry. He was always so brave. At that time funerals were held in homes and a floral wreath was hung on the front door to indicate a death in the household. Members of the family stayed up all night for the "wake." Mother was taken to the home of my dad's sister, Aunt Orie, for the service. Aunt Orie insisted that I go in and see my mother. But I did not. Dad and I had talked about it earlier and he understood that I wanted to remember her as I last saw her with her breakfast tray. I was so glad I had put a few flowers in a wee vase for her. Jack, who had come home for the funeral, also came to my rescue and sat in the kitchen with me so I did not have to see the coffin or hear the service.

Jack tried hard to lift Chick and me above the sorrow and sense of loss. He challenged us to a lemon-pop drinking duel by offering a quarter to the winner. (Lemon was the least favorite pop left over from our store's summer inventory.) Chick won the quarter, but after downing four or five bottles, I never again desired lemon-flavored pop.

Keeping House

Betty graduated from high school that year, so it was up to me to keep house for Dad and Chick. Since the Rural Electrification Program had not reached our area, we managed with propane and white gas. Even the iron had a small bulb for gas. I washed clothes by hand and how I hated those sheets and overalls. Dad insisted that I learn to make bread, since store-bought bread cost ten cents a loaf and money was scarce. I did not have to add salt to the dough, for my salty tears of self-pity took care of that. One day I was very proud of the many jars of green beans and bacon strips I had ready to cold pack. Dad took one look at them and said, "Janer, we have to do those over." I was upset to the point of heartbreak. Why did the beans have to be cut up? Why couldn't they be canned whole? He won the argument but I still do not understand the "why" of it. On one occasion I accidentally used plaster-of-paris instead of graham flour to make muffins. Chick took one bite and spit and coughed as if his life were threatened. Dad was not quite so dramatic, but I understood why he was unhappy. I had wasted precious sugar and eggs.

I felt sorry for myself on Saturdays when I had to do the washing, as well as clean the house. But I learned much and have enjoyed the simple life on the Island even more because of those experiences. If I worked hard on the weekends, I played even harder at school during the week, taking part in various sports and school activities. Dad attended many of those events. To see him flash me a huge grin after I sank a basket or hit a home run made Saturday's work tolerable. However, I missed my mother and our heart-to-heart talks. It was especially painful to jump off the school bus and dash down the hill, eager to share the highlights of the day—only to reach the door and realize she was not there.

Settling the Score

When Grandfather Jacobs lived with us at the lake, Chick and I often played a cruel trick on him. We were attempting to settle a score. Ruth was his favorite grandchild and we all knew it. He hardly had the time of day for the rest of us. He loved to fish and whenever he was getting his gear ready he would remind us not to let our dog out of the house. Dad always took our pet dog with him and just the sight of a fishing pole got Skippy excited. When Grandpa was halfway to the lake loaded down with his pole, minnow bucket, can of worms, and heaven knows what else, we opened the door. Out went Skippy, barking wildly and dashing after him. He usually ran between Grandpa's bowed legs, tripping him and causing his gear to go flying in all directions. On those occasions we did not appear at the house until Grandpa had retired for the night.

Lessons in Love

During this time I met Dick, the man who would become my husband thirty-seven years later. I was dating someone else, a local farm boy. Dick's wife-to-be, May, invited us to double-date with them. One night we drove to Fort Wayne to meet them and from there to the Bluffton Indiana State Fair. It was a long way from Bluffton to Knapp Lake and it was quite late when I returned home. I did not want to disturb Dad, so I took off my shoes and tiptoed up the stairs. However, I failed to miss the squeaky step. Dad said calmly, "Janer, what time is it?"

I replied, "LATE."

He said, "We won't do this again."

And I said, "No, sir, we won't."

My dream of having my own home and six boys for a basketball team looked quite possible during my senior year of high school. Because several of my classmates had announced their engagements to be married, I thought I too was madly in love with the farmer's son. I came back on another night, starry-eyed and full of plans for "our future." Dad asked me a simple but thought-provoking question: "Have you ever noticed how that young man talks to his mother and sister?" Of course I had not, for my ears only heard the sweet nothings he whispered. However, on my next visit to his home, I paid attention and did not like what I heard. In discussing it with my father later, he said, " A man will treat his wife the same way he treats his mother and sisters." I realized I did not want the young farmer's ring after all. I decided I would go on to college. (Of course I did get my six boys plus some girls when I married Sir Richard, with no morning sickness or labor pains. But more on that wonderful chapter in my life later.)

Mint Fields and Capsized Boats

Knapp Lake is in the heart of muck country. Muck, for any who are not familiar with the term, is black peat soil that is highly productive if properly drained. Farmers produced potatoes, onions, spearmint, and peppermint, along with corn. Chick and I worked in the mint fields weeding. Chick also had a small field of his own. It may be surprising to some of you to learn that mint is handled somewhat the same way as hay. It is mowed, windrowed, and dried. Then it is hauled dry to the distillery where live steam processes the hay into the precious mint oil for flavored candy, chewing gum, and medicines. The mint business is mostly gone now from that area. The stills no longer operate and I'm sure I'm not the only one who misses the scent of mint wafting through the air.

After a hot day in the mint field, we looked forward eagerly to a dip in the lake. One of our favorite activities was for three or four of us to stand up in a wooden rowboat, then brace our feet and rock back and forth until the water ran over the sides. We kept at this until the boat was full. It might flip over but it would not sink. We would then row about with a boat full of water, much to the amusement of onlookers.

As the Waterfront Director years later at a CGIT camp (Canadian Girls In Training) north of Toronto, I wanted the campers to know that you could not sink a wooden boat, and that if it turned over you could use it as a life raft. However, the Camp Director did not agree with me. As we were capsizing the boat, she screamed and ordered us to come in immediately. I never had the opportunity to convince her.

Not Just War Games

Brother Jack, the young sailor

High school was more than fun and games. Our history teacher made us keenly aware of events around the world. Names of cities, countries, and people we had never heard of appeared in our newspapers and class discussions. Germany was posing a threat to Europe. Hitler's "goose step" was no longer funny. And then on December 7, 1941, the

Japanese bombed Pearl Harbor. World War II was more to us than what we read in the newspaper or heard on the radio. War now surrounded our country on both sides, and our big brother Jack was out there in the middle of it. An October 1997 article in the *Milwaukee Journal Sentinel* captures what his life was like:

With His Luck Jake's Got To Give Again

Jake Jacobs has been giving blood since he nearly ran out of his own blood more than 50 years ago. He was born John W. Jacobs, but nearly everyone called him "Jake the cook" during his service years. When Jacobs joined the Navy in 1937 he was lucky that he was assigned to the U.S.S. Leary for only a few months. He wasn't on the destroyer in 1943 when it was torpedoed and sunk in the North Atlantic. Nearly 100 men died. And Jacobs was lucky that he was assigned to the U.S.S. Savannah for only a few years. He wasn't on the light cruiser in 1943 when it was hit by a radio-controlled bomb at Salerno Beach in Italy. More than 200 men died.

In 1941 Jacobs was assigned to the U.S.S. Casco, a seaplane tender. And the following year much of his luck ran out, but luckily not all of it. The torpedo that broke open a 40-foot-wide hole in the ship came as close to killing him as possible without doing it. Jacobs was blown against a bulkhead. "I fell and got caught by the arms in a hole. It was as black as pitch and I am hollering. All of a sudden someone who had a strange and maybe necessary sense of humor tapped me on the head and said, 'Jake, for God's sake, keep your voice quiet. You are waking everybody up.' Then he pulled me out of the hole."

The ship ran aground that day in the Aleutian Islands and Jacobs was transferred to a home on the beach, where an operating room was set up in the kitchen. "I lost the sight in one eye, my leg was bro-

ken, broken tail bone, broken ribs and shrapnel in my side." Jacobs ended up with an artificial hip and knee. His face was so broken up he had up to ten surgeries. He was in various hospitals from August '42 til May '43.

When he returned to Fort Wayne and stepped off the train, other young soldiers or sailors-to-be were waiting in the station with their families. At the sight of Jack swathed in bandages and limping on crutches, many of the mothers burst into tears and for the first time the young enlistees realized they would not be playing war games. Some would pay a high price to serve their country. In the summer of 1943 in Detroit, Michigan, he pushed blood donations and sold war bonds for the U.S. government.

And these days at the age of 76, Jacobs is still donating blood every eight weeks or so. "I just give blood," he said. "It's a payback. Somebody saved my life so this is what I do for somebody else. I try to talk everybody into it because when you give blood you are helping to save someone's life. Our grandchildren call and say, 'Hey, I just gave blood and I am calling you, Grampa, to tell you I am catching up.'" Jake has given 209 pints of blood and 14 pints of platelets in eight states.

Medals of Honor

I spent some time with Jack and his wife at their home in Texas in the winter of 1999. He was 80 years old and was shooting for 90, or even 100. Jack walks with a cane and cannot get up from the floor or the ground without help. His artificial hip has been replaced. As noted in the article, he had been a blood donor for years until prevented recently by health and age. He has always been a cheerful, optimistic soul. He was an avid camper and Boy

Scout leader and the high honors he received in Scouting, including the Silver Beaver, are of more value to him than his Purple Heart.

Chapter Four

Summer Jobs

(1942-1944)

COCKROACH DELIGHT

"This is my work, my blessing, not my doom."

Henry Van Dyke

I graduated from North Webster High School in May of 1942 and decided to return to Fort Wayne for a job. Since I was saving money for college, I knew I had to find something that would pay more than the mint fields offered. I soon found work as a maid at the Bass Mansion. My sister Betty had worked there prior to her wedding. I also knew the cook, Dotty Morrison, a friend from church. Made of limestone from southern Indiana, this home had been built long before my time and named for the man who also owned and operated the Bass Foundry. While this business had thrived in the early years of the twentieth century, the family had fallen on harder times by the time I arrived. Bass Mansion currently serves as the Administration Building of the University of St. Francis.

Royal Robes and Cockroaches

When I started my service as a maid, the staff consisted of only two others beside myself—Dotty, the cook, and a chauffeur/gardener. A separate part of the mansion contained the servants' quarters, where we had our own rooms with access to acres of beautiful grounds and a lake. We could walk to church; some distance from the church we could catch the streetcar to town. The pay was low, but we had room and board. And we staff members enjoyed one another's company. When the family was gone, Dotty and I put on our long, cotton housecoats and swished up and down the circular staircase like royalty. Dotty often played hymns on the grand piano in the ballroom while I shot pool in one of the alcoves.

She loves to tell the story about my cockroach dinner. Because the lady of the mansion was very frugal, the staff usually ate the leftovers, for nothing was ever wasted or thrown out. On this particular evening, only one serving remained of my favorite—the boiled cabbage dinner. Dotty decided that I should have it. Much later she revealed to me that she had fished several dead cockroaches out of the meal before she heated it up for me. It was difficult to keep the large buildings free of insects because we could not use insecticides of any kind for fear of poisoning the family dog.

When Dotty returned home to New York State to attend teacher's college, Beatrice was hired to take her place. I could not resist playing tricks on her, for Beatrice was a very prim and proper spinster. Each bedroom in the mansion featured a button con-

Bass Mansion

nected to a buzzer and signal light in the kitchen. One day when the family was gone, I pressed the button by propping open a bedroom door. The new cook was still not acquainted with the system, which by now was buzzing incessantly, so she dashed from the front door, to the side door, to the back door, and to every phone on the first floor, and then to the second floor, where she found me in stitches. She was not amused.

Labor Intensive

I later found a job with a tailoring company that manufactured heavy wool overcoats for the army. This was my introduction to a "sweatshop." The hours were long, the wages low, and the atmosphere most unpleasant. But I felt that since the war was ongoing, I was doing my "bit."

I was provided room and board with elderly friends who had a summer home at Knapp Lake. Their Fort Wayne home was within walking distance of the Wayne Knitting Mills, makers of women's fine hosiery. It was my good fortune then to find a job there. Working conditions were much better and the pay was unbelievable for that time. But it was shift work and it was hard. I worked on a footer machine, filling bars with very fine needles to make the foot of the stockings. Missing a needle created a run in the stocking, causing the knitter to groan and tie a knot in that item. We were paid by the piece (I should say the foot), and a runner cut down on our production and pay. Four of us filled twelve bars each as fast as we could to keep the machine running at top speed. It was some of the most intensive work I've ever done. I was only too glad to leave at the end of summer to fulfill my dream of college. The older women told me I was stupid to quit the good money. My older sister Ruth agreed. I was fortunate to be able to work there for two more summers. But how glad I was when that factory door slammed shut behind me for the last time and I never again punched a time clock.

An Important Decision

While working at these jobs, it was a real treat for me to be back home in Fort Wayne, attending the Fourth Street Wesleyan Methodist Church. Pastor Edward Smithee ('21) encouraged me to take an active role. I served as president of the youth group and taught a Sunday school class of boys. Remembering how faithful Pastor Uhrick had been during my own "wild" childhood, I followed his example by calling on the unchurched families in my old neighborhood. As a result Danny Wheeler ('68) is a Wesleyan minister today.

On one occasion after calling in a very poor elderly couple's home, I wondered if the Lord were leading me into ministry of some kind. Pastor Smithee urged me to attend the school affiliated with our church—Marion College in Marion, Indiana. He suggested that a year or two on campus would give me time to decide on a teaching career or some kind of church work. Accepting his advice proved to be one of most important decisions of my life.

Forsaken

Betty's husband, George Reed, had gone into the army, so Dad and Chick moved from Knapp Lake to Fort Wayne to live with my sister. A construction company hired Dad to do light jobs. During a heavy rainstorm he got soaked, caught pneumonia soon after, and landed in the Lutheran Hospital. One morning Betty phoned me at 2:30 a.m. to say that the hospital had called and reported that Dad was very low. We were urged to come immediately. While waiting for her to come and pick me up, I knelt by my bed and prayed a phrase from an old hymn: "Is your all on the altar of sacrifice laid?" Those words kept coming to me in my distress, for I was not ready to give my father up. He was only fifty-three years old and I had not yet started college.

When we got to his room, he recognized us and kept asking if we could see a light in the corner of his room. We could not see it, but did not dispute him. We prayed together and continued to sit by his bedside. In spite of the oxygen tent that covered half his bed, his breathing was very labored. It was not a pleasant sight, nor a soothing sound. An hour or so later, the room became deathly quiet. A nurse slipped in and turned the oxygen off. Without saying a word, she removed the tent and left. We kissed him goodbye and departed. Betty phoned Ruth and she contacted Jack and Chick. Then we made funeral arrangements. I left the hospital alone and spent the day walking and crying and praying. The bottom had dropped out of my world. My pastor and church friends had all gone to Marion for Harvest Home days (now called Homecoming). Never before or since have I felt so alone. Dad was my friend, my mentor, my inspiration. What would life be without him?

Later in the day I made my way back to our old neighborhood. I was soon balancing myself on the rails of the Nickel Plate Railroad where we had played as kids. As I prayed and committed myself to Christ, my faith took hold and the future did not seem quite so bleak. Psalm 27:10 came to my mind: "When my father and mother forsake me, then the Lord will take me up."

I would soon be off to college for a new beginning. I would miss my father terribly, but I also knew deep in my heart just what he would have told me: "Janer, you will make it."

Chapter Five

A Degree of Wisdom

(1944-1948)

We are Fearfully and Wonderfully made.

Psalm 139

"Blessed is the man who finds wisdom,
the man who gains understanding."

Prov. 3:13 NIV

The church gave me a royal send-off, showering me with gifts of clothing, bedding, and personal items. Betty gave me a handsome Bulova wristwatch. (Sometime later while playing touch football, I scratched the crystal on the rough brick wall of the college gym as I was trying to avoid a tap. How badly I felt. But even with a scratched crystal, my Bulova served me for years. I've always felt there's a fitting spiritual parallel to be drawn from that!) After packing all my worldly goods in an old, borrowed suitcase and two cardboard boxes, I boarded the Greyhound bus for Marion.

Velva Hathaway Bollinger ('48) promised to meet me. She was a member of the Albion Wesleyan Methodist Church and we had first met at our church youth rallies. She had started college the year before and agreed to help me settle in. As the bus approached the city limits of Marion, a comfortable and exciting feeling settled over me, a feeling that I was coming to the right place. After all these years I still experience that beautiful sense of coming home. The campus has changed in many ways but the feeling is the same. Talk about falling in love! I was enthralled with everything about the campus. My dream of going to college was coming true and I was overjoyed to realize that I had finally made it.

A Personal Touch

I enrolled in the theology department and was thrilled to sit under the teaching of Professors Elliot, Main, and Dayton. They were godly and knowledgeable men who challenged us "to study to show [ourselves] approved unto God" (2 Timothy 2:15).

During the basic speech course with Miss Laura Emerson, I immediately became aware that I needed her expertise. I soon dropped the words "chimley" for chimney, "ralroad" for railroad, "warsh" for wash, and so on. My diction and pronunciation left something to be desired, so she suggested that I enroll in her private speech classes. I have never regretted this decision. I gave my junior speech recital with Sheldon Duecker ('48), now a retired Bishop in the United Methodist Church. We did a variety of short readings. My senior recital was a forty-five-minute selection from the book *In His Steps* by Charles Sheldon. Many of the kids who wear the WWJD jewelry today probably don't realize this fad is the result of Sheldon's pivotal question in this book: "What would Jesus do?" I still use that reading in church services, camps, and retreats. Miss Emerson's patience, guidance, and personal interest did much to improve my self-image and confidence. I bless her memory.

The spiritual aspect of campus life was warm, vital, and most uplifting. The College Wesleyan Methodist Church was then THE church for students and faculty. There were few cars on campus so the majority of the students attended the campus church. It served as an inspiration and challenge for building character. It was a sacred temple where many hearts found God, renewed covenants, and received new blessings that spurred us to greater service.

The pastors and their wives took a genuine interest in the students. Dr. Allen Bowman, the Academic Dean, was in charge of the midweek prayer service. He made it a practice to fast and pray on Thursday. The depth of his leadership and teachings reflected his preparation and dedication.

Dr. Mary Dodd's ('21) Sunday school classes were rich and thought provoking. I'll never forget her series on the attributes of God. I served as devotional chairman for the class. Full-time youth pastors were unknown at that time. I had the happy privilege to meet with the young teens once a week. Most of them were children of the faculty. It has been exciting to watch the Bowman and Sheets children, as well as other youngsters from the faculty, become leaders in the church and community.

During that first exciting year of college, I discovered one subject that I did not enjoy. Unfortunately for me, conducting and sight singing were a "must" for all freshmen. Poor Professor Herman Baker ('24) never succeeded in making a "music" person out of me. One of my most horrible memories of that first year was attempting to lead the singing in the chapel, a requirement of the course. My ineptitude and the fact that my classmates were snickering in the front seats did not add to the solemnity of the lyrics in "At Calvary."

First Things First

The spiritual life of the college was also centered on the

Tuesday evening student conference, a service led by students and staff to meet the needs of the students. The student conference was also responsible for sending out gospel teams to represent Marion College in Indiana and surrounding states, as well as offering services for the local jail, children's home, the infirmary, and the factories. My team's leader was John Basham ('50).

We attended a series of meetings each fall and spring. Outstanding speakers from the Wesleyan Methodist denomination and other churches ministered to the students, staff, and the community. Every effort was put forth to challenge us to live the school motto: "First Things First."

The Gospel Team
l to r: Helen French Barefoot '49, Millie Jacobs Troyer '48, Ruth Huston Polston '49, John Basham '50, and Frank Simpson '52

My first camping experience as an adult came at the Wesleyan Youth Camp in Fairmont, Indiana. John Basham ('50) and I were asked to head up a recreation program. Those were the days when youth camps were more like mini-conferences or camp meetings. Churches had not yet become multipurpose buildings—heaven forbid!

After being rained out a few times, John and I thought we had a solution to the problem. Our friends, John and Mid Reed, were preparing crafts in the back of the Youth Tabernacle. Why not set up Ping-Pong tables and paint shuffleboard courts on the floor in the aisles? The campers would have more to do on rainy days than to mope around in their dorms. Reed agreed to assist us. We scrounged around the college and community for Ping-Pong tables, bought green paint (Eurekan colors), and burned the midnight oil getting our indoor recreation area ready. Imagine our surprise and chagrin to be told the next day by our conservative elders that we had overstepped the line.

The paint had to be removed and the tables had to go. I eyed the craft tables allowed at the back of the building and refused as a matter of principle to do any paint removal. The two Johns had paint under their fingernails for weeks afterwards. Looking at the multipurpose churches that abound today, I realize that once in a while we find ourselves ahead of the times.

An annual missionary convention at Marion College also challenged us to consider how God might want to use us in the future. I kept my heart open and prayed for a definite call to the mission field. I was so sure He would lead me to some exotic part of the world. The call never came. This was confirmed several years later in 1956 when I visited my friend Eva Gilger ('49) in Kenya. I observed every aspect of the mission station very closely and spent much time at the school and the hospital. One evening we were entertaining some of Eva's young teachers. One of them asked, "Did you come all this way just to take Miss Gilger home? Why don't you stay with us? We need you." As much as I was enjoying the experience, nothing "clicked." I knew at that moment that I had not missed my calling. By then I was involved in the work that would eventually lead me to All Tribes Christian Camp. The Lord has provided me with many opportunities to work with young people over the years and the enjoyment I experience has only increased with time.

Modeling Stewardship

The name of Dr. Charles DeVol ('26) is revered around the world. He was born in China to missionary parents. After graduating from Marion College, he returned to China to teach and preach. A world-renowned botanist who specialized in ferns, he returned from time to time to his Alma Mater to teach anatomy, botany, and physiology. The government of Taiwan recently recognized Dr. DeVol by issuing a postage stamp in his honor.

Dr. and Mrs DeVol

I was fortunate to sit under his teaching. During an anatomy class, he turned from the blackboard and said, with tears streaming down his face, "We are fearfully and wonderfully made" (Psalm 139:14). I shall never, never forget that.

Dr. DeVol taught us outside the class as well. One day I observed that he was making frequent stops as he crossed The Triangle in front of the Administration Building. As he approached me I inquired about his activity. "Trash, Millie. Trash. (Litter had not come into our vocabulary yet.) If we don't keep this campus clean, who will?" He drove home a point. Rarely do I pass litter of any kind without stooping to pick it up. (It is great for the waistline, too.) Those who have visited All Tribes Christian Camp know that "Reduce-Reuse-Recycle" is an important aspect of our purpose there, a concept that grew from Dr. DeVol's simple exercise in stewardship. It has always been difficult for me to understand how Christians can take so lightly God's command in Genesis 1 to rule over all the earth, not to destroy it.

Mrs. Leora DeVol ('25), our Dean of Women, took a personal interest in her girls at Teter Hall and taught me much about prayer. I, with others, bless the memory of the DeVols.

The Misplaced Briefcase

I took several psychology classes from Dr. C. G. Lawrence, a dear southern gentleman from Georgia. Talk about an absentminded professor! He had been known to drive downtown in his car and come back by way of the streetcar to South Marion. Other stories about him abound. Some students said he came to class one morning and set a six-pack of Pepsi on his desk instead of his briefcase. The briefcase had been left behind at Moon's Grocery across from the Administration Building on Washington Street.

The owner, Mr. Moon, told me this story about Dr. Lawrence. The professor had parked his car in front of the store and gone over to the Administration Building. When Mr. Moon was closing the store after 6:00 p.m., he noticed the car was still there. He phoned the professor to ask if he knew where his car was. "It's in my garage, of course," the professor said in his southern drawl. "Are you sure?" asked Mr. Moon. "Quite sure," Dr. Lawrence replied. That was the end of the conversation, but it was not long until the Professor shuffled up and drove his car away. I am ashamed to say we often imitated Dr. Lawrence and "chased" our books just as he literally chased his briefcase wherever he went.

Mr. and Mrs. Moon, by the way, were a Mom and Pop to scores of students. They had just the right words for homesick or heartsick students. Their little grocery store was a favorite hangout in the mornings if we overslept and missed breakfast. A sweet roll and a pint of chocolate milk held us over until noon and a wide variety of snacks and fruits were available to keep us going through the day.

Makin' Sunshine

In one memorable history class, Dr. Bowman may have altered the entire group's thinking about the weather. Several young men were planning a deer-hunting trip to Pennsylvania. They were complaining because it was raining. In a very serious manner Dr. Bowman turned from the blackboard, made a fist, and said, "I would be afraid to complain about the weather. The weather comes from God!" For the Nimrods this was a new approach to the subject.

Today, before I express myself concerning the weather, my thoughts usually go back to that history class. And I often quote the Hoosier poet, James Whitcomb Riley: "'Whatever the weather may be,' sez he, 'whatever the weather may be, it's the songs ye sing and the smiles ye wear that's makin' the sunshine everywhere.'"

Bird's-Eye View

One professor kept fit not by going to the gym, but by climbing three flights of stairs to the Crow's Nest in the Ad building, which was the biology classroom and laboratory. Margaret Hodson ('32) was a dedicated and capable teacher of Natural Sciences. I found her ornithology class to be very interesting, but I missed an early morning birding field trip because I knew something that she did not.

A few of us had planned to spend the night on the roof of Teter Hall. For obvious reasons, this was not general knowledge. We sometimes slept there to escape the heat or just for the fun of it.

Teter Hall

Many of the girls also sunbathed up there. But that particular night a hard rain drove us indoors. Certain the birding class would be cancelled because of the rain, we decided to sleep in the next morning. Later in the day Miss Hodson informed this absentee that the sun had shone brightly on the bird walk. I did not tell her how I knew it had rained during the night, or why I assumed it would still be raining in the morning.

Miss Hodson was also known for her kindness. She often allowed the young daughter of Dr. Glenn Martin to accompany her class on field trips. Adair Martin Morgan ('85) loved birds and the bird professor. One such field trip was designed as a bird identification test. The students were to identify the birds they saw and turn their list in after class. In her eagerness and excitement, the youngster kept calling out the names of every bird she saw. Once the students realized how much this little girl knew about birds, they kept very close to her. As a result, Miss Hodson had to silence her best student in order to preserve the integrity of the exam.

After a trip to Sierra Leone in West Africa, Miss Hodson took a special interest in our African students. She had much to do with helping them graduate from Marion College. As of this writing, she is the only professor I had as a student from 1944 to 1948 who is still living.

We students were most blessed to sit under the teaching of such fine professors. They were a godly and dedicated staff.

Paying Bills and Campus High Jinks

My hard-earned factory savings paid my school bill that first year, but I knew I had to work as well as study if I were going to graduate without going into debt. My first job on campus was serving as a waitress in the basement dining room of Teter Hall. I did not have far to "commute," since I lived on the third floor of the same building.

Meals were served family style and a family atmosphere prevailed. Different ones were called upon to bless the food. The fellows always seated the girls and served the food to them before serving themselves. Places were assigned and the food was always served in the same order. No one wanted to be the last one served. We called this "Starvation Corner." If seconds ran out on some items that person was cheated. We waitresses stood along the back wall with large aluminum trays in our hands, ready to meet the needs of our diners. It was our responsibility to cater to the students and faculty. Years later when the food service was moved to the Baldwin Food Center, Russell Baldwin, the school treasurer, gave All Tribes Christian Camp some of those trays, as well as several large cast-iron skillets.

In my opinion we ate well, but not all the students agreed. Churches, friends, and families donated large quantities of food to the college during the Harvest Day Festival in October. The offerings included fresh fruit, produce, home preserved goods, chicken, beef, and pork. This saved the school a large sum of money and made the donors part of the school family.

The head waitress was Marie Evatt ('45) from South Carolina. She also made the necessary announcements. During the winter we chuckled to hear her say, "If you are fixin' to park your car on Washington Street this evenin', be aware that the snowplow will be along later."

The laundry room was adjacent to the dining hall. (These two rooms later served as the Art Department weaving rooms.) A pile of old nylon hose had accumulated there. We waitresses figured out a "creative" use for those old stockings. Making ropes out of them, we tied the chair legs together at the Dean of Women's table, then placed empty aluminum trays in the seats of the chairs. As usual everyone came in and stood behind their chairs while grace was pronounced. Then when the occupants of that table attempted to pull out their chairs and sit down, the chairs would only budge enough to send the trays clattering noisily to the floor. The diners stood there helplessly. The frustrated Dean finally requested a pair of shears from the kitchen and they were able to proceed with the meal. In the meantime we waitresses remained standing innocently against the wall, hardly able to contain ourselves.

Another mealtime "episode" involved retaliating against certain young men on campus who had been turning out the lights incessantly and playing other tricks on the residents of Teter Hall. Five of us girls waited just inside the laundry room until everyone had started to eat their evening meal. We then dashed over to old

School Daze (poster)

Congress Hall, which was then occupied by sixteen of the men. Congress Hall was reputed to have been a part of the Underground Railroad during the slave days of the United States. [That building and the gym next door were later torn down to make room for the Howard ('40) and Marie ('42) Noggle Christian Ministry Building.]

We weren't thinking about history that night, however. We were on a mission. We soon had the dorm in shambles. Without doing any real damage, we emptied the dresser drawers, took down the curtains, messed up the beds, rearranged the furniture, and left little notes here and there. We then went next door to the gym to shoot baskets. When the fellows returned from their evening meal and observed the disaster, they suspected the non-students from the south end of Marion. Noticing us in the gym, they inquired if we had seen the culprits. We sympathized with them and turned our attention back to shooting baskets. Much later that evening they figured out who the real culprits were. They reported us to the Dean of Men, Professor Taylor, who sided with them and accompanied them to a conference with President McConn. After hearing their tale of woe, he thoughtfully rubbed his nose and said, "Don't you think the score has been settled?" Prexies sometimes have serious problems, don't they?

At that time a large blackboard in the main hall of the Administration building was used for all school notices. The morning after the "Congress Hall Incident," this announcement was scrawled conspicuously for all to see: "ATOMIC BLONDES STRIKE HISTORIC EDIFICE!" We should have suffered pangs of guilt at the next annual Easter Breakfast when those same young men served us in the dining hall. This was an annual tradition. I do remember the hot white cross buns, the delicious scrambled eggs, and the soloist singing "Up From the Grave He Arose." But pangs of guilt? No, I cannot recall one pang.

Getting Around

In my teens, I dreamed of having a sporty black car with a V8 engine. While saving money for college I discovered my dream car on a used car lot. Eager to share the good news with my dad, I went straight home. He wisely said, "Janer, if you buy that car, there goes your college education right down the drain." Going to college was a dream, too, and that was the dream that won over my desire for a car. In fact, I heeded Dad's words so well that I did not buy my first car until several years after I graduated from Marion College. I found it much cheaper to use public transportation, if not as convenient.

The streetcar was the transportation for most of us at Marion College. Campus parking was not a problem in those days because parents then (unlike so many of today's parents) did not buy cars for their high school graduates. The streetcar ran from North Marion to Teter Hall. Students who worked part-time in the downtown stores depended upon the streetcar for transportation. When the streetcar got to the end of the route, we were fascinated by how the conductor would pull the trolley cable to the back, then turn the seats around for his return trip. Sometimes we turned the seats for him.

One of my more memorable experiences as a student was having my tonsils removed. Miss Emerson had volunteered to drive me to the doctor's downtown office. I refused her kind offer and insisted on taking the streetcar. The doctor, using a local anesthetic, failed to freeze my throat adequately. As he operated I could hear and feel the cutting of the tissue. I gripped the arms of the chair until my knuckles turned white. After the ordeal he kindly suggested that I might want to spend some time in his waiting room before going back to the college. Generous of him, eh? As I staggered through the door, who should be waiting for me but my speech professor! Foregoing the streetcar, I let her help me to her car and drop me off at Teter Hall, where I crawled up the three flights of stairs to my room. Needless to say I did not complete my "to do" list during that particular Easter vacation.

We counted on the streetcar for our spring picnic at Matter Park at the north end of Marion. Of course the conductor stopped at all railroad crossings. Our school clown, Melvin Gentry ('45), who later became the pastor of the College Church, emphasized that fact by getting off the car half a block before the crossing, running up to the tracks, looking both ways, and theatrically signaling the smiling conductor across in safety. Our summer picnic was on a farm south of Marion at Deer Creek. Most times we walked to that site. These picnics helped to seal the bond among the students and faculty. I continually realize how my associations at Marion College have shaped my life.

Social Graces

Millie and roommate Velva

In an effort to help us get better acquainted and to develop our social graces, Marion College sponsored several events during the year. The President and Faculty Reception marked the beginning of the school year in the fall. All were expected to dress up in their finest and be introduced to (and shake the hands of) everyone in a seemingly endless line. After the second year some of us found ways to avoid this event, even though refreshments were always served. We were not *that* hungry.

The faculty ladies sponsored a tea each spring for the senior women. Gloves and hats were in order. Years later I had the honor of speaking to the group. I came all dressed up in my Girl Scout Leader's uniform, complete with beret and white gloves. The faculty ladies were impressed, but I doubt the seniors were.

Another celebration that comes to mind was the monthly Birthday Party. Each month, those born in that month got together and prepared a skit. They were also seated together and decorated their area appropriately. Before one of these events, I was shaking a rug out of the window of my room on the second floor of Teter Hall. The streetcar conductor was changing the trolley (the college was at the end of the line), when he spotted me and shouted, "The president has just died." That, of course, was Franklin D. Roosevelt. In spite of all our preparations, the college cancelled the Birthday Party. At first we were more dismayed and upset at having to cancel the evening Birthday Party, than we were about the announcement. We were young and didn't fully comprehend the seriousness of what was going on in the world outside our small campus. But he was the President of the United States, after all, and we respected the decision.

As a freshman I shall never, ever forget waking up at dawn the last day of school prior to our Christmas break. The junior and senior women were caroling in the halls, another annual tradition. The angelic sound almost convinced me I had died and gone to heaven.

Two campus literary societies, the Amphictyons and the Eurekans, were especially notorious. Formed originally to be strictly literary groups, over the years they had taken on other less noble pursuits. By the time I arrived on campus in 1944, they sponsored athletic teams and social events. We had many evenings of hilarity and fun under the two banners. The recruitment of new members was taken very seriously. Each fall the incoming students were rushed and courted. My roommate, Velva, was a loyal Amphic and had every reason to believe that I would become one too. However, while playing basketball pick-up games in the gym, I met some outstanding players who happened to be Eurekans. The rest is history. I turned out to be one of the most vocal and loyal Eurekans who ever walked that campus. Some Amphics accused me of even having green blood. Fortunately, my future husband Dick was also a devoted Eurekan.

I had been active in the Girl's Athletic Association at North Webster High School, so I decided to organize a Women's Athletic Association on campus. The girls responded enthusiastically. Other campus organizations included the Hoosiers (Indiana students), Buckeyes (Ohio), Wolverines (Michigan), Easterners, and Westerners. There was a Dixie organization, too, for our southern students generally came from Central Wesleyan College in Central South Carolina. Their southern expressions confused us all. (Central has since become Southern Wesleyan University, a liberal arts institution). Many of our students came from Miltonvale Wesleyan College in Kansas (until the school merged with Bartlesville Wesleyan College, now known as Oklahoma Wesleyan University). On rainy days in Indiana, the westerners would sing with fervor, "O give me a home where the buffalo roam and the deer and the antelope play . . ." They especially liked to stress that last line, "And the skies are not cloudy all day."

Groups also formed through the Art, Music, Science, and History Departments. The Forensic Club consisted of "invited" speech students. Their motto was: "Mend your speech a little lest it mar your future." I wondered if I would ever mend my speech enough to be accepted. During my sophomore year, I was honored to finally make it "in."

The Sports Connection

Dean Bowman approached me at the end of my first year and asked if I would consider taking over the student women's physical education program. A male student had worked with both the men and women in the past. This position would pay full tuition and room and board. I felt inadequate, but was challenged by the offer. I could also see how my background had played a big part in coming to this crossroads.

Miss Albert, my physical education teacher at Franklin Grade School, had first instilled in me the desire to go to college to become a teacher like her. (Although a smoker herself, she frequently reminded us that if we wanted to become athletes we should avoid cigarettes, tea, and coffee. I soon dropped my taste for the "weeds," and to this day coffee is distasteful to me. As for tea, one teabag will do me for at least a dozen cups, prompting my late brother-in-law Lloyd to accuse me of drinking "scared water.") You are already familiar with the tomboy inclinations of my childhood. I went on to play on every team possible in high school and college, making the all-star basketball teams for both schools as well. But to take on the Marion College Student Women's Physical Education Program? It was a challenge, indeed, but also an answer to some of my financial concerns. In addition to my campus job and activities, I also mustered the energy and time to work in several homes and to do some babysitting.

A physical education teacher in the local school system, Margaret Stone Stephenson ('37), became my mentor at Marion

College. I loved the classes and the girls. Due to World War II, many of our students had to work in factories in the afternoons. This meant 6:30 a.m. PE classes. I can still hear the groans of the softies who were out of shape! But I was in my element in the gym and on the field. Life was full and rich. Dr. Bowman thought I should pursue my M.A. and return to the campus to teach, but I did not feel led to take that course of action.

Although I enjoyed the sports, I still had missionary service or church work in mind. Since the college was only fifty miles from Fort Wayne, I returned to my home church regularly. The pastor invited me to preach many times and I also had the privilege of teaching the Young People's Sunday school class. My pastor suggested that I apply for a "local" minister's license, something that would benefit me later on, if and when I was ordained.

The Large and the Small of It

One very humiliating experience of my college days took place at one of our youth rallies in Indiana. I was taking part in a Bible quiz and misspelled Isaiah. My face turned several shades of red when someone said aloud, "I thought Marion College students knew everything!"

Eurekan Basketball Team
Back row l to r: Doris Powell Ferguson '48, Rosemary White Brown '51, Wilma Duncan Shirar '49, Clara Weaver Millet '50
Front Row: Mary Dutiel Deisler '51, Evan Gaberdiel Becker '48, M. J. Troyer '48

During my time there, Marion College had considerably fewer than 500 students enrolled. Everybody knew everybody and we were a family. The campus consisted of four buildings. Sometimes our small-school status led to derogatory comments; for instance, we were frequently referred to as South Marion U. We also had another problem. Marian College in Indianapolis, a Catholic school, caused more than a little confusion. In fact, one of their intended students enrolled in Marion and was a student with us for several days before she realized where she was. Wrong church, wrong pew!

Today, as Indiana Wesleyan University, the school has expanded to include more than thirty facilities. Enrollment has increased unbelievably. While this may make it more like a community than a family, IWU is highly regarded among private schools in Indiana.

According to the Bible, the fear of the Lord is the beginning of wisdom (Proverbs 9:10). Wisdom has been defined as the correct use of knowledge. It is possible to have much knowledge and little wisdom. It has also been said that the mark of an educated person is not so much knowing all the answers but knowing how and where to find them. In dealing with campers I have never been afraid to say, "I do not know." Instead I tell them, "Let's go and find out together."

The values acquired in a Christian college go far beyond book knowledge and learning in class. However, I feel strongly that those who fail to apply themselves to academics should stay out of college. Far too many people think that a degree or degrees will set them up for life. There is much more to education than the cap and gown, tassel and hood. Wisdom is not conferred with the degree.

From the April 1947 *Marion College Journal:*

"All right, girls, let's begin with a word of prayer." And the same words used to start her gym classes are characteristic of the entire life of Mildred Jacobs, better known to us as "Millie".

In the middle of May 1924, Millie made her debut into this world, gladdening the home of John W. Jacobs. In spite of the effect it was to have on her later life, she claims not to have even the remotest recollection of the occasion. Fort Wayne, Indiana claims recognition as Millie's hometown, being her birthplace and the scene of most of her subsequent life. For three years she lived in Webster, Indiana where she graduated from high school.

This active senior claims to have led a quiet, uneventful life. However, she did mention something about two brothers and a football. You may draw your own conclusions. Sports have claimed her interest from the start.

The highlight of her life thus far was the day she came to Marion College. Entering into campus life she chose the Eurekan Literacy Society and gave her allegiance, as she expressed it, "from head to toe." This is her third year as girl's gym instructor. Millie was influential in starting the W.A.A. But besides her sports activities she found time for forensic and senior speech recital.

At the top of her list of things that she likes was an emphatic expression of her love for Marion College. When it comes to food, she likes lemon pie. As is so often the case, those things she admires in others are her own dominant qualities. She chooses most of her friends from those who are sincere, purposeful, with Christ-centered lives. If you don't want to lose her friendship, don't chew gum in a public place and don't slam any doors!

Millie beguiles her few spare moments with a stamp collection and she likes to go on an occasional frog hunt.

This last summer she was camp instructor for a group of girls in Canada and she said that it was one of the most enjoyable events of her life, for in it she could combine her two outstanding interests — a witness for Christ and an outlet for sports activities.

The Lord willing, she plans to come back next year to get her B.A. degree. If you have not yet done so, make it a point to get acquainted with Millie. Her cheerful voice and hearty "Hello" can help cheer up many a discouraged moment in your life.

Chapter Six

Camp Wakonda

"Hey Ma, I wanna go, back to Ontario..."

In the spring of my junior year in college, one of my basketball teammates, Evan Gaberdiel Becker ('48), asked me to be her maid of honor. After the wedding rehearsal in Spencerville, Ohio, her father asked if I would consider taking Evan's place at their tourist resort in Canada that summer. My answer was short and to the point.

"Sorry, Dan," I said. "I have to work in the factory this summer."

He quickly replied, "I'll pay you every bit as much as the factory." I pondered my options. On the one hand, I had familiar Fort Wayne and the high-pressure, indoor, tedious work of the factory. On the other hand, I had the opportunity to leave the country for the first time in my life, work outdoors at a Canadian tourist resort for the same pay as the factory, and have plenty of time for swimming and fishing. How could I say no?

A Summer in Paradise

I traveled north by train. The Gaberdiels were late in meeting me at the station in Sault Ste. Marie, Michigan, so I walked about and studied St. Mary's River. On the other side of this river, which flows out of Lake Superior and down into Lake Huron, is the other Sault Ste. Marie, Ontario's twin. The twin cities are also known as the Soo. Small children often confuse the pronunciation with "zoo," providing some humorous misunderstandings.

The Gaberdiels arrived and took me across the river on a small car ferry. From there I noticed the famous Soo Locks. Few people realize that more tonnage passes through Soo Locks than through the Panama Canal. We cleared customs quickly and traveled Highway 17 east some fifty miles to Bruce Mines. The narrow, dusty road we traveled then was a far cry from what it is today. Now a paved, two-lane highway, portions of it are comfortably four lanes wide, with the entire length to be completed as a four-lane highway in the near future. On that trip I was struck by the many old cars in need of repairs. The war had ended two years before, but new cars as well as parts were still scarce.

Bruce Mines is a small community with a rich history. Some of the first copper to be mined in North America was mined there in 1846. I fell in love with the country. I had never seen so much water, so many trees, or so much rock. That rock is a portion of the Precambrian Shield, which exposes some of the oldest rock in the world. The Shield forms an arc from northern Ontario down to the state of Maine.

We crossed over to Gaberdiel's Island (now known as Peterson's Island) in a small motorboat and my things were taken to a private cabin. I saw immediately that I was now in paradise. During my stay that summer, the weather seemed to be nearly perfect. The only rain came during the night. Cool breezes swept in over the water and kept us most comfortable. They also served to remind me how much better I had it here than in hot and humid Indiana. Naturally there were some discomforts, as there are no matter where you live. But the perch fishing was superb and how we swam and swam and swam!

I became acquainted with the flicker when he woke me up each morning by hammering on the window screen of my cabin. My introduction to porcupines came late one night on a sleep-out. We were awakened by guttural sounds that escalated to horrible grunts and then fierce snarls. Slipping away from the huge, flat rock where we had been sleeping, we moved closer to the source of the sounds—a tall white pine where two porcupines were locked in combat. At least, we think they were fighting. It was hard to tell with all the quills!

The tourist resort was comprised of cabins. My work consisted of helping with cooking, washing dishes, and cleaning the cabins. Much of our time that summer was also spent clearing brush and building a boathouse. Using our small boats, we went back and forth to Bruce Mines to the little shops and the post office. We also traveled regularly to the Soo for supplies. The roads were primitive, so the few rainy day trips were often a challenge.

We attended the United Church in Bruce Mines and got acquainted with many people of all ages. I often played tennis with a university student who was home there for the summer. We hiked all over the area. Some of the early copper miners were buried in the village cemetery and we often thought of these first residents as we prowled around the old, interesting mine shafts.

A Foretaste of Heaven

It was while I was working at Gaberdiel's Tourist Camp in 1947 that I was first introduced to St. Joseph Island. We wanted some fresh vegetables and fruit, for which the Island was well known. We also wanted to attend an evening camp meeting service sponsored by the St. Joseph Island Free Methodist Church. We decided to take a ferry from Kensington Point across to the Island, an enjoyable ride on a beautiful, sunny day like this one. (On subsequent visits we sometimes went back and forth to the Island in a small motor boat. On windy days the choppy water made the trip a little scary.) I was intrigued with the cable that seemed to pull the ferry across with very little effort. We drove around the Island and found the veggies we wanted, including some famous St. Joe Island fresh sweet corn. We knew then why the Island was called "The Garden of Algoma."

Director's Camp at Camp Kalalla

We ate our evening meal in the dining hall on the church grounds and later attended the service in the tent. (It stood where the Tabernacle is now located.) I had read about the old-fashioned Methodist camp meetings held in tents, complete with hard, straight-backed seats, saw-dust trails, and a mourner's bench. We had all of that, plus hissing gas lanterns hanging overhead. The joyful singing of the old hymns was like a foretaste of heaven. For the life of me, I cannot recall the name of the speaker or the title of his message. However, the small cabins, the dining hall, the old outhouse down below the hill, and the scores of friendly people made a deep impression on me. (I well remember meeting the Hawdons, the Gilbertsons and Jean Connel—little did I realize then that in a few years I would become a part of this annual gathering.)

During the service there was a dramatic change in the weather. Perhaps that is why I cannot recall the service theme. We did not tarry long after the final hymn. We had no rain gear at all and it was raining cats and dogs. The road back to Bruce Mines was anything but smooth, especially that across Campment D'Ours Island. It was muddy and slippery and full of deep ruts, but we finally made it to the ferry. However, the scariest part of the trip was before us. We were waved on to the small ferry, boarding with fear and trepidation. Bolts of lightning made the night sky seem like day and we could see and feel the angry waves. Thankfully, we made the crossing safely. The storm had let up quite considerably by the time we reached our wee boat at the dock in Bruce Mines. We were wet and weary and glad to be home. Did we ever again return to St. Joseph Island? Of course we did—the sweet corn and those friendly Islanders were too good to forget.

An Intriguing Invitation

The United Church in Bruce Mines, a magnificent, hand-chiseled stone building, was built in 1905 by Methodists. These Methodists were descendants of the original Cornish miners to settle in Bruce Mines in the 1850s when it was one of the largest communities in Algoma. The Presbyterians united with the Methodists in 1917 and have worshiped there ever since.

I was honored to read a selection from *In His Steps* there one Sunday morning. Later in the service, the minister asked for volunteers to counsel at a CGIT (Canadian Girls In Training) camp on Lake McCarroll not far from Echo Bay. This invitation intrigued me, but I already had a job for the summer. On the way home from church, young Paul Gaberdiel shouted above the noise of the boat motor, "Why don't you go to that camp, Millie?" I pretended not to hear him. During dinner Dan said, "We are going on a family fishing trip. You may go with us, or take in that camp." Another easy decision!

A Look Back

My love for camping goes back to my junior year in high school. Some kind soul or organization paid my way to a YWCA camp at Winona Lake in Indiana. We could see the lights of the old Billy Sunday Tabernacle across the lake from our cabins at night.

What most impressed me, though, was our young tennis instructor and counselor, a senior at South Side High School in Fort Wayne. My admiration grew into a conviction: one day I would become a camp counselor too.

That YWCA camp also inspired a tradition that continues today at All Tribes Christian Camp. A Chinese counselor put a watermelon seed between her teeth and tapped the back of her head as if that motion were propelling the seed to the counselor across from her. All of a sudden the air was filled with flying seeds, sending the dining hall into frenzy—much to the dismay of the straight-laced camp director. That incident not only reinforced my desire to be a camp counselor, but also helped me make the commitment that camps should be fun. And what fun we have had with that game over the years. (However, I did make one change. The battles are held outside. Apparently there is some forewarning and preplanning. Recently I learned that a camper was saving seeds in advance so she would have enough "to get Millie good.")

Honor or Honour?

With that memory still warm in my heart, I arrived at Camp Wakonda in Ontario not knowing a soul. The staff and campers were so warm and friendly that I immediately felt at ease. However, I was puzzled as to why they smiled or chuckled whenever I talked. Of course, I had been smiling internally at their accents, not realizing that I had an accent as well. We were soon able to talk about the differences in our pronunciation of such words as "program," "house," "out," "about" and "khaki." And why in the world did they call table napkins "serviettes"? And why would you spell honor as "honour," check as "cheque," labor as "labour," theater as "theatre," and center as "centre"?

But the best was yet to come. I was the leader of a cabin of girls I had never seen before. In order to get better acquainted, I asked them to spell their names so I could memorize them. I asked Adelia to spell her last name slowly, and she said, "O-R-A-ZED-I-E-T-T-I." So I wrote down ORAZEDIETTI. After seeing my spelling, she repeated it and I spelled it the same way. She grabbed my pencil and wrote ORAZIETTI. That day I learned that Z is pronounced ZED! Fifty some years later, Adelia and I are still close friends and I am often reminded of the ZED incident. As I look back, those CGIT girls I worked with my first two summers had so much to do with my returning to Ontario. I am indeed indebted to them.

One morning someone said we were going to have porridge for breakfast. In my mind I envisioned some delicious concoction from the fairytale "The Three Bears." Imagine my disappointment to be served what I had always known as oatmeal. At another meal campers were anticipating Johnnycake. It turned out to be plain old cornbread. But there was one difference. Instead of serving their Johnnycake with soup beans, as my family had always done on wash days, the Wakonda campers poured corn syrup on their servings.

Another Tradition Born

From Camp Wakonda I carried another tradition to All Tribes Christian Camp. Each morning, we began our day around the flagpole repeating this "Salutation of the Dawn":

Look to this day for it is life,
The very life of life.
In its brief course lie all the
Verities and realities of our existence
The bliss of growth
The glory of action
The splendor of beauty.
For yesterday is but a dream
And tomorrow is only a vision.
But today well lived makes
Every yesterday a dream of happiness
And every tomorrow a vision of hope.
Look well therefore to this day
For such is the salutation of the dawn.

from the Sanskrit

Dining Lodge, CGIT Camp Kalalla

The director of the camp, Elizabeth Kerr Pearson, was in charge of all CGIT work in Ontario. One afternoon Betz asked if I would consider directing camps for them the following summer. They would pay me $15.00 for each ten-day camp, plus travel expenses. While this certainly appealed to me, I had to refuse, for it would not provide enough money for my college expenses. I fully expected to spend the next summer in the hot factory again. However, she asked if I would pray about it. Of course I did, but I did not see how it could happen. "O ye of little faith!"

During my senior year at Marion College, I often pondered Betz's offer to direct camps, but it always seemed out of the question financially. One day before chapel, my good friend Ellen Hovland Oldenburg ('46) from Wisconsin was sitting next to me reading her hometown newspaper. I glanced over and spotted a small quote in the upper corner. "Look to this day for it is life," it read. The words jumped off the page and into my heart! I knew then and there that I would be directing camps the following summer. A letter to Toronto was soon in the mail and within a short time I had a schedule and a travel itinerary.

A Whirlwind Year

However, the rest of the school year loomed before me. I had work to do before receiving that "sheepskin" in the spring. As I look back it was a whirl of activities. A very important dream was about to be fulfilled: I was going to graduate from college. I was greatly surprised to find myself listed in "Who's Who Among Students in American Universities and Colleges." The biggest surprise at the end of the school year was to read the kind words that my fellow students and faculty wrote in my "Marionette" (the school yearbook). I was impressed anew that we are a part of all those we meet. I owed them so much. They brought out the best in me.

I was privileged to speak for our class during our graduation ceremonies. My text was Luke 12:48 NKJV: "For everyone to whom much is given, from him much will be required." It had been a very special year and it was not easy to say good-bye to classmates who would soon be scattered all over the world, serving as teachers, ministers, missionaries, and in other worthwhile professions.

Knowing that I was embarking on a God-ordained path, I turned my thoughts to camp. Words are inadequate to express my joy upon returning to Camp Wakonda. Throughout that school year I had often found myself singing a favorite of the many camp songs I had learned at Wakonda: "Hey Ma, I wanna go, back to Ontario..." And here I was. Many of the campers of the past summer had returned. We still teased each other about our accents, but being outnumbered, I soon began to sound like one of them—at least I thought I did. Ending a sentence with "eh?" sounds better to me than "huh?"

The daily Bible studies, our quiet times during Morning Watch, Vespers, and services in our outdoor chapel overlooking the lake all aided us in learning the real meaning of our CGIT motto: "Seek truth, know God, serve others." The CGIT movement had been founded on Luke 2:52: "And Jesus increased in wisdom and stature, and in favour with God and man."

The campers and staff were most receptive and I felt as never before the calm assurance of being in the center of God's will. We sang, swam, boated, hiked, had cookouts, went on overnight hikes, and learned about His creation. It was glorious and confirmed that camping was for me.

Stepping Out on Faith

Before camp ended, the business manager, Nellie McLeod, and the music director, Edith Williams, asked if I would consider a job in the Soo. They were very involved in the CGIT movement which was sponsored by several church denominations in Canada and felt I could add a spark to the program. They wanted to organize groups in the city and down the line in Bruce Mines.

Of course, they explained, this would be a volunteer position. I would have to get a job to support myself. And what did they think that would be? They did not have any idea but were convinced I was needed in the Soo and that the Lord would work something out. I promised to pray about it and flew down to Toronto to direct another CGIT camp. While there I received a telegram from R. J. Smith, the general secretary of the Sault YMCA. Could I meet him for an interview? They were expanding their operation and they were looking for a Girl's Work Director. My friends Nellie and Edith had gone to R. J.'s office and convinced him that I was the person he needed. It did not take long for us to agree that we could work together. I had been praying seriously about my next step and since the door to the mission field had never opened, I felt this must be the direction I was to take.

Millie at the CGIT Ottawa Conference, 1958

I had only worked part time in the Physical Education

Department on campus. The Academic Dean, Dr. Allen Bowman, had urged me to go on for my Master's degree and return to Marion College after the summer. I had graduated without a debt, but there was no money in the bank for further schooling. And frankly I was tired of juggling studies and work. I felt then, and do now, that some actual experience before grad school is the better course of action. I have seen too many students go straight through grad school and come out with their heads full of knowledge, but woefully lacking in experience. All they had was theory. I was looking for as much experience as I could get.

I accepted R.J's offer of $1600 per year, although my teaching friends were earning in the $3000 range. Money did not matter then and it still does not today. God has always met my needs. He would and He had provided. For now I would be teaching physical education and swimming full time at the Y. Another "dream" was about to come to pass. I was on Cloud 9!

Chapter Seven

Lessons from the Y

"ARE SLEIGH-RIDES ALWAYS fun?

"Spirit – Mind – Body"

I had traveled all over the province by bus, car, train, and plane and had met hundreds of wonderful people in the camps. But now I was going back to actually live in Ontario. It was an incredible feeling. While I had grown up in the "lake country" of northern Indiana, those lakes were mere puddles compared to the North

Channel and Lakes Superior, Huron, and Michigan. The huge ships plying the waters and moving skillfully through the locks fascinated me. Precambrian rock seemed to be everywhere. The boulders I had known as a child in Indiana seemed like pebbles in comparison to the huge erratics left behind by the glaciers. The trees seemed to go on forever, with many growing within the city limits. Of all the trees, the white birch was my favorite.

Right at Home

Fort Wayne friends drove me to the Soo with my few worldly possessions. Mr. and Mrs. W. Ferris—the parents of one of my former campers, Lenore—rented me a room in their home on Wellington Street East. It was an easy walk to the Y from there. I ate most of my meals at Mike's on Queen Street or The Girl in Red Restaurant on the same street. I also had many delicious repasts in the homes of Wakonda campers and staff. The Soo people were most friendly and generous and I felt very much at home.

At that time, the Y was located at 123 March Street. It has since been replaced by The Soo Center Building, which contains several business offices. (Dr. Daniel C. Sharp, my eye surgeon, has an office in that building. Because of his skilled hands, I now have 20/20 vision as a result of lens implants in 1998, giving me greener greens and bluer blues.)

Fred Hickam had been managing the women's program at the Y on a part-time basis. His main focus was with the men and boys. If I thought I had been busy at college, I had a surprise in store. I jumped into the women's program with my whole heart and both feet and soon found myself busier that I had ever been in my life.

As we launched a membership drive, I was asked to phone a list of prospective members to see if I could persuade them to rejoin. On one occasion I dialed the wrong number and a very disgruntled woman said emphatically, "This is not the @#!?# residence, and you jolly well know it!" She hung up with a bang, but I persevered.

Our membership grew rapidly and the small pool and gym were soon overflowing. The program included swim and gym classes for all ages, a basketball team, as well as leadership clubs for girls in junior and senior high school. (One of those girls was Anne Abbott Hillstrum. After she completed college, she returned to the Y as a staff member and worked there until her retirement in 1999.)

Deep Water and Northern Lights

My job description included directing Y summer camps at Camp Pauwating on Island Lake north of the Soo. (This caused some Wakonda campers to think of me as a traitor. They could not understand my dilemma.) Ray Stortini directed the boys' camps. To help prepare me for the summer's work, he suggested we spend some time checking out the camp and the overnight sites. We canoed to Lower Island Lake, beached our craft, and hiked through the bush. Somehow we got turned around, for as we approached the water and looked across the bay, we saw our canoe on the far shore. Ray decided to swim over for it rather than go through the bush once again. From time to time I called out to him across the water but got no response. Fear gripped my heart. How would I ever find my way back to civilization, let alone explain how, as a waterfront director, I could have allowed Ray to drown? Sometime later he appeared on the horizon. He had been swimming underwater and missed my calls. (Judge Stortini now resides on St. Joseph Island—the home of All Tribes Christian Camp—and his grandson, Ben, has been one of our campers.)

On an overnight camping at Pauwating, the sky came alive with vivid colors and dancing lights. This was my first experience of the aurora borealis and to this day it was the most extravagant showing I have ever seen. This was also the first time many of the campers had ever seen the northern lights. Some of them were extremely frightened and had to be reassured. It took quite some time to get everyone settled down that night.

With All Thy Might

It was also during this time that I was invited to be the youth worker for the Free Methodist Camp Meetings on St. Joseph Island (the same camp meetings I had attended in 1947 when I worked at Gaberdiel's Tourist Camp). Not being musical or crafty, I did what I knew best. Our camping program included daily Bible studies and the study of nature. I also wanted the campers to learn the following poem.

Creed of the Out-of-Doors

I believe in the wonder of the out-of-doors, in the
inspiration of the stars, and in the
allurement of life in the open.
I believe in the strength of the hills, in the silence of
the night, and in the music of the birds and trees.
I believe also that my body was made for action, that
my mind was made for thinking,
and that my heart was made for loving
in unison with the life in nature.
I believe that to laugh and to sing, to swim and to
walk, to study and play, to eat and be happy,
to be kind and free, to grow strong and good
is my God-given right.
I believe, too, that God is as near as man: that I can
hear Him in the brooks and pines.
And that happiness and lasting peace are mine.
As I live in the atmosphere of kindness,
so near me in the life of the open road.

Carl Strolls

And I definitely wanted them to know Luke 2:52: "Jesus increased in wisdom and stature, and in favour with God and man." And Deut. 6:5: "And thou shalt love the Lord thy God with all thine heart, and with all thy soul, and with all thy might."

Rose and Bernt Gilbertson permitted us to use their property on Twin Lakes for swimming, cookouts, and sleep-overs. We hiked the surrounding area of the campground as well. The young people responded in a wonderful way, but they fell asleep during the evening sermon and that bothered the evangelist. He called me aside and told me I had to stop wearing the youngsters out during the day, for they were not hearing his sermons. I was quick to tell him just to be thankful that they were on the inside, in the pews. Other years they had been on the outside looking in. (I also wanted to tell him, "You put them to sleep, you wake them up!" But I refrained.)

John Knoll became the pastor in 1957. It was not long until the campgrounds took on a new look. He built the tabernacle and had electricity installed in the church, tabernacle, and dining hall. Cooking and serving meals became much easier for Dot Campbell, Annie Eddie, Rose Gilbertson, and others. These conveniences even included refrigeration!

The "C" in YMCA

During my second year at the Y, Gus Kalkin replaced Fred, who had resigned. At first, Gus startled me whenever he came into my office. My door was usually open and he would come in unannounced. Gus all but filled the door, for he was a broad-shouldered man and stood over six feet tall. In reality he was a big, lovable, teddy-bear type. I enjoyed working with him and we soon worked together like hand in glove. He and his wife had fled from the Communists

Millie at her desk

in Estonia. He loved to tell such stories as how he taught Prince Phillip to ski or the many times he had comforted the lad because the boys called him "Greasy Phillip."

Many of the Y members were also Wakonda campers. They all called me Millie instead of Miss Jacobs. I recall walking down Queen Street with a young lad. When he spotted his mother coming toward us, he introduced me as his good friend Millie from the Y. His mother was most indignant and told him to mind his manners. He was confused and hurt. I tried to explain that calling me by my first name was not a sign of disrespect. I have always tried to instill love and respect in those I teach, and I hope the name "Millie" is one remembered for that.

Pianists accompanied our rhythmic exercises. Rita was especially memorable, blessed with a sense of humor like no other. During one session when we were marching around the gym, the music suddenly stopped and she dashed out the door. We continued to parade on without a break. As quickly as she had disappeared, she was back, picking up the music where she had left off. I stepped aside and whispered, "What goes?" Never missing a beat, she said, "My uppers, Millie. I sneezed and out they came." Her quick exit was to wash them off.

This story always reminds me of an elderly Scottish lady I visited. I knocked on the door. She peeked through the curtain and then disappeared. After a bit she opened the door wreathed in a huge smile. "Me ivories, Millie," she said. "I forgot me ivories."

During one Married Ladies Class, we were flat on our backs doing floor exercises. I had often thought of pulling the firecracker trick on them. I could no longer resist. This was the day. I lighted a zebra cracker and tossed it into the air and kept on calling out instructions. The explosion reverberated throughout the gym, so that it seemed the roof and walls would come down. The ladies were on their feet like a flash while I remained horizontal. They soon caught on. Our French member, Clare Mairs exclaimed, "Millie-e-e, Millie-e-e-e. Don't. Me heart, me heart. It eez bad." She is still very much alive as of this writing and living in her own apartment.

When Clare first started classes she asked if I were a "Metadist." I said, "What?" She repeated it and someone across the locker room called out, "Dummy! She wants to know if you are a Methodist." When I replied in the affirmative, she said, "Too bad. You make good Catholic."

Her Bishop did not think so. I was deeply concerned about doing more than merely teaching swimming and fun and games. The Y triangle stands for Body-Mind-Spirit. Apart from living and setting an example, there was little time in regular classes to discuss spiritual matters. However, the pool was free for one hour on Saturday mornings. So I talked to R. J. about the possibility of inviting the younger girls for Bible stories and then letting them have the pool for the hour. He agreed. The response was gratifying. Many of the girls had never heard those beautiful stories before, so the group increased in size every week. One day R. J. said, "Millie, we have a problem. The Bishop has called and demanded I stop the stories." My righteous indignation boiled over. I asked R. J. if the C in YMCA really meant Christian. If it did not, I was resigning then and there. He said, "You really feel strongly about this, don't you?" The classes continued and we never heard from the Bishop again. I still hear from many of those girls, though, and they are grateful for that influence.

I was concerned about the young people's groups in the Soo churches and wanted more contact with them. I arranged to use a large room at the Y for hymn sings and fellowship after the Sunday night services in their churches.

I loved all the age groups I worked with, but the married ladies, the "Y Wives," were special to me. Many of them were busy mothers and had never taken the time to learn to play or swim. They were every bit as enthusiastic as the younger set, though. Our rhythmic exercises, badminton games, and swim classes were the highlights of my day. We also played golf at The Root River Course and had potlucks in various camps and homes. I have kept in touch with a number of these ladies and I consider them close friends some fifty years later.

It was at one of these gatherings north of the Soo that I dreamed about owning property in the area. I thought it would be neat to take up flying and have a fly-in camp. Dan Gaberdiel had offered to sell his island property near Bruce Mines to me for $10,000. That was certainly out of my price range on a $1600 yearly salary. (After many improvements that property is worth a good deal more now, but as you will see later on in this book, the Lord had the right property in mind for me.)

On some evenings, the Y Wives came into the Young Business Women's classes. It was not difficult to tell the married women from the singles in the locker room. The former did not have their husbands to assist them with the hard-to-reach zippers or buttons at the backs of their dresses or blouses!

Growing Pains

The old Y pool was a far cry from being Olympic size, but our enrollment grew by leaps and bounds. The only instructor and lifeguard, I had more children than one person could be responsible for. My request for an assistant fell on deaf ears until I pulled a drowning child out of the pool. We then hired Lillian Hunter, a former Wakonda camper, who was then a high school student. She was a decided asset. The entire Hunter family became special to me. Lillian's little sister, Ruth, later was our nurse at a Girl Scout Camp in New York State. Once when Ruth was a little girl, she plopped herself down on the tail of my skis and said, "Now go, Millie Jenkins, go!" One aunt, Ellice, was on the CGIT Work Board, and another, Dora, was the Sunday School Superintendent at St. Paul's Presbyterian Church where I helped with youth groups. Their homes on Wellington Street West and McMeekin Street were my second homes and I spent many holidays there. When it was time for me to take the road test for my Ontario driver's license, they loaned me their car. It became a tradition for me to take Christmas trees back to several of the faculty at Marion College during my Thanksgiving trip. The trees came from Dora and Ellice's sister, Kitty, who was married to Milroy Scott and lived out on a farm near the Airport Road. Kitty gave me the antique kitchen cabinet that is now in my porch. I miss those people very much.

During Easter Break, we gave free swimming lessons to non-members. Many of them were underprivileged and did not take our "shower before swim" rule seriously. I tested them by rubbing my thumb over their wrists. The dirt and grime flaked off one tyke's wrist. When I told her to take a shower, she rolled her eyes and said, "Your thumb's dirty." I was firm. "Back to the shower, kiddo!" I replied. "And be sure to use the soap." She did.

I was standing at the deep end of the pool when she returned. She jumped into the water feet first. She went down once, came up for air, and went down again. She came up a second time. The third time, I pulled her out by the seat of her pants. "You told me you could swim!" I admonished. "I can," she said, "but not in deep water."

Two of the first women on the Y Board of Directors were Mrs. Alex Sinclair, wife of Dr. Sinclair, and Mrs. William Brian, wife of Mayor Brian. They made an impact on the organization in many ways. Almost immediately, the entrance to the building and the main lounge received some much-needed attention, reflecting a woman's touch. Mrs. Brian frequently stopped by my office to see me. In reality, she was checking up on Millie. She knew my schedule as well as I did. Often I failed to take time for lunch, and dinner too, for the days were so full and exciting. In one session she drove home a point I have never forgotten. It undoubtedly accounts for my state of good health today. She asked me where I ate lunch that day. With a sheepish grin, I had to admit that I had not eaten lunch. "Millie," she said, "if you don't look after yourself, no one else will." Ever since that time, with few exceptions, nutrition has been important to me. I feel sorry for those who have not had the opportunity to learn that lesson from a Mrs. Brian, too.

The least enjoyable aspect of my work was putting out the Y monthly bulletin. Gathering the information and putting it together was not difficult, but running it off on an old worn-out mimeograph machine was horrible. I had ink under my nails from one issue to the next. If I were ever tempted to take up swearing again, that was the time.

Snow Stories

One weekend during the winter the girls' basketball team was scheduled to play in Sudbury. A storm warning and heavy snow prompted R. J. to cancel the trip, but the girls were so "hyped up" to go, that he conceded to their wishes. I didn't think we would get very far, but I knew I at least had to give it a try or I would not be able to live with them. We followed a snowplow to Echo Bay. When he turned off, we plowed on but ended up in deep snow in the Bar River flats a few miles east of Echo Bay. Fortunately, the train stopped in Echo Bay, allowing the team to return to the Soo. However, I stayed with the car until a snowplow and wrecker pulled me out. You may have thought I was stupid, but the team thought I was a "good sport." It was my first experience in heavy snow and I loved it.

In the winter Gus and I worked with the city fire department to make an ice rink next door to our building. We spent many late nights putting the finishing touches on it with an old garden hose. When I first moved to the Soo, I was fascinated by all the boys and men trudging down the streets with their heavy equipment bags, heading to and from hockey practices and games. It still intrigues me. Hockey is THE Canadian game. I remember how pleased I was when someone gave me a hockey stick and a puck as a joke. I prize them even today. I miss the voice of Foster Hewitt on the old radio favorite, "Hockey Night in Canada."

On weekends and in my spare time, I worked with CGIT leaders and groups. We offered seminars and workshops for the leaders and organized new groups in the Soo, in Bar River and in Bruce Mines. Echo Bay also had an active group. During one visit to Bruce Mines, I experienced snowshoes for the first time. The wife of the banker in that town and I snowshoed to Gaberdiel's Island. On the way back, I well remember her pointing to the roof and steeple of the United Church and then to the roof of the new Community Building and stating, "My heart is sad, for the Community Center has taken the place of the church in our community."

My first efforts at skiing took place when I was a child on the steep hillsides on the Nickel Plate Railroad near the Bass Farm. We used wooden barrel staves and held them on our shoes with rubber jar rings. That equipment left much to be desired. My friends in the Soo insisted that I learn to ski. That was not a hard sell. I was eager to really ski with the proper equipment. We did not have far to go to find a suitable ski hill in the city. As I drive about the Soo now, seeing housing developments on our old ski hills makes me sad. I had the fun of skiing at Searchmont, too, before the days when you had to stand in line for the tow lifts.

The Sleigh Ride

From the time I was a child, I had read stories about horse-drawn sleigh rides. The colorful pictures that accompanied the articles made me envious of those who lived in the north and could experience that kind of fun. Winter came early to the Soo that first year, and talk of skiing and sleigh rides soon followed. I could hardly wait. Late in October the snow was blowing down Queen Street like tumbleweeds in the west. Soon-to-be small drifts scurried here and there. Frost nipped my ears several times as I walked home from the Y late at night. I was delighted and thought it would never, never get cold enough for me. (As of this writing it still has not—even at -40 F. My friends will know I am getting old when I complain about the snow and the cold.)

The Young People from First Baptist Church invited me to join them for their winter outing. I accepted with readiness and dressed warmly enough to withstand the coldest weather. We went out on what is now Highway 17 north, past the old orphanage and The Davey Home. The Trans Canada Highway was only being talked about then. It was a picture-perfect evening and we had the road to ourselves. However, instead of singing—as I had expected—the fellows started to toss the girls off the sleigh. I resolved to remain seated on that bale of straw, no matter what. No one had warned me about this possibility, but soon I was flying through the air—not into the soft snowbank at the side of the road, but directly out the back and onto the hard, snow-packed road. The party continued on without me.

My right leg had bent under me and I could not move. I knew a bone had snapped. Ruth Tolley Amy, a former Camp Wakonda nurse, and one of the fellows ran back to check on me. I convinced them my leg was "broke." The fellow ran to a nearby farmhouse and phoned for a cab. We went back to the Tolley's house on Herrick Street. Ruth attempted to make me comfortable by elevating my leg and giving me two aspirins. By midnight we knew the hospital was my destination, for the pain had become unbearable. The X-ray department was not open at night, but at least they gave me some stronger medication. They placed a sandbag on either side of my leg and the pain became almost bearable. I slept until an hour or so later when I awoke with a scream. The offending leg was tucked up under me. An X-ray the following morning proved that I was right. The leg indeed was "broke" and a hospital stay followed. I phoned my sister, Ruth, and told her I was in the hospital. I can still hear her say, "You are where?"

I had worked with the Sunday school and CGIT at John Street United Church. Nellie McLeod, Mary Graham, and many of the Wakonda campers also attended there. Nellie's husband, Saul, was the lockmaster at the Sault Locks and once allowed me to open the locks for a small craft. Nellie and her brother, Earl Orchard, were known as "Mr. and Mrs. Camp Wakonda." Mary Graham was always a gracious lady and her family accepted me as one of the family. It was my privilege to conduct her funeral in later years. With this connection to the John Street United, it was only natural for the minister to call on me in the hospital. When he entered my room he exclaimed, "Millie, Millie, don't ever trust those Baptists! They don't even break the ice before they baptize you!"

My broken leg and hospital stay brought the Stewart family from Leeburn into my life. Helen Stewart, now Mrs. Ron McLeod, was my hospital roommate. Her twin sister Shirley and her mother visited Helen often and we have kept in touch ever since. For many years Shirley has taught religious education in the Algoma District schools. She has also been the heart of Galilean Bible Camp at Blind River and has been a strong religious influence on many young people in the area over the years.

Time-Out

Since I could not do my job at the Y with a broken leg, R. J. kindly suggested I take paid leave and go home to recuperate in Indiana. It was some time before I could put my weight on the walking cast, but as soon as I was able, I took the Greyhound bus from Soo, Michigan to Detroit, and then to Fort Wayne. Fortunately, the back seats of the bus were vacant, so I was fairly comfortable on the trip and could keep my leg elevated. I was back home in Indiana.

Ten days after my return to Marion, I was refereeing an Amphic-Eurekan basketball game in the college gym. I healed fairly quickly and returned to my duties at the Y. By the time the cast was removed, however, I had lost fifteen to twenty pounds.

It was while working with the CGIT in the Soo that I often traveled to Toronto by train to attend provincial meetings. It was a most pleasant journey. The train departed from the Soo at 5 p.m. As we slowly moved out, invariably someone would dash after the train to post a letter in the box on the side of the last car. We usually had breakfast in the Muskoka area and then arrived in Toronto at Union Station in time for our meetings the next morning.

At one of those sessions, I met Mrs. J. R. MacGregor, or Penny. She was the personification of CGIT and one of the founders of Camp Kalalla, the Ottawa CGIT camp. Camp Kalalla is located some distance from Ottawa in the Gatineau Hills of Quebec. As business manager, Penny offered me the opportunity of directing this camp for a season. However, I was obligated at the Y and was not able to accept the offer until a later time.

A New Direction

After three years at the Y, I no longer felt challenged. I had the inner conviction that my work was done. The programs were operating at full capacity and there were no plans to expand the facilities. My sister Betty was now involved as a volunteer in the Fort Wayne Girl Scouts. She informed me that the Allen County Council needed a district director. This, along with the opportunity to complete my B.A. degree, was the incentive I needed to leave the Soo.

It was not easy to leave. I was given a number of farewell parties and many tearful good-byes. Among the parting gifts was a three-piece set of luggage from the Y Wives Class. Those lovely women couldn't know then the mileage I would eventually get out of those suitcases!

Chapter Eight

Wearing the Uniform

(1953-1962)

Changing Currents

"On my honor I promise..."

As a child I didn't think much about Girl Scouts. Our neighborhood gang provided us with more than our share of group activities, competition, and camping. And besides, Girl Scouts didn't wear overalls—they had to wear uniforms and dresses!

My first real encounter with the organization came years later through my sister Betty. She was involved up to her ears as a troop leader, neighborhood chair, cookie chair—you name it, she was involved in it! Whenever I came home for a visit from my YMCA work, she shared her enthusiasm and entertained me regarding all the fun and many satisfactory experiences she was having. Naturally, her daughters and my nieces, Diane and Marjorie, were Girl Scouts.

My brother Jack, his wife Naomi and their children, John, Niles, Stephanie and Cindy, were also very much involved in Girl Scouts and Boy Scouts. Again and again I was asked, Why did I not join them?

When Sis realized my interest in YMCA work was waning, she urged me to apply for a position with the Fort Wayne and Allen County Girl Scout Council. Sure that I was qualified and that I would love it, she sent me an application form before I left the YMCA. However, I set the material aside. I had decided instead to complete the B.A. degree I had started at Marion College and then begin my master's degree at Ball State Teacher's College.

Shoveling Food In and Shoveling Snow Out

My college roommate Velva was teaching in Alexandria and found me a room with some of her teaching friends. Ball State was only twenty miles away. I could commute on a daily basis with a friend. When the teachers where I was rooming learned that I loved to cook, they offered me free room and board if I would prepare their meals. Of course I agreed. The best part of that deal was that they insisted on doing the dishes. The sky was the limit on the food budget, so we had some very exotic meals. It was a delightful experience and easy on my bank account.

The Alexandria teacher's group was fun as well as stimulating and included many evenings of interesting conversations. I came home from school one afternoon to catch Edith shoveling snow from the sidewalk. She had just celebrated her fortieth birthday, and I nearly had a fit. Forty and shoveling snow? That was a no-no. At that time, the news frequently reported the deaths of people over forty who had overexerted while shoveling snow. I gave Edith a jolly good scolding and relieved her of the shovel.

I chuckle now whenever I recall that incident. At seventy-seven years of age, I still shovel snow, chop wood, and do any number of very active tasks without a thought of that "fateful" number forty. Dick shoveled a lot of snow, too, during his eighty-two years. Times and conceptions do change.

Although my classes at Ball State were enjoyable, my financial situation did not allow me to enroll for the second year in order to finish my degree. Betty reminded me that the position in the Girl Scouts was still open. I submitted my application. Nothing else had opened up and I liked what I had read about the Girl Scout emphasis on character building and camping. However, the application process seemed long and arduous. I not only had to be approved by the local council but by the national council as well. This involved numerous forms and several interviews, but finally I was accepted. I felt comfortable with my decision and knew I was following God's will.

Sometimes Dignified, Sometimes Not

All I had to do was order my uniform from W & D's (Wolf & Dessauer Department Store, the store that carried Girl Scout uniforms and equipment), fill out a few more forms, and prepare myself for an orientation period. As part of the professional staff, I was expected to wear a uniform at the office and whenever I represented the organization. The uniform consisted of a smart green suit, white blouse, a green bow tie, and beret. I found wearing a uniform to be wonderfully convenient. I never had to waste any time in the morning trying to decide what to wear, and it was certainly easy on the clothes budget. I was also conscious that when I wore the uniform, I needed to remember who I was and what organization I represented. You can be sure I never jaywalked in downtown Fort Wayne.

One day my staff and I were carrying items from the office to

W & D's. We wanted to do several display windows for Girl Scout Week. It fell to my lot to carry the two eight-foot flagpoles and flags. Wouldn't you know I made an attempt to go through the revolving doors with those poles! It was the largest and busiest store in the city, so my struggle was conspicuous, to say the least. I wanted to drop dead on the spot. It was by far the most embarrassing moment of my life and I still blush when I think of my stupidity. Haste makes…

In Uniform

On another day I was walking briskly down a long hall at one of our local high schools. I was scheduled to speak to a group of girls who wanted to form a senior troop. I could hear the echo of my heels hitting the floor as I marched along. All of a sudden a handsome young male student appeared out of nowhere. He clicked his heels and gave me a smart military salute. I in turn clicked my heels and returned his salute. He gave me a million-dollar smile and went on his way. That made my day and almost made up for the revolving door fiasco!

A Bundle of Black Fur

During this time my sister's husband, George, was killed in a car accident. Betty needed some moral and financial support in raising my two nieces, so I lived with them for a year. The girls were a joy to me even though I had missed most of three very important years in their growing up. I was especially concerned that they had shown little or no emotion at their father's death. There were few tears and they were reluctant to talk about their father.

I thought a puppy might help, so I invested in a small black bundle of fur, a cocker spaniel. We named him Sir Reginald or Reggie for short. Marjorie, the younger of the two girls, and Reggie became fast friends. Early one morning I heard a sobbing sound. I found a little girl and a puppy curled up on a rug. My wee niece was crying her little heart out. The dam had finally broken. I picked the two of them up and carried them to a rocking chair. We sang and whispered soft love notes about her daddy. As we rocked and sang, I realized that both the little girl and the puppy had gone to sleep. I tucked them into Marjorie's bed and went off to work. The puppy was good for all of us.

Unsung Heroes

Betty remarried the following year and I moved out. In the meantime, Velva had changed school systems and had come to Fort Wayne. We decided to share an apartment and found one on East Wayne Street. It was within walking distance of the Girl Scout office, which was then located at the corner of Wayne and Harrison Streets in the old Central Building.

Hired as a District Director, I was in charge of several neighborhoods as well as the day and troop camp operations. I was soon off to East Lansing for a three-week orientation or basic training course at Michigan State's new Kellogg Center. The course was most enlightening, teaching us the history and both the inside and outside of the Girl Scout organization. We were also introduced to the very latest administrative principles, such as delegation of duties. I was surprised to learn that the Girl Scout training course used a lesson from the Bible to bring this point home: Moses and his father-in-law in Exodus 18:17-23. While I was familiar with this lesson from my own studies of Scripture, I was delighted to see so many in the class show new respect for the Bible, something they had thought of as just another book.

The course also greatly emphasized how to work with volunteers. They were and continue to be the very heart and soul of the organization. Our role as staff was to be facilitators. The Girl Scouts was not our organization—it belonged to the girls and leaders. We were there to assist them.

Lansing was full of spiritual lessons for me. I will long remember the Lenten communion service I attended with another student who was Lutheran. The minister delivered a very powerful message, then I knelt at the altar in that small chapel while he applied a cross on my forehead with a piece of charcoal. I had never experienced this Ash Wednesday tradition before and found it was most moving. Good Friday took on a whole new meaning for me after that.

When I returned to Fort Wayne I endeavored to put my training into practice. Most of my responsibilities involved working with adults. Training new leaders, the majority of whom were mothers, was stimulating and enjoyable work. However, this also involved one of my biggest problems: getting mothers to realize that their daughters were not the only girls in the troop! They had to be leaders of all of the girls. That problem holds true today. Mothers often don't even realize how they show favoritism to their own children. But in doing so, they alienate them from the rest of the troop. I'm sure this holds true in the Boy Scouts, as well as in other organizations in which parents take an active part.

Teaching women at the YMCA to relax and to learn to play was one thing. Teaching women such as these to serve was a very different matter, but still most satisfying. I admired the busy wives and mothers who juggled family responsibilities with leading a group of girls. But the women who volunteered and did not have children in scouting really caught my attention. They had no "vested" interest but simply served because they loved children. My hat went off to them. Still, I admired all of these women for giving of their time and energy.

Teaching our volunteers to say "No" was another challenge. So many of our brand-new leaders felt they had to respond to every request made by the girls, the girls' parents, and the council. I always told them a good leader had to know when to say "No." Sis never learned that lesson. She was available to the leaders in her neighborhood at all hours of the day or night. Her phone rang off the hook. I learned much from observing her, and in my training sessions advised my trainees to avoid phone calls that would disturb others at meals or late at night.

Volunteers are to be commended. Where would the Scouts, Guides, CGIT, schools, churches, and other organizations be without them? Every child needs a role model and leaders of these youth groups are in the perfect position to be just that. I have long maintained that the strength of any organization lies in the character of its leaders. God grant that we may be true to our trust.

I am reminded of an intelligent, enthusiastic woman who enrolled in one of our leader's courses. She seemed like a perfect candidate for a leadership position until near the end of the course. That's when she asked in all innocence how much and when the leaders were paid. I did not have to answer her. Another woman in the group said, "We get paid every day with satisfaction in sharing with the girls."

The first woman was incredulous. "You mean you do all of this for nothing?" Needless to say she did not return to finish the course.

No one has ever been able to calculate all the time and energy expended by volunteers around the globe. They deserve our respect and admiration

I think now of the scores who have volunteered at All Tribes Christian Camp as leaders, counselors, advisors, workers, builders, and encouragers. The camp is a testimony to many, many generous volunteers.

The Ultimate

The most enjoyable aspect of my job with the Girl Scouts was contact with the girls. They were the reason I had decided to don the uniform in the first place. Directing the camps where I would interact with them directly was the icing on the cake. The enthusi-

Millie greeting the girls. Sister Betty in white with her troop.

asm of the Brownies who attended our day camps made each session exciting. Since leaders came with their girls to our troop camp (Agnes McMillen Camp), I served principally as a resource person and activities coordinator for the various troops on the site.

When Gina Bond, the director at Camp Ella J. Logan, resigned to go to Burma, I was asked to take her place. I was flattered and elated. That meant spending most of the spring and summer living at the camp. Why would I not say yes?

I had just returned from a camping course at Camp Edith Macy, the national training center near New York City. One of our instructors was Catherin T. "Kit" Hammett, author of *Your Own Book of Campcraft*. She had written many books and owned her own camp in Vermont. (I had the opportunity to spend an afternoon with her there and I can point back to that afternoon as the moment I first dreamed of owning my own camp someday.) I also benefited from the camping expertise of Marie Gaudette, who was on the national staff of the Girl Scouts. It was hands-on camping as well as theory. While I knew camping was fun, I had been totally unaware of all its ramifications. I soaked up the Camp Edith Macy camping course like a sponge and could hardly wait to put everything I learned into practice at Logan.

(One of the highlights at Camp Macy had nothing whatever to

do with camping. On our day off most of the trainees trooped off to shop in New York City. A few of us chose to go to the Yankee Stadium to see a baseball game. We saw Mickey Mantle hit three home runs off Bobby Feller to beat the Cleveland Indians. We knew from the sound of the crack of the bat that the ball was going out of the park. I can still hear it.)

I accepted the challenge of Logan with enthusiasm but was surprised at the rundown condition of the camp. It took a great deal of hard work with the help of many volunteers to bring it up to safety standards. That experience taught me much about camp maintenance. No one thought to teach that aspect at Camp Macy. They assumed that every camp had full-time caretakers. Logan did not at that time.

While we divided our camping activities according to various age groups, we all came together for many meals at the lodge. The same was true of some campfires, although most activities took place in the individual units.

Our waterfront at Logan was one of the best. Cam and Brownie Parks from Garrett, Indiana had spent over a quarter of a century at Logan. Cam taught high school and coached, so he had his summers free. The campers all learned to swim, and many advanced to lifeguard status. Boats, canoes, and sailboats were available to those who were qualified swimmers. Canoe trips and overnights at a nearby island were a favorite activity. The longer canoe trips with Cam to nearby rivers or chains of lakes was the ultimate. Cam and Brownie touched many lives at Logan.

All went well there for several seasons. The camps were full each session. We even stopped advertising because satisfied and happy campers did that for us. I could not have been happier. And then came the bombshell!

The Next Step

The president, Evelyn Blitz, and the personnel committee wanted to come to the camp for dinner and a tour of the camp. Energetic and the epitome of dynamic leadership, Evelyn had a big influence on me. She seemed to know everyone in Fort Wayne. I admired her and we worked well together. The personnel committee was made up of men and women in the community who held positions in corporations and businesses. They advised us on any and all staff situations such as salaries, promotions, and contracts. We all enjoyed our meal together, after which we toured the various units. Then the committee asked the assistant director to take over my duties so that they could talk to me.

We sat around the fireplace in the lodge making small talk. They were all much too chatty, too flattering about the appearance of the camp, the meal, the well-being and happiness of the campers and the staff. I kept thinking, "Why are you here? Let's get down to business."

Finally the chairman cleared his throat and asked, "Have you heard the news? Our executive director, Helen Shaw, has resigned."

What? That was incredible. Girl Scouting was her life. She had been around for years. What was going on? They shared a few details and said that it had been her decision. Then they said, "We would like for you to make the decision to take her place."

I could not believe my ears. They wanted me to try to fill Helen's shoes. I thought up several reasons why I would not be able to handle the job, but they shot all my arguments down. They did not need an immediate answer, they said. I should take my time to think it over. However, they were convinced that I could do it and they saw no need to advertise outside of the council. Furthermore, the national staff member for our area was in agreement with them.

I do not recall hearing taps that night. I found an old stump by the craft lodge that was a comforting place to meditate. I went there that night to think and to pray. Did I want to get involved in administration to that degree? Could I handle it? What contact would I have with the girls? This would put me further away from our end product: the girls in the troops, the campers. Did I want the responsibility of supervising the clerical and professional staff? Could I challenge them enough to help them grow on the job? What about camping? In my mind, directing Logan had been ideal camping—the ultimate in camping!

On the other side of the coin was my own professional growth. I would need courses in administration and other aspects of the position to further qualify me for the task. I definitely would be stretched. And what an opportunity to help thousands of girls and leaders to fulfill their promise: "On my honor…" Was the Lord opening a new door for me?

In due time I gave them my answer. If I could direct Logan for at least one more year before accepting this position, I was willing to give it a try—with their support and the help of the Lord.

Leading Limberlost

For quite some time we had been hearing about the "Green Umbrella." The National Council was promoting the idea of consolidating smaller councils and lone troops into larger groups. Girls, leaders, and troops would all benefit from the move, they said. The proposed new council would include Adams, Allen, Dekalb, Huntington, Steuben, and Wells counties. Needless to say there were many late night meetings, discussions, misunderstandings, lessons learned, compromises hammered out, and new friends made before we became the new Limberlost Council.

Limberlost Council was comprised of eight thousand girls and two thousand leaders. Yes, there were many satisfying experiences. Yes, I felt as if I had two thousand bosses—all volunteers. No, I did not please them all, but I learned much. And I widened my circle of friends.

I still admire Ursula Miller, a vice president then, who was a major influence in my taking this position. She had a mind like a steel bear trap. I keep in touch with her and her own Girl Scout troop of seven daughters. Ellenore Bowyer was a capable neighborhood chairman and has remained a loyal friend. It was she who loaned me the money to buy property and build my dream home. Hy and Lorry Goldenberg from Huntington were also very special. (Hy left us about the same time as Dick.)

Rare is the fall trip to Indiana that I do not have dinner with Girl Scout friends Della Hutton, Hertha Moran, Helen Pickering, and

Betty Zern in Garrett. Several others are no longer with us.

As I look back, working with Mr. Mac, founder of Central Soya was a high point. Unlike Lee Beard, I knew Dale McMillen Sr. was a millionaire. We spent a great deal of time together planning and building a new lodge at Camp McMillen in honor of his wife Agnes. Details on that endeavor, the Girl Scout role in celebrating the 20th anniversary at Central Soya, the McMillan's 50th wedding anniversary, and his 75th birthday celebration—all on the same day—is a story all by itself.

It would take pages and pages to tell about all of my wonderful experiences with the camps in the Limberlost Girl Scout Council, as well as other councils. We saw much change and incorporated many new ideas. I can only mention a few memorable highlights.

After my trip to Kenya, Camp Ella Logan adopted a "Jungle Living" camp theme that summer. It was marvelous to see how creative the campers and staff members were in developing the agenda. Cam and Brownie Parks encouraged the beginner swimmers to swim above the imaginary crocodiles. The young swimmers did as they were told and their strokes improved greatly. The Jungle Bridge we put across one of the ravines added color and excitement. Nearly everyone had a hand in putting it in place. One heavy hay rope served as our walk. Two others were used for hand railings. Only a few did not venture across.

Roughing it

At a camp in New York, the council offered the girls a wide variety of programs. They could register for one of many ten-day sessions: back-packing or biking to the White Mountains; tenting and working on a nearby farm; riding and caring for the animals in a horse unit; living in a unit of covered wagons as pioneers among other units. It was a challenge to coordinate all of these activities. All of the food came from our camp kitchen and kept Bev Hill, our business manager, on her toes. The administrative staff was frequently invited to eat with the campers in their units. On our way back to our tents one evening, my assistant Tina Flook was heard to mutter, "What a burn-out!" The girls had burned every item on the menu, except the beverages.

The International Round-up encampments in Colorado and Vermont were undoubtedly the most stimulating and exciting Girl Scout events I have ever experienced. Can you imagine a camp of 10,000 men, women, and teenage girls from all over the world? It was a privilege to work under the direction of Kit Hammett once again.

An interesting aspect of the Round-ups was being on the sites while they were being set up. We watched those huge tent cities come to life. Ditch witches could be spotted here and there making shallow ditches to bury the temporary power and water lines. The PVC black plastic pipe had just come into use and men were fanning out in every direction with small handsaws fitting the joints together. I was intrigued and impressed.

Then came the United States Army with their olive-drab canvas tents, which were set up for our administrative areas. The girls soon followed with their smaller, more colorful tents. It reminded me of a huge flower garden. With the tents came thousands of excited teenagers. The camps came alive. Camps void of campers have never excited me.

The most important tent of all had to be the Army Field Hospital, staffed by military personnel. More than a few campers were treated for everything from broken bones to appendicitis. It was incredibly staffed and well run.

The avenue of fluttering flags, representing colors of every country included, stirred my inner being. Just to walk past those flags flapping in the wind gave me goose bumps. Other inspirational moments still linger in my mind. I will never forget a large chorus of girls in Colorado who sang "God Bless America." And the voices of the Von Trapp Family Singers in Vermont still ring in my ears. "Doh, a deer, a female deer . . ." and so on.

Another Dream Realized

We are all born dreamers. In fact, we can know we are "out of it" when we stop dreaming. Dreams about the future are as important to me today as they were when I was a child. The first one I can remember came when I was very young. My father's pilot friend flew him over our home in his plane. He had told me to watch for the plane at a certain time. When they swooped low over us, I well remember standing there with my hands in my back overall pockets, looking up, and saying out loud, "Some day I am going to fly an airplane."

That dream came to pass during the time I worked with the Girl Scouts. A friend had organized a "Wing Scout Troop," so I took lessons at the old Smith Field in Fort Wayne. As I was taxiing down the runway to take off on my first solo flight, I heard Wally my instructor hollering at me as he ran behind the plane. I came to a stop and finally heard what he was yelling: "Fasten your seatbelt!" It was dangling along the ground outside the door for all the world to see.

The thrill of actually flying all alone up there is beyond describing. Before a later flight, I called my nephew Chuckie and told him to stand out in his yard and watch for me. His family lived in the same neighborhood where I had once stood entranced with flight. As I flew over I could hear him yell, "Come down, Aunt Mildred! Come down!"

I often made a point of flying over the Girl Scout office in downtown Fort Wayne, then located at the corner of Wayne and Harrison Streets. I looked down at the old Central Building that housed our offices and realized how easy it was from up above to get the right perspective on some very tough problems we were attempting to solve.

With the costs of fuel, insurance, annual medical checkups, and owning or renting a plane, I soon discovered I had a champagne appetite on a beer income. But, I had experienced the thrill of flying a plane and realizing a dream!

Like my flying dream, I knew when it was time to take off my

Girl Scout uniform. After nine years of growing and giving, I sensed God leading me in a different direction.

Chapter Nine

A Year on the Island

(1963-1964)

"Out in the woods and fields with God."

M.J.T.

Few people I know "wear one hat." Most of us wear several hats or play several roles at the same time. So while I was involved in Girl Scouting, I also served as the president of Marion College's alumni association. After leaving the Girl Scouts, I enrolled at Indiana University to complete my graduate studies, but continued as alumni president of my Alma Mater.

The dream to take a sabbatical after my graduate studies took on tangible substance when I went to the Soo to ski during Christmas break. I was visiting in the home of Fred and Annie Eddy on Front Street. (That street no longer exists. The Doctors Building and parking lot replaced it.) Bernt Gilbertson happened to drop by. I asked him if he had a cabin for rent on St. Joseph Island the following year

"Sure," he said. "I have two, one right next door (a small home at that time, but since then enlarged by Greg and Henrietta Gilbertson), and another cabin three miles away."

Without seeing either cabin I said, "Save the one three miles away." The deal was sealed.

I knew absolutely nothing about the property or condition of the cabin. Later that summer, Meg and I stopped by to check it out. Although she simply shook her head, I thought it looked great. Of course, in my exuberance and anticipation I overlooked much that would need attention. What did catch my eye were some old magazines lying around. The cover picture of one issue of *Maclean's* (a Canadian weekly news magazine) featured a woman skiing. I wrote, "I'll be skiing you!" and tacked the picture on the inside door, saying aloud, "I will be back!" I still have that picture mounted on a board. And I have been "seeing and skiing" on this site for many years.

The Simple Life

Finally, my graduate studies were over. In the spring of 1963 I packed everything possible in my '59 Chevy and headed for St. Joseph Island. I do not remember all of the items I packed, but one was Reggie, my black cocker spaniel. This was Lady Regina, not Sir Reginald, the original Reggie who had remained at my sister's house. Another very important item was my Bible. I left the concordances behind, however. Professor Main had often instructed us to read the Bible and find the hidden meanings ourselves. The year on the island would give me the perfect opportunity to do so.

Ready for my year on the Island

I also took a salt block for the deer, a .22-caliber rifle and shells, fishing gear, and several cases of dog food. Although I fully intended to live the simple life, I did not expect my dog to. And I made sure to have a plentiful supply of candles and kerosene because there was no electricity on this property.

To dream about isolating myself for a year was one thing. To drive into the yard and actually be there was another matter. Reggie jumped out of the car and ran around barking like crazy. I did not feel like barking. In fact, I stood there and asked aloud, "Do you really know what you are in for?"

My work at the Y and with the Scouts had been demanding work, but very fulfilling. The year of graduate studies at Indiana University had been satisfying as well, but I felt the need for a complete change. I wanted to get away from it all. I wanted to read the Bible through in a quiet setting to learn more about my Creator and His creation. (I accomplished my goal of reading the Bible through in a year, but I shall forever be learning more about His Word and His glorious creation.)

My early childhood outdoor experiences, Girl Scout camping and CGIT encounters in Ontario and Quebec had whetted my appetite for more of the out-of-doors. Yes, I had read Thoreau, but mine was not an attempt to be a modern day version of him. I planned to bake my own bread and make everything from scratch. I brought no mixes or "instant anything" with me. I would fish and shoot rabbits and squirrels, and although I knew other game abounded, I had no desire to try beaver, coons, or skunks. I would forage for tender fiddleheads from young ferns, a delicacy that tasted like asparagus. I also noticed that asparagus from a neglected bed nearby had gone wild all over the property. And there was an abundance of greens for salads, as well as rhubarb, berries, apples, and pears to provide me with fruit. Since I was experienced in cutting my own wood, I figured that as much as possible I should be able to live off the land.

That first night I swept out the cabin's three rooms: a kitchen, bedroom, and living room. I also made a trip to the spring barrel for a fresh pail of water. (The property is blessed with many springs—at one time it was known as the Crystal Springs Farm. The springs provide water for the pond. A wooden barrel with an aluminum lid from an old washing machine is still in use.)

It did not take long to unpack the car and settle in. Reggie and I hiked about and I soon realized that cleaning up the property would be no small task. It would be a job just to pick up the old tin cans, bottles, antique apple crates, and trash of every description.

Following supper, we decided to bed down for the night. Rose had not yet delivered the promised bed so I unrolled the sleeping bag on the floor. Reggie curled up beside me, but wasn't quiet for long. She kept busy most of the night trying to catch the mice that scampered back and forth across the sleeping bag! The next day I covered the mouse holes with the ends cut from the dog's food tins, then set some traps.

Not Exactly A Recluse

I soon realized that I would never be completely alone and isolated. Often in the weeks that followed, I had help cutting wood. My neighbors, Elgin and Donna Eddy, had planted a garden for me before my arrival that first spring. It flourished and added a welcome variety to my wild foods. (What fun it is now to have their grandsons Joshua and Matthew as campers.) Generous friends dropped by to see what I was up to and were quick to lend a hand. Later in the fall they would bring gifts of venison, moose, and bear meat.

Bernt had never mentioned how much rent he was going to charge me, so when he dropped by one day I asked him. He said, "Millie, if you will teach the Young People's Sunday school class and meet with them on Friday nights there will be no rent." That was good news, for I had just completed my master's degree and had no gainful employment. Glancing around, I asked if he would mind if I cleaned the place up.

"Do what you want," he said, "for it surely needs some work."

Seven trailers and two truckloads later I could begin to see a difference in the place. Each day I was up at the crack of dawn. There was so much to see and do. The teenage boys from St. Joseph Island Free Methodist Church who helped me could never catch me eating breakfast. One day Gordie Hawdon asked why I got up with the chickens, for his mother never got up that early. I was quick to respond, "I don't have her four boys to wear me down." The young men were good company. They helped me cut wood, carry rails down from the orchard, and do many other odd jobs.

Next I had my eyes on the old barn. The front was not bad, but the back was a dangerous, tumbledown mess. Bernt agreed I could burn it after a heavy snowfall. "Aha!" I thought. "A perfect Friday night activity with the teens." With this in mind, I began clearing the barn of anything valuable. I removed old horseshoes, several old wooden barrels without ends, and a hand plow or two. One of these plows we placed prominently on the property. Painted on it are these words: "He that putteth his hand to the plow and looketh back is not fit for the kingdom of God" (based on Luke 9:62). This reminder helped to hold me steady. Four of the horseshoes from that barn later graced the screen for the cabin fireplace. Jimmy Harten, who was then the village blacksmith, made the screen for me for $11.00.

With the arrival of December snows, the stage was set and the Young People readily agreed to a Barn Burning Party. I informed the Volunteer Fire Department, then baked dozens of sugar cookies and mixed gallons of hot chocolate. We made a ceremony of starting the fire. The boys made small fires inside the old barrels. The draft inside them made them look like funnel stacks. Soon the flames were licking through the staves and bungholes. For a moment I was back in my childhood, taking straw sips from old LeMay's cider barrels. Once started, the flames were soon shooting high into the air and lighting up the whole area. It was glorious—even better than any display of Fourth of July fireworks. My father would have loved it.

However, that fire was only the beginning of many fires that would be needed to rid us completely of the unsightly barn. On my fortieth birthday, Bev Hill and I lit the final clean-up fire. I felt that the saying I'd often heard over the years was true: Life does begin at forty!

My Own Piece of Paradise

The first group of campers in 1963 numbered about a dozen. Our camping activities were sanctioned but not sponsored by the local church. This was my idea and something that seemed quite natural, considering my background, the beautiful setting, and my dream to someday have a camp of my own. As I was soon to learn, the word quickly spread! The first service project the campers tack-

Bible study with my first campers in 1963

led at the camp was to build a pulpit and cross for our outdoor chapel. In the process of building and handling the birch wood, I exclaimed, "I just love white birch trees!" A girl responded, "My mother says you can't love nuthin' that ain't got a soul!" We held vespers every Friday night before our athletic and social activities, and we always used the outdoor chapel when weather permitted.

The second project was to replace an old broken-down wire fence along the road. In addition to the rails the boys carried down from the old orchard, Bernt sent over a truckload. Seeing my intense interest in the property, he frequently offered to sell it to me. I always put him off. "Bernt, I am all but broke," I would tell him. "No way can I afford to buy this place." One day while I was working on the fence alone, a man stopped by and asked, "Lady, is this place for sale?" Without even thinking, I responded, "No, sir." Immediately I knew in my heart I would be buying it. I was hooked and somehow was sure that this property would be mine. After all, I had that dream to consider: the property was not only a perfect personal retreat, but had the potential of being developed into a full-fledged camp.

Now I felt obligated to Bernt—for I had possibly lost him a sale—so I invited him and Rose over to discuss the purchase. He suggested I borrow the $4000 asking price. On a later trip to Indiana, I checked with bankers Bob Bradley and Lloyd Beattie. Both men had served on the Finance Committee at the Girl Scout Council. They wanted to help, but international banking laws prevented them from making personal loans. They suggested I get in touch with Mr. McMillen, the generous benefactor I had come to know through the Girl Scouts. They were sure he would loan me the money. However, there was no way I could take advantage of a professional relationship to obtain money for anything personal.

My good friend Ellenore Bowyer, who was involved in Girl Scouting, worked in a bank in Monroeville, Indiana. She had kept Reggie for me while I was studying at Indiana University. We discussed the matter at length and she proposed that I offer Bernt $5000 in U.S. currency, with $500 down and $50 monthly payments with no interest. The Canadian dollar was worth $1.10 in

U.S. currency at that time. My payment would be in Canadian funds.

In the meantime, I had signed a contract with Marion College and now headed up the Program of Progress, raising funds for the new Science Hall, Library, and Baldwin Food Center. Soon after I would become the first full-time alumni director. I made my offer to Bernt and Rose over a spaghetti dinner at the cabin. He said, "Make it $60 per month."

I replied, "If you knew how much I was going to make at Marion College, you wouldn't trust me with even the $50 payments."

Bless his heart, Bernt said, "Make it $40."

Ellenore loaned me the $5000 at 6% interest. I was ecstatic. I was now the proud owner of one hundred acres of paradise. Life indeed began at forty!

"Dunroamin"

This purchase would make more of my dreams possible. Someday the log cabin that Dad and I had talked about would rise on this site. I knew that many of my past efforts would also bear fruit. At Ball State I had taken a teacher's course on creative crafts, something that would be indispensable over the years. I still use the first cutting board I made at Ball State—a hard maple board in the shape of a pig.

I like to name things. I had pondered the name "Dunroamin" for the cabin. A key fob (identification tab that hangs on a keychain) would say "Dunlookin," and I thought I might name my canoe "Dunworkin" when I got one. Even if I didn't yet have a "Dunworkin," the other two quickly became reality. I cut my signs from quarter-inch yellow plastic. For one period of my life it looked as if I actually were "Dunroamin." However, I did not take into account my thirst for travel. It was too soon to know how far I would travel in the next three decades. But with all my trips since, my friends jokingly refer to my place as "Stillroamin." (Later I was fortunate to marry a man who was as willing to travel as I was, although he refused to go to Alaska with a tent in the trunk of the car!)

Gradually specific areas around the camp received special names. Many have asked why we named the pond Placid Pool. My good friends, Howard and Marie Noggle and their teenage daughter Carol visited me. The name Placid Pond did not suit Marie. On a quiet evening she looked at the peaceful water and said, "Let's call it Placid Pool." And so it is.

When the senior Noggles left, Carol stayed behind to share a few weeks of the simple life with me. She was good company and we worked well together. We constructed a simple shower with four poles and some old canvas. During the day an old tank acted as a solar heater for the water. A garden sprinkler served as our showerhead for evening showers.

We made a sundial by painting white numbers on an old tire. Eventually that first sundial would be replaced by the lovely bronze version I gave Dick one year for Christmas. We secured it on a portion of a concrete pillar I found on the property. The inscription says it best: "Grow old along with me. The best is yet to be."

Carol and Sandy Gilbertson Wilson became good friends and the three of us had great fun pitching our tent and enjoying cookouts on the old D Line Dock when it was still open for camping. Carol '70 and Dean Dayton '70 later spent a portion of their honeymoon at the new cabin.

What's a Nice Girl Like You . . .?

Before the pond became Placid Pool, it was an unsightly, neglected mess. An old boardwalk out onto the pond was tempting, but very unsafe. I decided to remove as much of it as I could. I labored diligently days on end in old gym shoes and jeans. Late one day I fell into the water, but kept on working in the frigid water. When I finally finished for the day, I shed my wet clothes and saw that I was as red as a boiled lobster from the cold. As enticing as it looks on a hot day, the spring-fed pond is much too cold for swimming. Several people predicted that I would "catch my death," or suc-

Cleaning up the pond

cumb to pneumonia, but I persisted in my task and never had so much as a sniffle.

When I later moved to the property, I decided to get rid of the weeds in the pond, something that proved to be quite a task. We used rakes, forks, and hooks. Bev Hill ('70) was the champion weed puller. Many were the cold hours we spent removing them. Although they do make wonderful compost, it is an ongoing struggle to keep them in check. Man-made ponds created from swamps have a natural tendency to revert back to their natural swamp condition. The use of nontoxic chemicals in our case is impractical due to the ever-moving water from the springs.

Pastor Allan Hyndman brought his chain saw over and assisted me in removing many of the old posts and planks. Al and Viv were special. They appreciated my work with the Young People and helped me out in many ways. Since I did not have a telephone then (and not until recent years), they received my personal calls. Regardless of the time, day or night, they graciously delivered the messages. I shall be forever grateful.

Bernt stopped by one day in a very serious mood. He said, "I have a problem, Millie. People keep asking me about you. I don't know what to tell them. Really now, what is an intelligent woman like you, with a master's degree, doing here?"

I answered, "Tell them anything you want; you don't have to defend me."

During my later years on the Island, district reporter Ada Tranter wrote about me in *The Sault Star.* She had a quick mind, a gift with words, and I enjoyed her wit immensely. She was the only person I ever saw sit down to a manual typewriter and write out polished articles on the first try. In her "purple prose" she wrote her impressions of me:

> *"Miss Jacobs carries her own water from a spring in a picturesque dell; does her own washing beside the pond. (No, not on the stones, but in an early-century wooden, hand-turned washing machine.) A covered wagon is located near a campfire, on which by some mysterious process she can cook to perfection a whole chicken in thirty minutes.*
>
> *"And Miss Jacobs is no recluse. A charming hostess, the cabin is the center of social activity, frequently full of houseguests. Evenings are cozy beside the open fireplace by candlelight, with bowls of apples and nuts, and books . . . and the almost-forgotten art of conversation.*
>
> *"She was the valued member of the girls' ball team this summer, takes full part in community life, and acts as supply in the local Free Methodist Church. An all-round athlete, there are few situations with which she cannot cope. She is an excellent shot, and no mean wielder of a pony chain saw. She can skin a skunk or a rabbit; and in winter is completely mobile on skis or snowshoes."*

The Ben Franklin

As winter approached, my wood supply became a concern. I had saved every stick of wood while cleaning up the place and had chopped it up for kindling. It was piled along the path to the outhouse that was located just behind the storage shed (now called Meg's Place). At that time the old sawmill was in operation at the corner of the Hilton Road and Highway 548. Hardwood slabs were available in abundance, so I filled my car trunk frequently and added more to the woodpiles. Later in the fall, Gord and Jerry

Hawdon and Bob and Jim Dennison helped me cut up some hardwood logs. Although I had a cookstove in the kitchen, I knew it would never be enough to keep the cabin even close to comfortable during the winter.

The Ben Franklin stove

Since I was serving as the president of the Alumni Association that year, I made a few trips to Indiana for board meetings. On one journey I ordered a Ben Franklin stove for the cabin's bedroom. I paid for it at the Fort Wayne store and was told I could pick it up at the Chicago warehouse to save shipping costs. I was also told the men there would load it for me. I parked at the loading dock and went in with my receipt. The man asked where I had parked my truck. I replied, "What truck? I have a '59 Chevy with a huge trunk." He was most unhappy and declared I would break the springs.

"I will take that responsibility," I replied. "I often haul three good-sized women in the back seat." That irritated him even more. The real problem was that he did not want to take the stove out of the box and put the individual parts in the trunk. He ultimately did, of course, and I headed north.

That Ben Franklin has been a beautiful stove. With the two doors open and a screen in place, it threw out a lot of heat and helped to keep the cabin comfortably warm. Being able to see the flames added much to my enjoyment as well. (The same stove now graces the corner of the master bedroom in the new cabin—our home—that replaced the old shack in 1967.)

Renewed Appreciation

After doing some alumni work in Marion in November 1963, I decided to visit my friend Eva Gilger, who was studying in New

Orleans. Marie Noggle took me to the bus station. Just as I was purchasing my ticket, the station became very quiet and subdued as the radio blared forth the news that John F. Kennedy had been shot in Dallas, Texas. I boarded the bus and traveled through the night. At every stop along the way we tried to get an update on the news. As the bus carried its somber passengers south, I was reminded of President Roosevelt's death when I was still in college. While that had been a sad occasion and had prompted the cancellation of our campus festivities, still this assassination was very different. It was incredible, unbelievable that a modern American president could be cut down this way. This was not a banana republic—this was the United States of America! How much we took for granted in our country.

Traumatic events have a way of juxtaposing themselves with lesser, even humorous events, events that somehow are remembered with equal clarity. On that journey I also recall a breakfast of huge, fluffy, hot griddlecakes. The butter melted on contact. The pitcher did not indicate the kind of syrup, but I poured it on generously, only to discover that it was not Canadian maple syrup or even Mrs. Butterworth's. It was strong sorghum molasses! Even though I had been fascinated with a horse-powered cane press that I had seen along the way, I did not like the sorghum—and could not eat the pancakes.

Eva went all out and took me all over New Orleans and the South. We crossed Lake Pontchartrain and went to Biloxi, Mississippi for our Thanksgiving dinner, dining on shrimp rather than the traditional turkey. I was intrigued with the small leaves of the Live Oak and the fact that these oaks remained green the year round. Spanish moss mysteriously draped many trees, and cypress knees—looking like hooded monks—poked up out of the swamps.

Eva took me with her to say good-bye to some of her missionary friends and coworkers. Bound for Kenya, they boarded a small foreign vessel at the mouth of the famous Mississippi River. I inquired about the old junk lumber of every description that had been lashed to the top of the hold. Surely it could not be intended for construction? No, Eva told me, it would be used as firewood for cooking in Kenya. Wood was scarce there and this mismatch of scrap lumber was preferable to dried cow dung. I had an immediate and renewed appreciation for the vast wooded areas of St. Joseph Island.

Under the Stars

It was so good to return "home" from that trip and know there was no reason to leave all winter. Meg was scheduled to come from Massachusetts to the Island for Christmas. I had met Meg at the International Girl Scout Round Up in Vermont. We had also attended Kit Hammett's camp together. She was a high school guidance counselor and avid camper. I had seen for myself how well she worked with campers and how they loved her spirit. We had talked about camping out in the snow and were determined to give it a try on this visit.

Meg arrived in good spirits. We spent the afternoon preparing the shelter where we planned to sleep outside that night. We placed our skis at an angle near a rick of wood. An ample supply of pine and spruce boughs for our bed and the roof, as well as cozy sleeping bags, assured us of a comfortable night out. It all looked so tempting, and I could hardly wait. But first we wanted to observe our traditional lobster dinner. Our gourmet meal by candlelight did not disappoint our taste buds. I had also made several small plum puddings for gifts, keeping one for our meal. I molded them in one-pound Maxwell House coffee tins, which were the perfect size, and I kept the tins to use year after year. I steamed them on top of the old cook stove and the aroma that coursed all through the cabin set my mouth to watering long before I had a chance to taste them.

I suggested that we retire early. I wanted to get as much mileage out of this sleep-out as I could. We would be challenging Old Man Winter in a new way. We had both camped extensively, but had never slept out in the snow. I settled in first. Meg kneeled down at the entrance with her sleeping bag, but came out with those famous words: "No room in the inn!" She turned and went back to the cabin. I could not believe my ears. I was disappointed for her, but I was determined to stay. It was a night to remember. I saw the stars twinkling through the pine boughs. I agreed with the Psalmist: "The heavens declare the glory of God; and the firmament showeth his handiwork" (Psalm 19:1). This was my first winter camp, but it would not be my last.

A Fitting End

That holiday Meg and I snowshoed and skied around the bush. We also pulled each other on skis behind our cars. Don Gilbertson and his crew had made a fine ski hill in the gravel pit across from the Eddy Farm on Hilton Road. (Before they removed so much gravel in later years, we could even see the lights of the Soo from the top of that site.) Don used some of their road building equipment to pack the hill. It was almost as good as The Landslide ski hill in the Soo. The moon was so bright that week that we drove home without turning on our headlights.

Winter of 1963

That seemed a fitting end to my first year on the Island. The brilliant moon illuminated everything around me—the past, the present, and even the future. It shone on what I had accomplished, alone and with the help of others. It reflected the projects underway and the lives of young people being changed. And it glowed with the bright hopes of tomorrow. Yes, this year had certainly exceeded everything I had dreamed it would be.

Chapter Ten

Lost and Found: One Personality

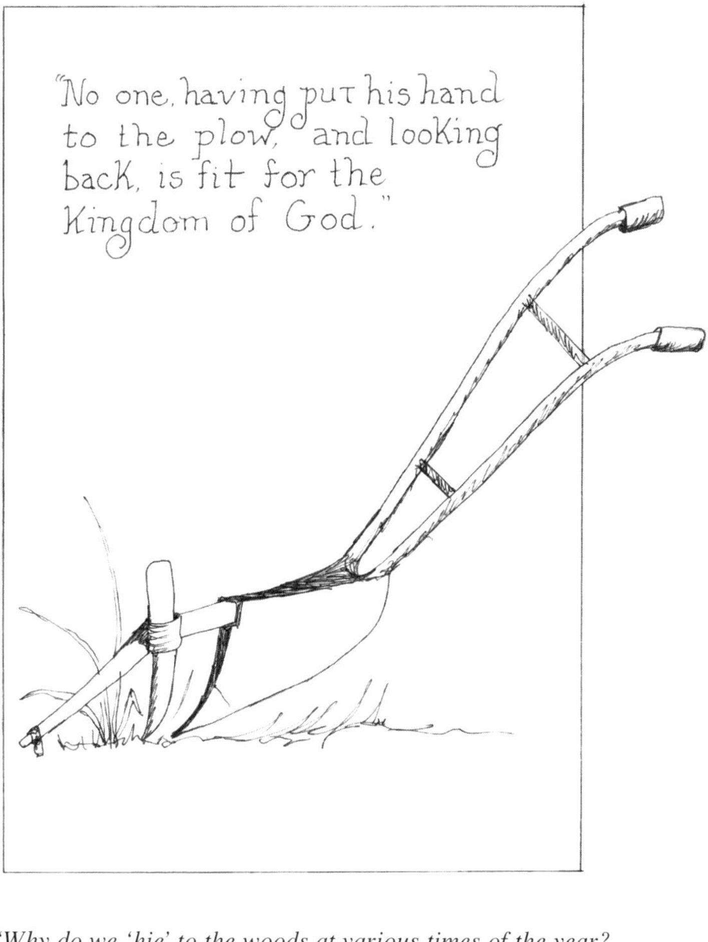

"Why do we 'hie' to the woods at various times of the year? Methinks it is the call to nature, to the earth, the call of God Himself. Here one can live creatively for a time."

Journal of Millie Jacobs

The following article was written by James L. Huffman ('63), a professor at Wittenberg University in Springfield, Ohio. Used with permission.

Dusk was closing in on the cabin in which I was staying. Surrounding hills and trees, cutting off the sunlight, hurried the falling darkness. Instinctively, I reached for a light switch on the cabin wall, but I reached in vain. There were no lights!

For the first time, I realized that I had entered a new world. I had come into a world without electricity, without running water, without the usual store-purchased foods, without radio, telephone or newspaper. Yet, I had found a world of quietness . . . simplicity . . . and peace.

Away from the rollicking screech of the city, I was sharing, for a couple of days, the "simple life" experiment of 40-year-old Miss Millie Jacobs, a highly sociable, intelligent, former Girl Scout Executive from Indiana.

For several years, while directing Limberlost Girl Scout Council in Fort Wayne, Indiana, and serving as alumni president of Marion College, an Indiana liberal arts school, Millie Jacobs had dreamed of experimenting for a year with the "simple life." Like Thoreau, she wanted to reject life's fringes and find out just what was important—and necessary—to satisfying existence.

"Next year is my special season," she told friends in 1962. "I am interested in making the most of the essentials, in growing a bigger mind, in enlarging the soul."

Consequently, late in the spring of 1963, Miss Jacobs completed work on a master's degree at Indiana University and headed north for St. Joseph Island, Ontario. There, in Lake Huron, she settled among 1,400 people who populate the 300 square miles of the Island (five persons per square mile!).

But she became a distant neighbor, even by St. Joseph Island standards. For she chose as her home, a rundown cabin two miles from the nearest human being.

In November, I visited Miss Jacobs. By then she had been living the simple life for five months. She had grown her winter veg-

The Shack and the Plow

etables, fished and hunted for much of her meat, won a place in the hearts of Islanders who met her. And, doing these things, this adventurer had allowed much of the Island simplicity to creep into her soul.

For years I had known Millie as a dynamic, personable leader, always interested in community and academic affairs. When I met her that day in Canada, though, she had become a drastically different person—affable as ever, but somehow changed.

Gone was the social correctness that demanded nothing of her dinner guests but relaxation. In its place she had developed the art of making guests share her experiment.

In fact, as soon as I entered "Dunroamin" (the name she had given her cabin), Millie handed me an empty water pail. Then she kindled a fire in the kitchen range to remove the tinge of coolness from the air, picked up another pail and led me out the door toward a spring near the cabin.

As we stepped from the cabin into the midday November sunlight (no snow as yet), Millie made it clear that she had fallen in love with the out of doors. "Look!" she exclaimed, throwing out her hands in a gesture that swept the entire landscape. "What does it do to you?" Obviously, what it did to her exceeded expression.

At the foot of the hill on which the cabin was located, she pointed out the source of her water supply, the source, as well, of many hours of soul growth. A friend had named it Placid Pool. Spring fed and about the size of two tennis courts, the pond had been the scene of many hours of contemplation and activity for Miss Jacobs. Here, she had learned to work—and to live.

Millie laughed as she told me about one Placid Pool experience. Last fall she decided that an ancient catwalk across the pond detracted from the pool's natural beauty. So one morning she decided to remove it. Section by section, she did her work, cautiously balancing on one plank as she tore out the next. At the end of the first day she had not touched the water once.

But things changed during the next morning of work. She had little more than started when a section collapsed. Splash! Miss Jacobs found herself deeper than her waist in spring-fed, 44-degree water.

Yet she was determined to complete the job as swiftly as possible and decided to stay in the water until the work was finished. So she did, working and shivering for two hours in the bone-chilling pond.

"Didn't you freeze?" I queried.

"Freeze? You should have seen me. I was numb. I looked like a robot walking to the cabin later. I had to pick my legs up mechanically every step I took." She added triumphantly: "But I didn't catch pneumonia!"

Her experiences at Placid Pool have not all been work, though. At times she goes out to just sit and stare. On a clear night, the reflections of a million tiny stars pierce the glassy surface. "Here," Millie says, "I find the satisfaction of . . . oh . . . just being here."

Long hours beside the pool and working over the wood-fire stove in her cabin have convinced this modern Thoreau that "the best things in life cannot be hurried. Look at the sunset and sunrise, for example," Millie points out. "Man in town puts on a flood light. Here I do the natural things, which can be done without a light. When it is light enough, I do other things naturally. That is the reason women do not bake bread anymore," she explained. "Baking bread is not hard. It just takes time."

One afternoon, while she was baking bread, I sat and queried Miss Jacobs. One question was uppermost in my mind. Why had she come to "Dunroamin"?

The reasons against such isolation were myriad. All her life she had worked with people. Now she was avoiding them. This abrupt change did not make sense to me.

Was it a "back-to-nature girl stunt"? She said not. And it obviously was not. For, rather than emphasizing the crude, she was continually making improvements. A shed needed new roofing so she put it on. Junk had surrounded her old cabin and she carried the refuse away. Outside she had planted two picturesque flowerbeds.

Further, Millie was temporarily rejecting civilized society against the opposition of many friends. Some had called her selfish for isolating herself for a year. A singer feared she would lose her voice. And a foreign friend commented: "Yee—no water, no lights! In my country we do not have it. Something ees wrong with you, no?"

Even one of her closest friends wrote: "I love the North Land, but not to that extent. I am glad electric lights and inside 'greenies' are here to stay."

Obviously, Miss Jacobs had not come for mere adventure or travel, either. She had had that without giving up life's luxuries. For six years she had served as executive director of 10,000 girls and adults in the Limberlost Girl Scout Council, working with a yearly budget of almost $100,000. During that time she did a great deal of camping, and in 1956 she toured Africa and Europe. Always, there was time in Millie's life for recreation.

"Have you come because of your love for Thoreau?" I asked. "Did you want to imitate him?"

Her reply was pointed. "Definitely not! If my life seems a bit like his (and who could deny it), it is because there are just certain basic necessities in life. A search for simplicity always arrives at some of the same points."

"Actually," she said, "inspiration for the experience came several years ago on a Canadian ski slope." She and her friends were skiing in Ontario one day when it suddenly hit her that she would love to spend a year in the area—living in the raw. That night at dinner she joked with the owner of a St. Joseph Island lumber mill, Mr. Bernt Gilbertson. She told him her inspiration.

"You don't by any chance happen to have an unused cabin around?"

He surprised her, "Yes, I surely do. In fact I have two; which one do you want?"

The fanciful subject was abruptly dropped. "But dreams do

come true . . . if we do something about them," Miss Jacobs contends. A few years later, her dream became reality.

Frankly, though, I still had no answer to my question of how much sense the experiment made. So I probed further. "Why?"

She went on with a few stock answers. She was doing three hours work toward a doctorate. This involved compiling a camper's cookbook, with such specialties as milkweed and fern shoots, cattails and watercress. Further, she was collecting wood samples to help campers identify trees more easily. She mentioned that sycamore trees remind her of long winter underwear, an identification tag unusual enough to help campers remember it.

Miss Jacobs added that she had needed extra time in order to set up some improved organizational plans for the Marion College Alumni Association. In three years as president of that group, annual giving had increased from $7,000 to nearly $50,000. The organization was on the move, but she must devote more time and energy to the cause.

She added another reason for the experiment: "I want to prove that the simple life can be lived in the twentieth century."

In all these replies, however, Millie did not seem truly frank. Clearly, she was not "coming clean."

Finally I asked: "Does the basic reason have anything to do with 'losing your soul' to really find it?"

She started. Then she lowered her head and was quiet. At last Millie spoke, subdued and totally sincere. "I suppose . . . to be honest . . . you have hit it . . . These are the things people do not talk about much. The quest to really know ourselves, to know God . . . I do not think we ever arrive spiritually, but I need this and I wanted it."

"And what have you found?"

Most of her answers she did not express orally. But they were there—in her life, in her habits, in her sense of appreciation.

For example, she had come to love nature so much that conservation was now an obsession. Time and time again during my stay she spotted wasteful or destructive rubbish left by nearby lumbermen or construction workers. Her response was always the same:

"Unforgivable!"

Everywhere, she picked up discarded lumber scraps or misplaced planks or logs. A portion of her winter wood supply had been collected from scrap, which had fallen off island lumber mill trucks.

Even water was precious to Millie. Carrying pails of it from the spring rather than turning on a spigot would make one think twice before wasting a drop of it. And her old kitchen stove served as a heater, a cook stove, water heater, and for old paper disposal. Food was composted.

When it came to protecting trees and wildlife, Millie Jacobs went to the extreme. My first afternoon there, a young Islander, Gordie Hawdon, came over with a load of sawdust for an icehouse which she was building in the hillside above Placid Pool. She spotted a tiny spruce tree near the spot where she wanted the sawdust unloaded. "Please do not hit the tree if you can help it," she pleaded. "Of course, if you can't avoid it, I guess I can't have my cake and eat it too." The tree was spared.

The soul-enlarging results of Miss Jacobs forsaking complex society also showed up in her growing familiarity with nature. She said, "It's to get better acquainted. My desire is to feel at home and at ease with nature." And she did. When asked by friends if she were not afraid to stay there alone, she replied, "Afraid of what? Actually I feel safer here than in the city. What is there to make one fearful?"

Ever and again, during my stay on the Island, she would lift her head during a conversation and listen. "It's an evening grosbeak," she might say. Or: "Listen to the phoebes." And as she listened, a gleam lighted her eyes.

The Island had clearly increased Millie Jacob's ingenuity, though it had not been lacking before. Her comment here: "This throws you on God and your own resources."

For example, she either killed or grew most all of her food. In fact, the only canned goods she brought to the island were for her dog. Shortly after arrival, the dog had died, so she returned the case of dog food.

"It is so much more fun to make your own foods," she contended. "These you create. I can't stand mixes." As a result of this simplicity in food, her store-purchased items (flour, sugar, yeast and such) cost her an average of 17 cents a day. She commented that Thoreau spent about 27 cents a week for food while he was at Walden Pond. "Not far off, considering the change in times," she said. On one occasion she barbecued crow.

Making cider the hard way

"Did you enjoy it?"

"Not really. The meat is dark and I kept thinking about it being a scavenger . . . too big a mental gap to overcome." She added, "It might be good if one doctored it up and played with it, especially the breasts."

Eventually, she said, she intends to eat porcupine and skunk, "Just to see how palatable they really are."

Above all others, Miss Jacobs said one phase of her life at "Dunroamin" had been most important. It was the time "to be still . . . and to know . . . to really know that God is in His heaven and all is right with the world." In November she used some of this time to read the entire Bible through without interruption by other reading matter. It took her about 55 hours, and she remarked: "Oh, there's so much truth. You get saturated."

Even the world around Miss Jacobs had become symbolic of the realm of the spirit. For example, a decaying, horse-drawn, one-blade plow outside her west window daily reminds her of a favorite Scripture phrase: "He that putteth his hand to the plow and looketh back is not fit for the kingdom of God." This had become her St. Joseph Island motto. Each morning the rising sun enshrouded the rustic tool in radiance and symbolism. Contemplating from her breakfast table, she said she was challenged to maintain her simplicity.

Millie reveled, as well, in the symbolism of birch trees. A few hundred yards from her cabin, three slender birches rose from one base. "Look at them," she solicited, "don't they remind you of praying hands? See their fingers stretched to heaven?"

The quietness and soul contentedness have made her fond of Clarice Bowman's statement: "He who learns nature's inmost secrets somehow finds her vastness creeping into his soul."

Surprisingly, though living alone, Miss Jacobs came to consider sharing and helping others among life's most rewarding necessary values. Her helpfulness showed up each evening when she walked two miles to her mailbox, carrying a gun as she went in case she saw game food. Her way passed a neighbour's broken-down rail fence, and on each trip, she stopped to mend one or two sections of it. During these walks she also trimmed and cleaned the secondary growth around some birch trees which lined the road.

Consistently, Millie allowed no room for selfishness in her own life, either. This lesson came early in her stay at "Dunroamin." In June her dog encountered a swarm of bees and never recovered. For years she had been her closest, most constant companion.

"The loss hurt deeply," she confided. "She had more zest and curiosity about life than any human being I have ever known." But she did not grieve long. Instead, she said that the dog's death showed her that "to be sad is to be selfish." And selfishness she deplored.

Occasionally friends visited her for a day or two. Although these visits robbed her of some of her time alone, Millie did not usually begrudge that time—especially if the visitors were close friends. "What a shame not to share these experiences," she said. "I am just here to live a simple life. There is no virtue in secluding myself to the extent of barring friends." When they did come, she put them to work and expected them to live just as simply as she. Miss Jacobs said she felt that if they would leave a part of themselves at "Dunroamin," their experiences would be richer for it. She enjoyed referring to a professor who visited as my "Ph.D. Waterboy" (Dr. Allen Bowman).

Apparently her philosophy was valid. The professor wrote: "Our short stay on St. Joseph Island did something for us. It was an inspiring experience. It helped us to realize anew the incidental nature of all our modern gadgets and the supreme importance of the external verities."

One guest, 15-year-old Hoosier Carol Noggle, wrote: "I can think of many things that have changed my outlook . . . the lofty trees, the majestic waters, the humble and loving roads . . . it might be of interest to you to know that 'if and when' I get my doctorate the following weeks are going to be spent on St. Joseph Island."

Combining all other elements, Millie Jacobs had found contentment in life's bare necessities. During her last year of work it occurred to her in a supermarket one day that "there wasn't a thing in the store that I wanted that I couldn't get and that at home there was not a thing that I needed."

Yet, she knew there was more to life than she was deriving from it. So a year later she packed what she could in a car and went North. Now, she commented: "I do not miss the things back home a bit. Our fathers had an element of peace of mind and security. I have found that here."

On my last afternoon there, we went out and looked at Millie's washing machine—a 1906 model and wooden. She carried water for it and turned both the agitator and wringer by means of a hand-crank. Friends frequently offered to do her washing. But she always replied: "Nothing doing. That would be cheating. I came here to live the simple life; this is a part of it and it is fun!"

As we talked that afternoon, I asked if there had been any disappointments.

"Only one," she said. "My time here is too short. A year can slip by all too quickly."

Later in the afternoon, we climbed the surrounding hills to look at "Dunroamin" from a higher perspective. In the far distance we could faintly see the North Channel in Lake Huron. But for now we were content to feast our eyes on the cabin, Placid Pool and peace…

Completely enraptured, I sighed: "Oh, how I'd love to spend a year this way myself, but . . . "

"Ah," Millie interrupted, "there's an island for everyone—if he is willing!"

Chapter Eleven

Building the Cabin

1967

"The wise woman builds her house . . ."

Proverbs 14:1 NIV

In 1839 one could have purchased 100 acres of land on St. Joseph Island for five shillings per acre. In 1856 the government offered the same land for twenty cents an acre. The Homestead Act of 1868 made it possible for hardy souls to claim 100 acres free if they had at least fifteen acres of land cleared within five years. They also had to build a home—at least 16 ft. x 20 ft. and fit for habitation.

The History of the Land

Henry and Margaret Gilroy came to Lot 10, Concession N in Jocelyn Township (the present site of All Tribes Christian Camp), sometime in the late 1890's. We don't know how much they paid for the property. They cleared the front parcel of maple, beech, and ironwood, which are the dominant species of trees here, and then proceeded to plant an orchard of apples, plums, and pears, as well as grape vines. They also kept bees. Henry owned the first fruit sprayer on the Island. It took two men to operate it, but they made it pay by hiring out to other orchard owners. The fruit trees were purchased from Tait's Nursery, which was just a few miles on up the mountain. (Our so-called mountain is 1400 feet above sea level. The major portion of the Island is 600 feet above sea level.)

From Gothic to Hangout

The Gilroys built a log cabin just north of where the All Tribes Camp Amphitheater now sits. Some of their lilacs, hops, and a huge old gnarled apple tree are still growing there as a testimonial to their vision and hard work. Later they built a nine-room frame house covered with clapboard. It featured two gothic windows, hardwood floors, a huge kitchen, and a spacious living room and parlor. The stairs rose from the middle of the house and led to at least three bedrooms on the second floor. The Gilroys kept their cream separator in the kitchen during the summer and in the basement during winter. They also stored their apples and vegetables in the basement. They hand carried water from a spring for drinking and for the animals. (We have piped water up to my cabin from the same spring, but in the place of spigots we use a small pitcher pump.)

T.T. Barnes of the of the Barnes Drug Store in Sault Ste. Marie purchased the place from the Gilroys. Barnes hired Guy Workman, an uncle of Mrs. Barnes, to take care of the property. John McMaster remembers Guy hauling loads of apples in a buckboard pulled by a single horse to the wharf in Richards Landing. When the larger crop came in, Emerson McDougal would come from

Hilton Beach to haul it away with his red International truck. As a small boy, John was impressed with the truck's wooden wheels and solid rubber tires. He also recalls the sound of a wrought iron dinner gong calling the farmhands to meals. John was delighted when I recovered the gong from a pile of trash on the pond bank. After I had cleaned up the gong, George Hadden bolted it to the pond gatepost. There it was readily available for use but not easily removed.

After Mr. Workman died, a Mr. and Mrs. Jackson came from the Sault, along with a nephew, Sam Holden, who lived with them. He was an inventive lad who was ahead of his times. He rigged up a turn signal for his old flivver. (I well remember putting my left arm out of car windows to signal a turn. I could hardly believe my eyes when I first beheld an automatic turn signal. No more wet or cold arm. By the time I finally bought a car, automatic signals were in!)

When the Jacksons returned to the Sault, their son Jack moved in. He was married to Blanche, a sister of Roman Aikens. Del Haight, grandfather of Donna Hadden (Mrs. George) was next to buy the place. He decided to make a commercial trout pond. In the mid-forties he hired Reg Hawdon, John Hyndman Sr., and others to make a dam. They drove wide elm planks by hand along the Hilton Road side of the property. Some of these planks can still be seen today. To fill in behind the planks, they took sand from the gully west of the cabin and wedged it behind the boards to reinfoce the dam. To this day the overflow of water goes under Hilton Road, meanders over to the A Line, and under the K Line near Kent's General Store. From there it makes its way to the Huron Line and on across several farms until it reaches the St. Mary's River. Interestingly enough the water level in the pond never varies.

While Del was in residence, the large home burned down. He then built a small cabin, insulating it with cardboard and old newspapers. (This is the cabin I called home in 1963. Yes, the wind and cold went right through the walls. When we tore a portion of the cabin down, I was not smart enough to keep the newspapers for their historical value. All I could think about was to get rid of them—there were zillions of flies hibernating between the layers of paper!) When Del vacated the place, Dave Reed lived there for a time. He was a mill hand for the Gilbertsons.

In the late 1950's, the Gilbertsons bought the 100 acres principally for the timber. They sold the logs to Soo Mill in Sault Ste. Marie. Several more mill hands came and went. Don Gilbertson told me that when he and his cousin Ron Hawdon were in their teens, they used the house for a hangout on weekends.

Go North, Young Woman, Go North!

The property's camping history probably unofficially began with Rose Gilbertson, who cleaned up the cabin and sponsored various activities there for the youth from the Island Free Methodist Church. One scheduled skating party never materialized. Don and his team of horses, Queen and Lady, went through the ice as they were clearing the snow for the rink. He well remembers those few very chilly hours. With no little effort, the trio and their equipment made it out. And Don lived to tell the tale!

Kay McMaster, John's wife, contributed the following about the individual who "relieved" the Gilbertsons of that particular piece of real estate:

> *"Next came this young woman* (I was forty) *from the United States who bought the property. She set out to build a log cabin. In the winter of 1966, the Gilbertsons took out the long straight spruce logs (from Vi Kent's lot at the corner of Highway 548 and the Hilton Road). George Hadden and John built the cabin that summer. John's last job there was building an outdoor privy with a picture window overlooking the pond. That was in 1967."*

A "Kit" Wouldn't Do

During a flight delay in Atlanta while I was attending an alumni chapter meeting, I used the extra time to draw up a rough sketch of my dream cabin. That simple plan remained tucked away in my billfold until the spring of 1966. I had paid off the loan on the property, so 1967 seemed to be the year to build a log cabin.

Canada would be celebrating her 100th birthday. Everyone seemed to be planning or doing something special to commemorate the occasion. I decided a rustic log cabin would be my contribution to the cause. While I was intrigued by the "A" frame structures I had seen at various ski resorts, I kept coming back to my dream of a log cabin. Ellenore was willing to float me another loan at 6% interest and my pennies were mounting.

In discussing my plans with Bernt and Rose, Bernt said he just knew he had the answer. He was affiliated with Soo Mill and Ian Hollingsworth. Both men had previously owned my 100 acres, of course. Bernt explained that the mill produced log home kits. The logs went through a lathe and came out smooth and of uniform size, ready for erection. In my mind's eye, however, I saw rough logs, not a factory product. Bernt insisted on the "kit," asserting that it would be cheaper and faster to build. During our last conversation regarding the plans, he pushed a bit too hard. I remember Rose standing up and saying, "Bernt, if Millie wants real logs, that is her decision. I don't want to hear another word about this. Let her alone." And he did.

But where would we get real logs? And who on the Island knew how to build a log structure? Someone suggested George Hadden. He was a carpenter and might be interested. On a trip to the Island I stopped by to see him. He told me he wasn't sure he could handle it. He had never worked with logs and they were much different than two-by-fours and siding. He did look at my crude plans and agreed to go over my books and articles on log buildings. I could tell by the wee grin on his face and the twinkle in his eye that he was weakening.

On my next trip up from Marion to the Island, George gave me his answer. He would give it a try if he could have a helper and if I would supply the logs. I had already surveyed that situation. Vi Kent owned a stand of spruce a mile away. The Gilbertson men would cut and peel the logs and Johnny McMaster agreed to assist

George. We would begin building in early summer of 1967. I was overjoyed!

While I worked through the winter at Marion College, the logs were cut and piled near the road. There are no words to describe my feelings when I came up in the spring and saw that beautiful mound of logs. My mind went into overdrive. I could begin to see the cabin. What I could not see was all the hard work that would go into its construction.

The logs next went from their pile along Hilton Road to Ashur Bookman's mill on the F and G, a concession road about four miles from Hilton Road. There they were sawed flat on two sides and delivered to the cabin site. Ashur's work was nearly perfect. There were only three or four places where we had to shim the logs to make them fit. Between each log we put two strips of oakum, hemp rope soaked in oil. Also used to caulk boats, oakum repels insects and absorbs moisture. As the logs went up, we hammered in ten-inch and twelve-inch spikes every three or four feet to make the sides more solid.

I had taken the summer off to oversee the building of the cabin and I felt I had to make every moment count. I believe I did. (At the end of nine weeks, I returned to the campus. Ruth Bowman, wife of Dr. Allen Bowman, said I looked like a brown piece of string.) I found myself doing everything that George and John did not want to do. At least that is the story I always tell. They came at 8:00 a.m. and left at 4:30 p.m. Before leaving at the end of each day, they would suggest various projects they thought I could handle to help speed things up for the next day's work.

Darkness comes late in the northern summers and so my work-days were long. I nearly killed myself but I was in my element. Nothing equals the feeling of having an active part in seeing a dream come true. They say a dream is only a dream until the foundation is laid. I was working on the foundation, plus. I was a Pepsi guzzler then, and I often remarked that my share of building the cabin was done on Pepsi and prayer. The two kept me going.

We all worked very hard that summer. We did not have electric lines into the site then. I remember one hot afternoon when John

The Log Cabin

was sawing the rafters by hand. He looked up with perspiration running down his face and remarked, "If you get hydro in here within ten years, Millie, I will shoot you dead!" I had managed without electricity during my year on the Island and did not intend to spoil the cabin with the likes of this modern invention. Heaven forbid! But why we never rented a generator for the job, I will never know.

The Proof's in the Pudding

My plan for the cabin included a pudding stone fireplace. This stone is unique to the Island and the surrounding area. It is composed of bright red and brown jasper pebbles mixed with pebbles of white quartz and cemented together by white quartzite. The early settlers called it pudding stone because it looks like a plum pudding that is full of fruit and nuts. Due to the prominence of red jasper, it is also known as bloodstone. From the first time I saw a pudding stone fireplace in the home of Ollie Hawdon (now owned by Brent and Janet Gilbertson), I knew I wanted one like it.

I had even begun to collect pudding stones in preparation for the future. They were much easier to find then, for the roads were gravel and the grader often brought them to the surface. During my year on the Island I often hiked to the Island Free Methodist Church two miles away. As I walked I had a marvelous time discovering the stones, which I then hid and later retrieved with my '59 Chevy. It took a toll on my car, though, for by the time I had them all collected the weight of the stones had caused the floor boards to give way. I repaired the floor with pieces of plywood and old carpet. This kept the dust out of the car and our feet off the road. The car was eight years old and only had 146,000 miles on the odometer!

Everyone advised me that Ralph Nelson, Sr. was the man to build my pudding stone fireplace. He had constructed many in the area, and they were not only beautiful but also functional. Being on the Island only once a month made it difficult for me to contact him. Later I learned that he had been away honeymooning with his third wife. George finally contacted him for me.

We had poured the footings and fireplace slab, as well as the walls for the 6 ft. x 6 ft. x 8 ft. cistern. I had dug the hole for the cistern by hand over the Fourth of July weekend. One evening I was sitting on the back stoop reflecting on the project and wondering if a fireplace would ever materialize. A car drove in and a handsome, elderly man walked over to me. Immediately I said, "I assume you are Mr. Nelson. I am Millie Jacobs," and I reached out to shake his hand.

A strange look came over his face and he blurted out, "Good God, I expected an Amazon!" The men had told him that I had dug the cistern by hand, but he did not believe them.

It did not take us long to get down to business. He had come to tell me that at seventy-six years of age, he was too old to build a stone fireplace. I would have to settle for a brick one.

Mr. Nelson departed saying, "You get the bricks, mortar, and sand and we will talk business. But forget about those stones." I was more than a little disappointed. I was devastated. What about my beautiful collection of pudding stones?

In a few days he returned to say that he had changed his mind. If I wanted a pudding stone fireplace so badly, he guessed he would have to do it. BUT I would have to hire an assistant for him. He did not want to be bothered with paying wages, insurance, and so on. After a long pause I asked, "Would I do?"

Chuckling, he replied, "Anyone who can dig a hole like that cistern should be able to do the job." I could have hugged him. This marked the beginning of our mutual admiration society and a beautiful friendship that would span sixteen years.

When I asked how he wanted to be paid he said, "You can pay me when we are done." We were working one Saturday morning when his son Francis came by to see if I wanted to go flying later that day. Francis owns the only airstrip on the Island. When Ralph heard the invitation, he stood up and said, "If you are fool enough to go with him, pay me now."

Once Ralph started on the fireplace, I was busier than ever. He taught me to mix the mortar to his exacting specifications. I handed him the stones as he selected them for a proper pattern. In between I did odd jobs for the other two men, but when Ralph yelled "MOR–TAR!" I was johnny-on-the-spot with the next bucket of mud.

First Things First

During that busy summer my godchildren, Beth and Brad, came to spend some time with me. The children of my college roommate, Velva Hathaway, and her husband, Harry Bollinger, they are an important part of my life. (These were the godchildren who accompanied me to my parents' graves. See Chapter Three.) I was at the hospital for both their births. Each time, new father Harry was so nervous I had to put the dimes in the pay phone so he could announce the good news to his parents and friends. I spent much time in their home when they were growing up. Their parents have been most generous in sharing them with me and allowing me to take them on many jaunts. They are like my very own.

Brad was five and Beth was seven that summer, and they were delightful company. We had an understanding that they would have to entertain themselves during the day. We would have a picnic lunch at noon at the tree house that George had built for them in a nearby apple tree. (Visiting campers and children still enjoy the tree house some thirty years later.) Saturdays were for swimming and hiking, if we did not have to go to the Soo or Kent's for more supplies.

However, sometimes the construction got in the way of our schedule. When we were ready to put the beams up, we realized we were four short. The Gilbertsons were able to get the logs, but I had to peel them before Monday morning. I started to work on them early Saturday morning, with a promise to Beth and Brad that we would have a picnic and go swimming in the afternoon. In anticipation, they had donned their bathing suits before breakfast and monitored my progress very patiently. But at one o'clock that afternoon, Beth could restrain herself no longer. "Mern," she asked, "is George working for you, or are you working for him?" That did it. I put down my drawknife and we were off. By getting up very early Monday morning, I was able to have the logs ready for the men to put in place later that day.

One evening when we were cleaning up the scraps left on the construction site, Brad discovered some candy wrappers. He looked up and said, "Those guys don't believe in keeping America beautiful, do they?" I reported Brad's remarks the next day. We never found litter again on the construction site.

(Speaking of litter, we have taken great pride over the years in having a litter-free camp. Clever signs pertaining to litter can be found around the grounds today. In 1994 our seventh and eighth graders in VBS expressed it well. They painted a plastic tombstone with the words: "Here lies mankind buried under his own trash." I tease the campers about shooting "litter bugs" on sight. We must look after this special world He has created for us.)

Despite the constant infusion of black flies, mosquitoes, and sand flies, log by log the walls went up. When we were ready to put the top logs in place, the men said that we had reached a day of decision. The plan called for a simple five-foot overhang in front, such as graces an Adirondack cabin. John suggested making it long enough for a garage. Horror of horrors! A garage attached to my log cabin? George thought a screened-in porch would be more practical. About that time another swarm of "skeeters" hit—it would be a screened-in porch!

We extended the logs for a nine-foot porch. I shall be forever grateful for that change. A year later Ralph built a four-foot high stone wall on three sides, incorporating a stove and baking oven on the west end. For all those who have been asking over the years, yes, the oven works. George put in copper window screens and made shutters to fit the openings. We installed a loft at one end and placed a bale of straw and some mattresses up there. George made a solid, movable, cedar ladder for easy access. Beth and Brad, the grandchildren, and other campers have loved sleeping up in that loft.

The Eye of the Beholder

One day when Ralph was working on the fireplace from inside the cabin, he got up from his knees and looked beyond me. Without any explanation he said, "For two cents I'd quit right now. I should walk out of this place straight away!" When pressed for an explanation of his outburst he responded, "I have worked so hard to make this place beautiful and look what that guy is doing!" George was putting up kitchen cupboards made of barn boards. "Whoever heard of spoiling a place with material from an old chicken house?" Thank the good Lord he cooled down and stayed to finish his work.

After the fireplace was finished, Ralph began erecting a brick wall as a partition between the bedroom and the kitchen. It was to be an aesthetic feature as well as a safety feature, for the cook stove would be against that wall. I also wanted a four-foot-high brick wall in the corner of the bedroom where I intended to put the Ben Franklin stove. When I asked about that project, he replied, "No sir-ee, Bob! When this wall is completed next week I

Millie's cookstove

am finished!"

On Saturday I mixed up a bit of mortar and laid about a dozen bricks to start my desired wall. The following Monday morning he took one look at my handiwork and yelled, "Who did that?"

"I did," I answered innocently. "Why?"

"Tear that out of there and mix up some mortar. I don't want people to think I did that!" My psychology had worked.

Earlier when we were doing the outside of the fireplace, I frequently carried the stones and buckets of mortar up the high ladder. One day I was hurrying and went up with a rock under one arm and a bucket of mortar in the other hand. As I was ascending the ladder, he peered down. "Great Scott!" he said. "Is there anything you can't do?" In a few minutes he put me to the test. He pointed to an unusually large stone and said, "I need that one."

I replied, "Sir, that stone is too heavy for me. If you want it, come on down."

He slapped his knee and said, "Good girl! You are smarter than I thought. It is the smaller one next to it I need." He got it!

We were nearing the end of August and the cabin roof was not shingled yet. I expressed my concern to George. "No sweat!" he said. No sweat? I thought. It will take some time to shingle a 24 ft. x 45 ft. roof with wide overhangs.

A few days later George came in with the forest-green shingles. Behind him came a procession of four or five pickups. They backed up to the cabin, carefully spacing their trucks. They then pulled out planks and laid them across the truck beds. From there the men could reach the roof. By mid-afternoon the job was done. No sweat! I could not believe my eyes.

A Fireplace for All Seasons

As must be evident to the reader by this time, I do not wait patiently for things to happen. So, once Ralph had finished the new fireplace, I was most anxious to try it out. Ralph said I must be patient and let the mortar set and dry. One day at long last he said, "I think tomorrow will be the day!" When he arrived the next morning at 7:30, he saw smoke coming out of the chimney. I was just finishing my breakfast, which I had cooked over the first fire in my new fireplace. Ralph slipped in through the door and caught me red-handed! But he admired my spirit, just as I admired his. We remained friends for the rest of his life and I grew fond of his family as well. He died at the age of ninety. He had come to the Island as a small child, and he taught me much about the history of the area and the people.

Hy Goldenburg, who had been on the finance committee for the Girl Scout Council in Fort Wayne, procured the metal Heatilator for my fireplace. It came from the Majestic Furnace Company in his hometown of Huntington, Indiana. (A fireplace without a Heatilator is for decoration only and produces little useful heat.) That fireplace has served us well. I cannot begin to count the number of cups of hot chocolate I have made for campers and friends over fires in this fireplace. More than a few "smores" (toasted marshmallows and a square of chocolate bar between two graham crackers) have been created and consumed. As well, mountains of popcorn, bowls of chestnuts, and countless meals have been made and shared by this fire.

To me a fireplace is for all seasons, but I enjoy it most of all on dark, rainy days or during howling blizzards. The crackling flames speak peace to my heart. Often as I sit and gaze into the fire, I can see the faces of former campers in my mind's eye. Thank God for memories.

The Single Life

It seems my unmarried status puzzled a lot of people. My old .22-caliber rifle intrigued the men who had shingled the cabin roof. When the men asked if I ever used it, I replied, "How do you think I have remained single so long?" They thought that was some joke! (Eleven years later, after my marriage to Dick, one of those roofers, Elgie Reed, stopped me in Richards Landing and asked, "What happened to your gun?" It took me a few minutes to catch his meaning—how had Dick gotten past the gun?) I did use the rifle, of course, for shooting squirrels and rabbits. They are delicious when fried nice and brown and served with mashed potatoes and gravy.

The builders also wondered why I wanted such a small window bed made. They suggested larger dimensions, possibly for a time in the future when I would marry. However I convinced them it was for solitary use, for I was happy being single. After all, I had a great job, could travel when I liked, and was even able to help build my own cabin. Did I really need a man?

They thought otherwise and tried to introduce me to every bachelor on the Island. One such effort was sneaky but hilarious. George usually paid for the materials he needed and then I would reimburse him. One Friday afternoon he gave me an invoice for a very small amount, one owed to an unmarried man on the Island. George insisted it had to be paid on Saturday. I was puzzled but obediently made my way to the man's home and settled the account. George could hardly wait to see me on Monday morning.

"Did you see him? Did you pay the bill?" he asked.

I replied, "How desperate do you think I am?"

When I shared this story with Dick much later on he said, "They just didn't look far enough."

I am still deeply impressed by the way George and John and Ralph put themselves and their talents into their work. I am proud of the cabin now and they were proud then, and rightly so. In fact they were so pleased that on Sunday afternoons and many evenings they came by with their friends to show off their handiwork. The Centennial Log Cabin going up on Hilton Road seemed to be the talk of the Island. I could hardly believe the flow of traffic and the comments of the sightseers.

I was especially surprised and pleased with one visitor. A timid figure came slowly down the lane. When she came into full view, I saw her light hair and sunburned nose. It was Bonnie McPhee Nelson, a camper I had known at Camp Wakonda thirty years earlier. (We called her "Rudolph" then.) She was now Ralph's daughter-in-law. Ralph had talked so much about this Millie from Indiana that she had to come over and check me out. It was a pleasant surprise for both of us.

Taking Care of "Business"

The cabin was all but finished. It was time to think about the outhouse. We were going to use up some short logs left over from the main construction. I had told the men I wanted a picture window in the outhouse facing the pond. No problem, they said with a grin. But the day I brought the window to John he said, "My gracious, Millie! You were serious, weren't you?" The window went in.

The reason for the window? The only things I have ever disliked about camping are the dark, smelly johns, greenies, kiboes, latrines or whatever you choose to call them. (More recently we have added another outhouse with a window at All Tribes Camp, but the campers have insisted on a curtain for that one. We also have three wee-wee teepees without doors, but they face the bush—why not breathe fresh air and enjoy the scenery? I have tried to improve some outhouses along the way by having campers paint the interiors with white paint and then adding colorful polka dots.)

When John finished building the facility behind my new cabin, I immediately papered it with pictures, poems, cartoons, and the like. George's mother, Winnie Hadden, came by one day to have a "look-see." She was impressed and especially liked the idea of the big window. She said to me, "There'll be no constipation here." And then she added, "But one thing thou lacketh." She returned later with a Sears catalogue.

When Dr. Bowman made his first visit, he said in all seriousness, "You are going to put a curtain out there, aren't you, Millie?" We teased him about being wary of the birds, squirrels, and fish.

A "Flush" of Memories

All of this reminds me of the original outhouse on the site. It was a rickety, old thing out behind the storage shed (Meg's Place). The door wouldn't shut and the porcupines visited it frequently. (For the uninitiated, porcupines love the taste of salt, something they can find in urine splashed on the seat or the surrounding boards. The residue of sweat on ax handles and canoe paddles is also prized.) Quite often we had to sweep out Peter Porkie's quills and droppings. This mess upset Beth more than a little, especially the quills on the seat. One morning she stomped in and shouted, "He did it again, Mern!"

I said, "Let's fix him. I'll write him a note." So I wrote. "Porcupines Not Welcome!" About that time she realized I was teasing her.

"Mern," she said, "porcupines can't read." We continued to sweep up after our prickly visitors to the outhouse.

When I was a child, my Dad built an outhouse for his truckers—a six-seater! Come to think of it, I do not recall ever seeing the workers standing in line.

A Dream Come True

The end of summer was approaching and we were running out of time. More help was needed, so we hired Ross Armstrong. He was a real "go-for" and we all worked well together. With this extra help, we were able to finish on time.

We completed the finishing touches on the cabin over Labor Day weekend in early September. I reluctantly locked the door before heading south to begin work once again in Marion. I lingered outside and thanked God for a dream come true. The logs glistened in the morning sun. I took numerous pictures and as I turned to leave I committed the place to God. I recall praying this prayer: "It's yours, Lord. If for any reason it burns down or is destroyed, give me the grace to accept it. And thanks again for allowing me to realize another dream." The protection and use of it were in His hands.

I had promised to prepare a turkey dinner for the three men who had worked so hard on the cabin. Their wives and Ross would also be included. This was scheduled for my return during the American Thanksgiving holiday in November. I could tell by the looks on their faces that they just knew I had never taken the time to learn to cook. They had another "think" coming! When the time came, I fulfilled my promise and prepared a turkey with all the trimmings. During the meal Ralph said, "Well, boys, she can cook as well as she mixes mortar or pounds nails!"

I cooked two turkeys that weekend in the old wood stove. I had promised Beth and Brad that they could come up and see the "finished product" in November. They rode up with me when I returned, and Dr. and Mrs. A. Bowman came with Velva and Harry. Needless to say they were impressed, but it was especially interesting to observe the children's reaction to the new log cabin.

Brad was sad to see the old, shaggy shack deserted. He recalled many delightful times there. Beth, though, was more interested in checking out every detail of the new cabin. We had to light the kerosene lamps and at least a dozen candles. During her inspection, Beth spotted a log with a saw cut in the middle of it. George and I had agreed we could not afford to replace it with a new log. We figured we could live with a wee error like that, for no one would be likely to notice it. But Beth saw it. She said, "Even big people make mistakes, don't they, Mern?"

I returned at Christmas, too, bringing Bev Hill with me. Bev had spent a portion of the summer with us and had done a lot of work staining the logs and applying paint. She had taken her share of ribbing from the men, too. She was not an early riser, and George had delighted in starting his chain saw outside her bedroom window for her morning wake-up call.

During the Christmas holidays, we skied and snowshoed and tried to relax in front of the fireplace. I emphasize "tried," because we also kept busy trying to keep warm. The cabin was very damp because the logs had not yet had time to be completely seasoned. Worse still, although we had been generous with the oakum during construction, we had overlooked the corners and around the doors and windows. There was a hard, cold wind that holiday, which made locating the neglected spots a little easier. Much of our entertainment consisted of poking oakum. Needless to say, we also burned an inordinate amount of wood.

The climax to the year of the cabin came on New Year's Eve. George and Donna Hadden, Don and Ruth Gilbertson, and thirteen other couples came over for a snow machine party. We roared around the Island at a fast clip. It was cold and exhilarating. The moon was full and every detail of the trees and bushes stood out. We came back to the cabin to share food and memories around the fireplace. What a way to close out the old and welcome in the new! This was to be an activity we repeated for several years.

What a joy it was to finally be able to use my dream home! And what a joy it was, and is, to share the cabin with friends. Sharing my home and my heart has always been very important to me.

Relaxing at home – still as enjoyable as in 1967.

Even today, memories surround me. The Kitty Hunter Scott antique kitchen cupboard and Dr. and Mrs. McConn's old oak icebox are on the porch. Ralph made a table from a barrel Don Gilbertson had used for oats for his horses. George welded old tractor seats on five-gallon milk cans to use as seats. A woven wire and metal hammock, which was used in a ship on the Great Lakes, hangs at one end of the porch. That area is much appreciated in the summer. Late in the fall the shutters go over the screens. The hammock and some of the seats are stored in the loft and two ranks of wood (what Canadians call a cord of wood) come in for use in the kitchen range during the winter, for I still cook with wood. There is nothing like the special flavor of many of the foods I make on a wood stove.

The inside of the cabin has many built-in features, too, including a beautiful, wide window seat that overlooks the pond on the east side of the cabin. This is made possible by a large 46 by 70-inch thermal windowpane, plus a window at each end. George built the seat large enough to be used as a bed. It is delightful to awaken there in the early morning and from the comfort of bed observe the outdoor activity.

Proverbs 14:1 says: "The wise woman builds her house." I do

not know how wise I am, but I am grateful for all who had a part in building the cabin and who donated antiques to furnish it. To live in one of my dreams is the ultimate.

In the fifty-plus years since I first came to the Island, I have seen many changes. Access to the Island has progressed from two small ferries, to one larger year-round ferry, and now to the beautiful Bernt Gilbertson Bridge. Seeing the narrow gravel roads become blacktopped highways has not been hard to take. The biggest change is the influx of new people. At one time we knew almost everyone, but that is no longer true. It is delightful to continually meet new people who love the Island as we do.

Chapter Twelve

More Than Just My *Alma Mater*

(1961-1971)

"Cheer, cheer for Marion College!"

Original School Song

In 1961 I was elected the first woman president of the Marion College Alumni Association. At the time I was working with the Girl Scouts in Fort Wayne. The professional training courses I took in administration, finances, and public relations for the Scouts proved to be just as invaluable for the association. Since I had served on the alumni board before becoming president, I was accustomed to hearing the "naysayers" and their negative message: Our alums were too busy; did not care about getting involved; were not loyal. The excuses for not supporting the college went on and on. I was determined to prove them wrong, and with the help of many, I did.

Since I lived in Fort Wayne at the time, only fifty short miles separated me from the campus. I was a frequent visitor and organized several active committees to facilitate our work. I realized the importance of involving alums beyond the city of Marion. Consequently I traveled around Indiana, Michigan, and Ohio to organize or revitalize alumni chapters.

Administration building with Teter Hall in background.

Filling Big Shoes

It soon became evident that we needed a full-time director to coordinate all of our activities. I was honored to follow Dr. Clarence Huffman ('44), who not only had worked with the alumni earlier, but had also taught classes. When I was elected president,

I also felt awed to follow in the footsteps of such fine men as Dr. Donald Porter ('29), Dr. Charles DeVol, Dr. Howard Noggle, and others. They gave me their full support. Howard was the Director of Church Relations at the time and his office was adjacent to mine. His support and friendship over the years have been invaluable. I have always loved his letters and notes, which invariably close with, "Your friend in the Faith."

Howard was and is still called "Mr. Marion College." Although he thinks I gave him that title, he carried it long before I knew him. On a few occasions I have had the honor of being tagged "Miss Marion College." Shortly after I came on staff, Howard told me, "I am at your service. I will be pleased to march in your army." What a man, and what a blessing his life has been to so many.

My work as the director went beyond my wildest expectations. To work side by side with my former professors and several classmates, as well as to socialize with them, was a very satisfying experience. It was wonderful to see and feel their overall concerns for the students and the school—my Alma Mater.

In her delightful book, *The Lord, The Landmarks, The Life,** Dr. Mary Elder ('45) has recorded the early days of the school in a wonderful way. She depicted the early struggles and dedication of the faculty and staff who gave so much. In doing so, they and their families suffered more than we will ever know. Dr. William McConn, John and Horace Williams, and many others brought the college through the difficult years of the Great Depression. Over a period of time, John and Horace alternated donations, each giving $1000 every other month to keep the school going. Because of such dedication, Marion College fared better than most private schools in the state.

We hear many complaints today about the high cost of tuition. Many are unaware of the extent to which the average student is subsidized. This money comes from the alumni, churches, friends of the school, foundations, estates, and other groups and organizations. Our present faculty also contributes indirectly, for they could be earning much more by teaching at state universities.

Turnabout's Fair Play!

Coordinating and working with the faculty was a very important aspect of my job. I entertained many of the faculty and their families earlier in my Fort Wayne apartment. I made it a point to invite all new faculty members and their families in for a meal. There was only one stipulation. The children had to learn the school song "Cheer, Cheer for Marion College" and sing it before arrangements were made for the visit.

One of my classmates, Dorothy Newby ('48) married Gerald Smeenge ('50), who had returned to the campus to teach in the Art Department. In due time the trio of Smeenge daughters stood outside my door singing all three verses of the school song. Later during our meal, Gerald offered to do any signs or posters I might need for my alumni work. I took him at his word and sometime later requested several charts. He completed them and I arranged to pick them up at their home. When I arrived, young Gretchen opened the door. I asked for the material but Gretchen had a surprise in store.

"Sing 'Cheer, Cheer for Marion College'," she stipulated.

I replied, "Gretchen, I don't have time to play games today." I was on my way to an alumni meeting and was in a hurry.

She insisted, "And sing all three verses, Millie!" I obeyed, and she handed me the artwork.

Keeping In Touch

Early in my alumni work I was fortunate to attend a National Meeting of Alumni Directors with Claude Rich of Indiana University. He was known as "Mr. Alumni, U.S.A." and rightly so. Indiana University had one of the best alumni programs in the country. I had first met him when I was a grad student at IU. I valued his advice and hung onto his every word. At the national meeting, I picked his brain again. He strongly advised me to be in touch with as many students as possible. If they were to support their college later as alums, they needed to be sold on the school while they were still students. That truth is good yet today.

In my travels I have met a few disgruntled alums and other constituents. I remind them that their loyalty to the school is more important than any slights or misunderstandings they might have encountered along the way. The school is much larger than the persons who might have offended them. Only small people hold grudges and withhold support.

One of our best public relations persons on campus was Marie Noggle. In the bookstore she had contact with all of the students and left her stamp upon their lives. If ever there was a "mother confessor" on campus she was the one. She loved the students and they loved her. I often challenged the faculty and staff members to imitate her and to keep in mind that the students were the only reason for our being there.

I worked before the days of the computer. In one drawer of my desk I kept all of the alumni names, recorded alphabetically as well as by class and present location. I referred to these cards frequently. Our alums then were numbered by a few, not many thousands as they are today. My period of service was ideal. The classes from 1920 to the 70's were small and I knew most of our alums. I could call or write to them when I needed assistance of any kind. Rarely did they refuse. When sending out a bulk mailing, I made it a habit to add a personal note to our military personnel and to the missionaries who were serving overseas. Since each piece of mail that I sent out requested a return or response for one reason or another, I was able to keep my files updated.

One alumnus on file was Navy Captain John Neff. A favorite student of Dr. Dodd and Dr. Porter, he had been on campus before entering the Naval Academy at Annapolis. (Imagine my delight years later when I married Dick and learned that I had become a cousin-in-law to John!) The intimacy I was able to establish with our alums remains an important facet of my life. During our extensive travels together, Dick and I met with alums from Alaska to Mexico, as well as Africa and Hawaii. While we were in Hawaii, Captain John gave us a special tour of the USS Arizona Memorial.

I felt I had the best job on the campus—no grades, no discipline. The students all called me Millie. I shared my love of my Alma

Mater with them and challenged them to be the best they could be. We had a mutual love affair. (When I had the privilege of speaking to them in chapel one fall, I offered a five-dollar bill to the student who could spell and define Alumni, Alumna, Alumnae and Alumnus. Son-in-law Alvin Wooters ('74) and others still talk about that challenge. I was more than pleased to part with my money.)

Important Team Members

The capable secretaries made my work much easier. Our first secretary was Joyce York Ott ('46). She was a jewel and served us well—with her quiet, personable manner, she was just the person we needed. In fact, she was too efficient. We lost her to Dr. Burns, our Academic Dean. She went on from that office to later serve several of Marion College's presidents. The sudden senseless deaths of Joyce and her husband Ellman ('45) in an auto crash have been difficult for me to accept.

When Joyce moved to Dr. Burns' office, Jean Strawser stepped in—or to be more accurate, jumped in to take over as my secretary. We were a good match for one another. She was clever, a ball of energy, and we had fun working together. When I was traveling, she handled phone calls and correspondence as if I were there. I think of her fondly, especially at Christmas when I remember how she beautifully decorated all of the office doors on the first floor of the Administration Building. Each had a different color covering and a special bow to make them look like a huge parcel.

While I am on the subject of office secretaries, this is a good time to toss a bouquet to the present alumni secretary, Carolyn McGhee. She has served under five Alumni Directors. Dick could never figure out why they did not promote her to the director's position. She has held the association together through phonathons, homecomings, graduations, and you name it, as well as the day-to-day operations of the office. She was married in May 2001 to Dow Chamberlain, the brother of Daniel Chamberlain, president of Houghton College. I wish them well. Cindy Ruder has recently taken her place and is learning the ropes fast!

Special congrats also to Bill Westover ('78), who has been named as our new Alumni Director. Along with my good wishes, I trust they will be used for many years to advance the kingdom through Indiana Wesleyan University.

A Concrete Idea

Along with excellent secretaries, an active alumni board, and committees, students have helped with everything from mailings to homecoming. For our Jubilee Homecoming we decided to use antiques for most of our decorations—with accents in gold, of course. Someone suggested we fill large milk cans with cattails and adorn them with golden bows. But where would we get the milk cans? I had to be out of town for some alumni meetings and did not have time to search for them. Imagine my surprise when I returned home and entered my drive. My car headlights illuminated a huge pyramid of milk cans and cattails! Lorna Shelton Bennett ('71), Allen Costello ('74), and others had come through again.

I am grateful to former President Dr. Woodrow Goodman ('39) for excerpts from his memoirs regarding that celebration:

Jubilee Year

"1969-70 was the fiftieth year of operation for Marion College. Our theme for the year, 'Tradition Touching Tomorrow,' was found on campaign-style buttons, the title of a brochure, and in other publications. The concept was that the present moment was the link between our past and future. Homecoming 1969 was an important part of that celebration. In the morning Baldwin Center was dedicated. At noon there was an old-fashioned ox roast. For the evening meal students, faculty and alumni came together. Approximately six hundred persons were served in Baldwin Center that night. The program featured pictures of the past and dreams for the future. A recep-

tion was held to honor Dr. Mary Dodd who graduated in the first class of Marion College and who returned after graduate study to teach at her Alma Mater for forty-six of the fifty years."

My idea to put a replica of the campus arch on the Court House Square involved more than I anticipated. We were granted permission to erect the two large brick posts, if we would set them on concrete footings. That seemed fair enough. I went to Teter Hall where some of our young men lived at that time, called upstairs, and said that I needed help. Dick's sons Jim ('73) and George ('70) and a few others responded. When I explained the situation, Jim and the others said, "We're out of here!" I did not really blame them. George and two of his friends finally agreed to go with me to do the job. By the time we got to the courthouse it had started to rain. An "alum" was going to pour the footing the next day, so we had to complete our part that evening, rain or no rain. Before we were finished, we were soaked to the skin. However we were pleased and surprised that neither the police nor any other officials questioned what we were doing. After we completed our task, we picked up some pizza and Pepsi and went tired, wet, and hungry to my home. After the fellows left, I had a hot shower and fell into bed exhausted. My portion was done. Another group had volunteered to lay the bricks and duplicate the sign. The completed sign was a real attention-getter. In this attempt to link the city and the college, the city of Marion certainly knew we were celebrating our 50th!

Marilyn Birch, my physician friend in Sierra Leone, wrote the following regarding our work in the rain: "Your putting cement work up in the rain in the heart of the city says something else about concrete ideas! You're a nut, and probably glad of it, eh? There are such things as first-class nuts and I'm quite sure you would qualify."

George and his friends probably thought I was a nut, too. However, in 1977 when Dick and I announced our engagement, George was heard to say to several, "Do you know Millie Jacobs?"

"Yes."

"Have you heard she's getting married?"

"NO! To whom?"

"My DAD!"

Previous to the early sixties, annual membership dues of a few dollars per year financed the alumni activities. President-elect Goodman sent a message to those attending the May 1960 alumni banquet, soliciting their help in future activities for accreditation, for institutional growth, and for the development of income.

Again I quote from Dr. Goodman's memoirs:

> *"Total gift income to Marion College in 1959-60 was $26,268. About $20,000 of the income came from the church budget assessment of $3.00 per member per year."*

Alumni support was one of my earliest goals. The alumni officers organized a campaign for 1960-61 with $16,000 as a goal. That was achieved and a new goal of $25,000 was set for 1961-62. By 1963-64 the alumni giving topped $50,000. The 1963-64 totals for class participation listed 650 donors, up 77 from the year before. The percent of participation was 27.3 and the average gift was $47.98. Total cash gifts from the alumni came to $31,184. Gifts-in-kind, with $8,650 in pledges, brought the total to $50,029. The response was excellent considering the number of alumni and the short history of the alumni fund."

Carolyn Wilhite ('29), a local school principal, was the effective chairman of that campaign. When the association was revitalized and we were actually raising money, some of our members wanted to form a corporation separate from the college. They wanted to control all of "our" money. Dr. Goodman and I successfully resisted this proposal. I have always believed the alumni association exists to serve the school, not to dictate to it.

Pushing Hard

During my tenure as alumni director, I was able to visit the Island one weekend a month to continue improving the property. However in order to do that, I pushed myself the rest of the month. Sometimes, I pushed myself too hard. While I enjoyed the solitude and change of pace on the Island, I often took faculty or students along with me.

I traveled extensively to hold alumni chapter meetings and to make other contacts for the school. Over a period of time, I flew or drove from coast to coast and north and south. I well remember driving one afternoon on an East Coast interstate highway. I had been up late the night before in a meeting and wondered to myself if I would ever make it to this scheduled appointment. I felt ever so weary and discouraged. A Scripture came to me: "But David encouraged himself in the Lord his God." (1 Sam. 30:6) I did as he did and had a wonderful time with the alums, prospective students, and their parents.

In 1965 we started the annual phonathon. Benny Meadows ('55) and Dave Spargo ('52) were invaluable to the effort. A number of our older alumnae graciously served us snacks each evening. Other alums did our recording and mailing. This new endeavor was exciting and satisfying but very stressful. The phone system was not as efficient as it is now and we did not have calculators, much less computers, for tabulating. I worked late each evening after the phoning to record the number of calls and the amount of pledges, the refusals, maybes, etc. Along with raising thousands of dollars for scholarships, we took the opportunity during the phonathon to update alumni addresses and other information. We emphasized the need for giving rather than the amount of giving, and that each and every gift was important to the total effort. We also stressed that before foundations, corporations, and other potential large donors decide to give to a school, they should first examine the commitment of the school's own alumni to supporting their Alma Mater.

The Door Is Always Open

Pre-Christmas exam time was special on our campus. The alumni board members and I baked mountains of cookies, made stacks of sandwiches, and prepared gallons of tea, coffee, hot chocolate, and wassail. The students wolfed our food down as they crammed in knowledge for their exams. I did my alumni work during that period at home by catching up on phone calls, correspondence, and planning future events. The students could drop by any time during the day and up to eleven o'clock at night for a chat and a snack. One way or another, I became acquainted with most of the student body.

During the year, too, my home and my office were always open to the students. My den was reserved as a place of relaxation and solitude. One day Dale Spaulding ('67) came by and asked, "Millie, may I have the privacy of your den? I want to give Roxie (Hoke '67) her diamond this weekend." That was the night she consented to become Mrs. Spaulding.

Another time I looked out and saw three or four fellows picketing my place with empty signs. They walked back and forth for quite a while before I inquired about their actions. Russ Cooper ('65), who later became a faculty member and is now with Wycliffe Translators said, "Millie, we are looking for a place where we can sit down and discuss something other than girls, sex, and cars. May we come into your den?" So in they came, free to discuss whatever they had in mind.

During a rare winter storm which closed down the campus, Russ trudged through the snow to my home and borrowed my snowshoes and sleeping bag. With these he hiked to his uncle's farm near Gas City, where he camped out overnight. I am not sure why I loaned the sleeping bag. I have always told my campers that there are two things I refuse to loan—my sleeping bag and my toothbrush. He brought back the sleeping bag with a damaged zipper. Years later when he returned to his Alma Mater to teach, I imposed upon his new wife, Mary, to replace the zipper in the bag. I am so glad he got a spouse who could sew! During that same snowstorm, by the way, I had the fun of being pulled around the campus athletic field on my skis behind Deanne Dayton's Volkswagen bug.

Although I gave myself to the students, they also gave much to me. I was well looked after. Early one morning I glanced out of my window to discover Dan Barker ('68) and Mark Abbott ('68) at my car. They had spotted a flat tire and saved me the trouble of taking it off. They were even ready to take it to Joe Clement Sr.'s service station to have it repaired.

Bev Hill, a former CGIT camper and counselor from Ottawa, roomed with Laura Mangus ('69) in Shatford Hall. They did their best to try to make me beautiful each week by doing my hair—and they also saved me a lot of time and money. One day they found two gray hairs and were determined to dye my hair the very next week. "The rest of the students would never see Millie Jacobs with gray hair!" they claimed. I flatly refused their offer—after all, you can only fool part of the people part of the time. Laura was dating Richard Gaddis ('70), who was working at the General Hospital. We three would often pick him up at the hospital on Friday afternoon and then we would head for the Island for a short weekend. It was fun to share the cabin and Island with them.

My home on campus was a second home to the international students. Since they prepared a meal there once a month, the ethnic aromas—or should I say "bouquet"?—permeated my home. I especially enjoyed taking some of these students on their first outings to supermarkets, malls, through automatic car washes, and to Bollinger's Farm near Fort Wayne to see sheep, turkeys, dogs, and cats.

Hilda V. Clarke ('68) was often seen—and heard—on campus. The president and nearly everyone else knew her. She came from Honduras to study English and music. Now teaching at White's Residential and Family Services near Wabash, Indiana, she is making her presence known there as well. Hilda is a good friend. She traveled to the Island to sing at my ordination, later sang at our wedding in the College Church, and again at Dick's funeral service.

Making a Point

When I sometimes had differences of opinion with students, I tried to settle them in unique ways. It bothered me to see them taking shortcuts and wearing unsightly paths on the campus lawns. I was reminded of a similar situation at Ball State University when I was doing graduate work. The president told us, "If you want this campus to look like a cow pasture, I will help you." He then put cow manure on the unwanted paths.

At Marion College some of us had already posted clever signs like "Your Feet Are Killing Me" and "Robins Only" around our campus. This didn't seem to be working, so I fetched several bushels of bovine scat from Deer Creek farm and scattered it on their paths. The next morning I found most of the manure on my front porch! My strategies did not always work. But I still wonder: how did they know?

One Halloween eve I frustrated them. I had heard that some of the young men were going to kidnap a Volkswagen Bug from the Shatford Hall parking lot near my home. So I turned out my house lights early that evening and waited and watched. Soon a group of students arrived and surrounded the car. I flipped on the porch lights and they scattered like scared rabbits. I repeated this exercise several times before they finally gave up.

Another group of men/boys masterminded another prank. One of them managed to secret himself in the chapel before it was closed for the night and then later admitted his cronies. They unscrewed all of the pews from the floor and turned them completely around. However, they could not resist bragging about their adventure when they went back to the dorm. Soon word reached the Dean. The pranksters were ordered to return the pews to their original positions and then later appear before the Administration Committee. Finding themselves in trouble, they came to my office seeking my help and sympathy. I said, "Get out of here and go face the music. You have pulled one of the best jokes ever and couldn't keep your mouths shut." (During my last phonathon, I enjoyed reminding a medical doctor of his participation in that event.)

One of my more unusual experiences with students involved Frank Van Order ('73). He was a nephew of Lema Hicks Van Order. I was then renting a wee house on Selby Street from the college. (Carmin Hall now stands there.) Frank was working for the school's maintenance department. He knocked on my door with the announcement that he was there to paint two rooms for me.

And then he said, "This is not going to be a very good day. I hate painting." I made him a proposition. If he would polish all my silver—and I had a lot of it in the china cabinet—I would do the painting. We had a wonderful day. He even got a free lunch out of the deal.

A Reason to Celebrate!

Marion College achieved accreditation by the North Central Association of Colleges in 1966 during the presidency of Dr. Goodman. Our application in earlier years had been denied; however, the effort continued. Finally we were so confident about being accepted that we started making plans for a celebration. President Goodman and Dr. Maurice Burns, Academic Dean, were in Chicago for the final consideration. Russell Baldwin, the Business manager, was waiting at the college phone for the expected good news. We had stationed students at every fire alarm on campus, ready to pull the handles as soon as we heard the exciting news.

When the call came, I raced to the Crow's Nest and climbed the ladder to the bell tower. The alarms went off below and I rang the bell above. (At that moment in the history of Marion College, I had the highest physical position on campus!) The celebration had begun. We made posters and banners and prepared a bonfire with the mountains of materials we had accumulated for that purpose. That night on the athletic field we had a real fire. We had reason to celebrate. The faculty could now take greater pride in their teaching, and the students' credits would be accepted at other universities.

We continued to celebrate the next day. Led by the police and the hook-and-ladder truck from the fire department, we paraded noisily down Washington Street, around the Courthouse Square, and back to the campus—faculty, staff, students, alums, and other friends. We met in the old gym for a time of praise, singing heartfelt songs of thanksgiving. Howard Noggle and others expressed our gratitude to God in prayer. A quartet composed of Byron Tippey ('47), Jim Luttrull, Gerry Smeenge, and William Fessenden ('32) ended the celebration with the hymn "To God Be the Glory for Great Things He Has Done."

The Color of Change

Accreditation brought many advantages and changes to our campus. Intercollegiate sports were now an option—really a must, if we were to attract students who wanted to teach physical education or participate in sports beyond Amphic-Eurekan competition. As is true of any change, not all Marion College supporters were ready for intercollegiate competition. Black and red were our school colors. Many thought we needed to change those—we needed brighter colors to enhance uniforms, banners, flags, and so on, so they said.

One of the most interesting faculty meetings I ever attended involved that issue. Many alums felt strongly that some things should remain unchanged, that some traditions were worth fighting for. Not surprisingly, one of those happened to be Dr. Mary Dodd, who was a member of Marion College's first graduating class. She was soft spoken, but as you will note, strong willed. She was proud of her long, reddish brown hair and she happened to be an Amphic. Amphic colors were brown and white in contrast to the Eurekan's green and white. On occasion she would flash the Amphic badge hidden under her lapel. Helen Hacker Shellenbarger ('44), the alumni president at that time, and many others were in agreement with Dr. Dodd.

When the issue of school colors first surfaced and Dr. Dodd knew there was a possibility of change, she asked if I would assist her in doing some research on the subject. Together we examined all of the old *Marionettes* and *Journals* and other documents from the earliest days to the present time. Just as she had said, the first student body of Marion College had selected red and black for the school colors. She had been one of those students. A lawyer might have been proud of our research efforts, for we found many facts to support our stand on the issue.

We took our findings back with us to the faculty meeting on school colors, presided over by Dr. Goodman. Those in favor of changing our colors presented their arguments. All the while Dr. Dodd sat quietly drumming her fingers on the chair back next to her. Finally Dr. Goodman said, "Would you like to speak to this issue, Dr. Dodd?"

She was short and to the point. "All I can say, Dr. Goodman, is this: if these Johnny-come-latelys want to change everything about this institution, they should go and start a school of their own."

A vote was taken and the colors red and black were retained. Later, of course, the colors would change. With the introduction of intercollegiate sports, the Amphics and Eurekans gradually faded. But strong feelings among former members still remain.

Although the Amphic-Eurekan societies were eventually dropped from the campus scene, they did not leave quietly. A mock wedding of the two groups was held. The service included these words: "Dearly beloved, we are gathered together in the sight of the faculty, some fortunate alumni, and in the presence of this company of students to join these two friendly rivals into one great unified school spirit."

Later there was an all-school contest to choose a name, mascot, and emblems for the school teams. We became known as the Titans. That was later changed to the Wildcats. We won our first intercollegiate soccer game by defeating Bethel College of Mishawaka with a score of 5-2. The Titans also won the first Wesleyan Basketball Tournament Invitational in 1968-69 under coach Paul Mills. Paul is now the president of Oklahoma Wesleyan University.

When I am asked if all these changes bother me, I respond, "No, change is inevitable and when we cease to change we cease to grow." Along with Dr. Jim Barnes ('65), I am more concerned that we continue to "Keep First Things First."

Storm Damage

In 1965, the Palm Sunday tornado caused extensive damage in many parts of the state. Considering the widespread destruction of property, human casualties were surprisingly low. We were in College Church when the lights went out and the police advised us to remain in the building until traffic could move once again. A few of the girls had decided to stay in Teter Hall instead of attending the evening service. The severe rattling of the windows and the howling wind frightened them. Later, they surveyed the devastating destruction only a short distance away. I wasn't surprised to see all of them in church the next Sunday evening.

To my knowledge only one Marion College student was seriously injured. Jane Fulk ('67) and her husband to be, Gerald Hewson ('65), were driving along 45th Street at the edge of the storm. Jane suffered a bad head wound, but Gerald was only slightly injured. The Wesleyan Church Headquarters building was badly damaged, as was the south end of the city of Marion and surrounding areas. Benny Meadows ('55) and I had met on Friday afternoon to plan the upcoming phonathan. His home was severely damaged. However, during the storm he was in the College Church—with our phonathan plans in his inner coat pocket. We were extremely grateful!

The power outage and so much disruption did not allow me to do my work at the office. With the president's approval, I gathered up my papers and portable typewriter and went to the Island. Using natural daylight or candlelight at night, I prepared the next issue of the *Marion College Alumni Bulletin*. That left my home in Marion available for three African male students who stayed there and cooked their meals on my propane stove.

An Abiding Love

The great love I have for this university must be very evident to the reader by this time. Although at the time of this writing my home may be 514 miles from the center of the campus, Indiana

Wesleyan University is never far from my mind nor left out of my daily prayers. I could write another book filled with stories about my contact with faculty, staff and students, and I would not miss homecoming for anything. In fact, I care enough about this school to will the bulk of my estate to the Canadian Campus.

A handsome black chair embossed with the college seal sits in front of my desk here in the cabin. On the wall above the desk hangs a plaque given to me by the alumni association in 1972. These are symbols indicating that I have been recognized as a distinguished alumna. If there should be any truth to that, may God have the glory.

*_The Lord, The Landmarks, The Life_ by Dr. Mary J. Elder commemorates the Diamond Jubilee Celebration (1920-1995) of Indiana Wesleyan University. Printed by IP Graphics, Plymouth, IN, 1994.

Chapter Thirteen

A Difficult Transition
(1971-1972)

"What reasons endeavor cannot bring about, often time will."
T. Fuller

The transition from Marion Campus to the Island came much sooner than I anticipated. When I had worked at the YMCA and again with the Girl Scouts, I instinctively knew when it was time for me to move on. Marion College was different. Signing my contract as alumni director, I felt that I would spend the remainder of my career life on the campus. I was thrilled to be back at Marion

College and I truly loved my work. But I must have loved it too much. I guess in a sense I was married to my job and it showed. I gave my all to my work.

The Camel and the Straw

The encouragement and support of the students, staff, and alums kept me going at a much faster pace than I realized. I managed on less and less sleep and seemed to work endless hours. Deuteronomy 33:25 says, "As thy days, so shall thy strength be." I took that Scripture too literally. Friends expressed concern about my weight loss, but I shrugged off their comments. It has always been easier for me to gain weight than to lose it, so that didn't seem like much of a problem to me. My chief concern was that my energy level wasn't sufficient for all the projects I was handling.

My good friend Dr. Marilyn Birch suggested that I have a check-up at Marion General Hospital. Marilyn had returned from her missionary work in Sierra Leone, West Africa, and was working on an assignment at the Wesleyan World Headquarters in Marion.

She had given me a few sleeping pills, but I could not handle the side effects. The sleep was not worth the "hangover" that accompanied the pills. A complete medical check-up along with several X-rays merely revealed that I had extremely low blood pressure and low iron. The doctors prescribed weekly iron shots and suggested I slow down and lighten my workload. But this was one of the busiest times of the year. Homecoming 1971 was at hand. How could I possibly slow down?

Planning for Homecoming was the straw that broke the camel's back. The parade, campus decorations, and the banquet plans were all in order when my world caved in. My kind friends, Sam and Ethel Good, had an isolated cabin on Deer Creek away from the campus. I was familiar with the cabin, as it had been the scene of numerous, intimate faculty dinners. I collapsed there in the quietness of that refuge.

No one except the administration knew of my whereabouts. My

only visitors were my godchildren, Beth and Brad Bollinger. They raised my spirits but couldn't cure my exhaustion.

At the time, my friend Eva Gilger was in Marion on business at the World Gospel Mission. Planning to drive to her home in Kansas for a few weeks before she returned to Kenya, she invited me to spend those weeks with her. I accepted somewhat reluctantly because I dreaded the long drive. We had made that trip several times before and we always drove straight through. She promised that this time we would take our time, stopping along the way as needed. Her physician gave me the necessary iron shots and Eva proved to be a capable nurse and cook. However, the change of pace and her loving care did not bring me out of my breakdown.

A Comforting Companion

I have yet to mention my huge black cat. Originally named Tar Baby, he had grown into Tar Man. Eva was not a cat lover but agreed to take Tar Man to Kansas with us. Unfortunately, he disappeared from Eva's home on the eve of Halloween. We searched for him late into the night to no avail. A black cat missing on Halloween? I was sure I'd seen the last of him. But he surprised us by showing up on the porch the next day.

Dr. Goodman had previously suggested that I take some time away from the campus. My sister Ruth and several others offered to care for me, but my heart yearned for the quietness of my cabin. When Eva made her flight plans to return to Kenya, she arranged for me to fly out the same day for Sault Ste. Marie, Michigan. For the flight to the Sault, I rented a pet carrier for Tar Man and attempted to sedate him. He awakened long before we landed in the Sault. Who knows what he must have been thinking in the cargo hold, but he was one wild piece of luggage when I picked him up!

Fred and Donna Gibbs, pastors of the Sault Ste. Marie, Michigan Wesleyan Church, met my plane, took me home with them, and tucked me into bed. We had become good friends on previous visits, when I had spoken to their church about Marion College. Later, the young people from their church were frequent campers on the Island. One of them, Roxie McKiddie Halvorsen, now serves on the camp's board of directors.

The next day they helped me pick up groceries and supplies before taking me to the Island. The Gilbertsons met us and made sure the cabin had wood and water. Shocked when she saw me, Rose said I looked like a walking skeleton. After that, she and various relatives checked on me often.

When everyone left and Tar Man and I were all alone in the cabin, I breathed a sigh of relief. For weeks my family and friends had showered me with love and attention. Of course, along with the expressions of concern came endless advice and suggestions as to what was really wrong and what I should do about it. Tar Man's companionship was a delightful contrast, one that allowed me to truly relax. Unlike dogs, cats make few demands, but provide plenty of entertainment with their antics. I found his presence to be comforting.

In the Valley

I knew I was not functioning properly. I knew I could not sleep. I knew I did not have any energy, and I knew that people upset me. I well remember thanking God for the peace and quiet of the cabin. I was alone, but not alone. At the cabin, I did not have to answer to anyone but God. I was certain that in a very short time I would be my old self again. I would return to campus. The students there would put the wind back in my sails. Those thoughts gave me hope. God's promises were as true today as they were yesterday. "All things [do] work together for good" (Romans 8:28).

I was also encouraged by the support of my friends at Marion College. The following article appeared in the January 1972 edition of the *Marion College Alumni Journal*:

> *"Millie Jacobs has been given sick leave for an indefinite time to permit adequate convalescence. Last September she suffered from extreme exhaustion and was released from her work responsibilities in*

Once again . . . the simple life

> *early October. Medical tests have been negative in regard to several other possible diagnoses.*
>
> *"To make the most satisfactory and quickest recovery it seems best to release Miss Jacobs from any deadline of responsibility or set time for return to campus. Hopefully in a few months she will be able to resume her activities as Director of Alumni Relations.*
>
> *"In the meantime, Millie is making her home on St. Joseph Island, a Canadian Island near the Soo. She is making slow but steady progress in her recovery. Let us support her in our prayers."*
>
> *Dr. W. I. Goodman.*

I had often encouraged others with Paul's words: "I have learned, in whatsoever state I am in, therewith to be content" (Philippians 4:11). I had always been content. This too would pass and I would be back on campus. I was determined to eat right, follow the doctor's orders, and make an effort to get outdoors every day.

The local doctor agreed on the iron shots, but thought I should also take some sleeping pills to get back on track with my sleep pattern. (I heard later that he was a pill pusher.) Perish the thought! The very idea was an aversion to me. My mother and others I had known had become addicted to sleeping pills. I had always counted myself lucky that I never needed to take much medication, and I certainly did not want drugs in my system now.

Looking Up

I spent much time reading and praying in the window bed that overlooks Placid Pool. It had always been conducive to quiet meditation, but especially now gave me such a sense of serenity. When I am on my knees in prayer or meditation, I can see such a long way into the distance from that vantage point.

My energy level was too low to allow me to get very far from the cabin at first, but each day I took a few steps more. Setting my sights on two spruce trees at the far end of the old orchard, I chose certain rest stops and then paused to study my surroundings and contemplate His goodness. And gradually, day by day, I felt myself grow stronger—but it was oh, so slow.

Generous friends saw to my needs. Don Gilbertson usually took me down to Richards Landing for my shots. His family continued to bring in my wood and water. Bert, another friend, owned the hundred acres across from me. He was timbering there at the time and pulled out treetops for friends to saw up for my firewood. The Gibbs from Sault, Michigan, brought meals to me on their day off. (Donna makes the best chicken curry I have ever eaten.)

With weekly iron shots, the surrounding peace and quiet, and no phone calls or demands on my time or energy, I began to recover. In spite of my progress, however, several specialists advised me against returning to the type of work I had been doing. I was devastated. What would I do? I was in my late forties, so opportunities were limited. Furthermore, throughout my professional life I had always worked with young people. They were my inspiration and my light. But I wondered, would I ever have the energy to do that kind of demanding work again?

My heart was broken. I could not see beyond my life on the campus. But an amazing thing began to happen as I recovered. Groups of campers began to come for short periods of time, staying only as my strength permitted. These visitors said they wanted to help me. Slowly, too, my self-confidence returned. From time to time I was invited to direct CGIT and Free Methodist camps here and there around the province.

God seemed to be opening a door for me. Was camping to be the next phase of my life? When I purchased the property in 1963 from Bernt and Rose Gilbertson, I intended it to be a camp, something that would minister to others—especially young people. I was well aware that in the near future there would not be very many hundred-acre parcels of unspoiled land left in this world that could be used solely for outdoor activities.

Dr. Allen Bowman, academic dean of Marion College, and Russell Baldwin, business manager, along with their wives had been frequent guests at my cabin. They were impressed with the property and its potential for camping and college classes.

In 1967 I discussed with Russell the possibility of donating the property to the college. He appreciated my generosity but suggested that I include this decision in my will, just in case I needed money or changed my mind in later years. They say it's a woman's prerogative to do that very thing.

But in 1972 my life had taken a dramatic turn and I was facing in a new direction, confronting a new kind of ministry. What I take so much for granted now, some thirty years later, seemed such an uncertain future for me then. But God was faithful and gave me the inner assurance that this indeed was the way, walk ye in it.

And I took great comfort knowing Jesus ministered in the out-of-doors.

Christ Was the Outdoor Son of God

My master was a Man, who knew
The rush of rain, the drip of dew,
The wistful whisper of the breeze,
Night's magic and its mysteries.

He was a Man of sun and stars,
He knew the Pleides and Mars,
The star trail called the Milky Way,
The crescent moon, the dawn, the day.
His feet were stained by dusty ways,
His cheeks were brown as summer days;
His skin had the look of one
Who knew the blazing balm of sun.

He walked alone upon the sea,
Spake peace to wave-washed Galilee,
All shores and seas were in His thought,
This Man, God bred, star led, sky taught.

To Him there were no sweeter tones
Than water washing over stones;
To Him no splendid symphony
Like murmuring, blue Galilee.

His hair and heart were washed with showers;
He loved the fields and flowers;
The sea and tree, the star and sod;
He was the Outdoor Son of God.

—William L. Stidger

Chapter Fourteen

A Woman's Place

(1971-1977)

"Here am I; send me."
Isaiah 6:8

When my strength began to return in the mid-seventies, I took a more active role in the Island Free Methodist Church. I served as the Christian Education Director, which included teaching the adult

Sunday school class and working with the young people. On Sundays I frequently filled the pulpit for Pastor Ralph Byggdin and often led the midweek prayer service. I was also invited to speak at other area churches, retreats, and conferences. As I became involved in the Western Ontario Free Methodist Conference, many asked why I was not ordained. They knew I had a degree in theology and they pointed to the similar doctrines and practices of the Wesleyans and the Free Methodists.

Ordination—Why Now?

I could have pursued ordination in The Wesleyan Church. Women had been ordained in The Wesleyan Church for well over a hundred years. In 1853 Luther Lee, one of the Church's founders, preached the sermon at the ordination of America's first woman minister. For his text he used Galatians 3:28: "There is neither Jew nor Greek, there is neither slave nor free, there is neither male nor female: for ye are all one in Christ Jesus."

While I was attending Marion College as a student, I worked toward a Bachelor of Theology, as well as a Bachelor of Arts. Many urged me to be ordained. During that time, I also prayed for a call to go to Africa as a missionary. That call never came. In my heart I often thought if I went into ministry, I would like to serve in some remote area in the mountains of Kentucky or Tennessee or the far north. Professors and well-meaning friends urged me to be ordained to preach or to go into full-time ministry or to pastor a church. But I did not feel God leading me in those directions. However, I did learn how to quiet myself before Him, to search His Word for that inner conviction and assurance of His will in my life.

Africa may not have been the place He had in mind, but it became very clear that working with young people was my calling—and ordination was not a requirement for that. There were many doors to present Christ and I did not feel the need of a "tag" to open any of them. Ordination was not necessary for my happiness or for me to feel "complete." Before I actively sought ordination, a friend reminded me in a letter that I had already been ordained by God. We are all ministers whether we are ordained or not.

But the combination of increased involvement at the Island Free Methodist Church while establishing my own church youth camp brought the issue of my ordination into clear focus. I saw that being ordained would increase my capacity for service in the operation of our new camp, especially in working with the various groups who come to the camp. (As well, another privilege that comes with ordination is the ability to officiate at funerals and weddings. Being acquainted with the Island since the late 1940's, I have seen all of the Island church ministers come and go. It has been my honor to officiate at many funerals and weddings for those who did not have a minister.)

The Trouble with Women

Over the years the pros and cons of ordaining women have filled volumes of books. As a student of His Word—benefiting from both individual and group study—I have come to the conclusion that ordination for women is consistent with His teachings. Many are convinced that even though the New Testament writers believed they were reporting God's will when they issued their demands and prohibitions about women, they were really victims of cultural bias.

Many Christians are not happy with such dismissal of those biblical instructions. To hint that the writers of the New Testament epistles might be wrong about something so basic as the relationship between men and women would contradict their view of Scripture as God's infallible Word.

Such people are often suspicious of any attempt to interpret texts in a manner that explains away what they take to be the "clear meaning" of these verses. However, whoever reads the Scriptures must do some interpreting. Scriptures must be taken in context, both in the context of where they appear in the chapter and in their context as statements made to specific people in specific times and places. Those who oppose the ordination of women generally select certain

Scriptures (regarding the position of women in the home, church, and world) that support their particular stance toward women.

I have made an effort to live by Colossians 3:15-17: "And let the peace of God rule in your hearts, to the which also ye are called in one body; and be ye thankful. Let the word of Christ dwell in you richly in all wisdom; teaching and admonishing one another in psalms and hymns and spiritual songs, singing with grace in your hearts to the Lord. And whatsoever ye do in word or deed, do all in the name of the Lord Jesus, giving thanks to God and the Father by Him."

What Did Paul Mean?

A look at some of Paul's most famous passages may shed some light on this issue. In 1 Corinthians 11:5-6 he discusses head coverings for women: "But every woman that prayeth or prophesieth with her head uncovered dishonoureth her head: for that is even all one as if she were shaven. For if the woman be not covered, let her also be shorn: but if it be a shame for a woman to be shorn or shaven, let her be covered."

Is it fitting for a woman to pray bareheaded? If we are honest we must say, "Perhaps not in Corinth in the first century, but in the twenty-first century, yes." Most churches have long since decided this was a cultural prohibition relevant only for the time in which it was written, not a decree of God laid down for all time. Often Paul's concern is with decorum, with the impression the women will make on others. His concern is for modesty and propriety. Never is a woman to engage in conduct or appearance that is not fitting.

Then consider 1 Corinthians 14:34-35: "Let your women keep silence in the churches: for it is not permitted unto them to speak; but they are commanded to be under obedience, as also sayeth the law. And if they will learn any thing, let them ask their husbands at home: for it is a shame for women to speak in the church." Again, very few churches take this literally. If they did, there would be no women teaching in our Sunday schools, certainly no soloists in our choirs, nor any women missionaries sharing or praying with us.

And how do we interpret 1 Corinthians 11:5, "But every woman that prayeth or prophesieth"? Here is full proof that women were praying and prophesying in public. It is difficult to imagine how women could prophesy if they were to be silent. The New English Bible avoids this by saying, "Women shall not address the meeting." But how do you explain the possibility of their prophesying without "addressing the meeting"? In short, we simply cannot take these passages at their most literal meaning—they cannot be understood without interpretation of some sort. Interpretation must involve looking at the context as it relates to all of Scripture.

In 1 Corinthians 14:26 Paul takes up the matter of conducting meetings. "How is it then, brethren? When ye come together, every one of you hath a psalm, hath a doctrine, hath a tongue, hath a revelation, hath an interpretation. Let all things be done unto edifying." It is important to remember that Paul is dealing with a problem church. The women had been calling out, even heckling the speakers. In first-century Corinth, respectable women did not even speak publicly to their own husbands.

Paul is clearly speaking to married women, for he says they can go home and ask their husbands. The single woman, the woman who lives alone was not common in that early society. The church will have to decide the role of single women today, since the New Testament writers never thought to talk about it or, if they did, it was not recorded for us.

Paul discusses church offices in 1 Timothy 3. He gives the criteria for what kind of men should be office holders. We have evidence that he would not have approved of women in such positions. Or do we? The question probably never occurred to him. With few exceptions, women were not trained and did not take part in public kinds of services. When Paul thought about leadership, he thought in terms of men, quite possibly not because there was anything wrong with women assuming leadership, but simply because so few women would have been capable.

Phoebe must have been one of the few who held some kind of leadership position. In Romans 16:1 we read: "I commend unto you

Phoebe our sister, which is a servant of the church which is at Cenchrea." He goes on to say in verse two: "That ye receive her in the Lord, as becometh saints, and that ye assist her in whatsoever business she hath need of you: for she hath been a succourer of many, and of myself also."

A Question of Interpretation

Paul exhorted women not to admonish their husbands publicly. In 1 Timothy 2:11 Paul refers to meetings where unbelievers might be present. He told women to keep their places as the law directed, not because Christians had to live by the old law, but because the women had been talking out of place. He did not want their behavior to bring disrepute upon the church. Allowing the women to question publicly or to admonish their husbands would appear to be letting them domineer over their husbands. His admonition here has nothing to do with the function or ruling of the church or being active in benevolence.

A problem in interpreting this text is the Greek word translated "domineer over." This is the only time that the word is used anywhere in the entire New Testament. It is related to the word "master" or "autocrat," and could be properly translated "be master over." Whether having some kind of official authority in the church would automatically make a woman domineer over her husband is debatable. It seems quite feasible that there is a sense of "domineering" that has nothing to do with official positions of leadership. Instead it refers to a situation between people that might be unhealthy if the woman were doing the domineering.

Some who insist women may not have authority in the church argue their case from the headship of man. But in every case in the Bible where headship is mentioned, it refers to marriage relationship, not church order. The question of a woman's relationship to her husband is quite different from the problem of the woman's role in the church. The two should be kept distinct.

In Ephesians 5:22-23 we read: "Wives, submit yourselves unto your own husbands, as unto the Lord. For the husband is the head of the wife, even as Christ is the head of the church: and He is the saviour of the body." But in verse 21 we read: "Submitting yourselves one to another in the fear of God."

The Greek word "submit" is sometimes translated "obey" or "to be submissive to." But whatever we take it to mean, the point is that a woman's relationship to her husband's authority is very much like the relationship of all Christians to one another.

Remarkably Different

Any discussion of the role of women in the church should include Christ's life and relationship with women. In a world that gave women very little respect—where the orthodox Jewish male thanked God every morning that he had not been born a woman—Jesus was remarkably different. He did things that were unheard of in biblical times: talking at length with a Samaritan woman; telling Martha that Mary was following a better way when she sat and listened to Him in the same room with men.

Not only was He different, He was astonishingly radical. He refused to condemn the woman caught in adultery. He permitted the woman with the issue of blood to touch Him, even though this violated strict laws concerning uncleanness and propriety. Even more radical than these examples, he sent Mary to tell His disciples that He had risen from the dead. It was unlawful for a woman to bear witness in a court of law in Israel because her testimony was considered unreliable. By appearing first to Mary and by suggesting that she was a reliable witness, Christ once again demonstrated that He considered women to be equal to men.

The New Testament does not record any situations in which Jesus acted as if women were inferior, or as if they ought to be home rather than following and listening to Him. To us today this seems like perfectly natural behavior. But in a day and age where women were not often allowed public roles, when even speaking to a woman in public was not considered respectable, Jesus modeled extraordinary behavior.

Some have asserted that while women may be equal, they have

different roles. As an example, they point out that Jesus did not give leadership roles to any of His women disciples. Of course, women could not have had leadership roles in that day. Traveling about in mixed company or going on teaching trips with the male disciples would have branded them as loose and immoral women. But He certainly did all He could in that time and place to establish the equality of women.

We have no substantial evidence on either side of the issue to know whether Jesus would have given women leadership roles had He come in a different age, or whether He would have insisted that leadership roles were only for men. We do have a clear picture that He did not consider women to be inferior in any way and that, contrary to the strict rabbinical law, they should be permitted to study the Scriptures.

Jesus encouraged women to learn about Him and His teachings and to follow Him, to take up their crosses, to let their light so shine that men might see their good works, and to glorify their Father in heaven. He went on to say: "The harvest truly is plenteous, but the labourers are few; Pray ye therefore the Lord of the harvest, that He will send forth labourers into His harvest" (Matthew 9:37-38). He also said, "For whosoever shall do the will of my Father which is in heaven, the same is my brother, and sister, and mother" (12:50).

Working or Quibbling?

If as Christians we take the story of the talents in Matthew 25 seriously, we must admit that it is an act of disobedience to God to allow one's talents to go unused, wasted, or hidden. The demand to grow and develop and use one's gifts applies to women as well as men.

Our Lord demands that the church use every talent and all her strength in advancing the Kingdom. She must go dynamically into the world, working and praying mightily that the church develop and grow as much as possible so there may be even greater maturity and ability for the Kingdom work.

In Philippians 1:27 we are admonished to "stand fast in one

spirit, with one mind striving together for the faith of the gospel." Paul goes on to say later in this letter: "And I entreat thee also, true yokefellow, to help those women which laboured with me in the gospel, with Clement also, and with my other fellow laborers, whose names are in the book of life" (4:3).

It is evident we have more to do than quibble over an issue which has so much Scripture to support the work of women in the church. Let us work together to advance the Kingdom.

I like something I once heard Karen DeVes say (my paraphrase):

> *"In allowing women's abilities to go unused, the church is depriving itself of a source of leadership and growth, and a deprivation it cannot afford. Christians must take seriously Paul's vision of the church as one body in which each member has a part to play. Nothing in that vision suggests that women must be all hands and hearts. Women can be feet and lungs and brains and muscles in the church just as surely as men."*

The Whole Counsel

I am glad that the Free Methodist Church has long recognized women in the ministry. Ordination for women was fully granted at the General Conference in 1911. However, it was not until 1974 that ordained women could become senior pastors.

I fully believe with many others that if we hear the whole counsel of God through Scripture, women are set free to worship and to serve. The language of Scripture has been used too long to rob women of their place in the church.

Our emancipation comes from Acts 2: 17-18 NIV. "In the last days . . . I will pour out my Spirit on all people. Your sons and daughters will prophesy . . . Even on my servants, both men and women, I will pour out my Spirit in those days, and they will prophesy."

Any other texts must be squared with the above if we are to be true to the teachings of Christ.

My preparation for ordination was not directed to pastoral ministry. I took the required course in Free Methodist church history and discipline. And I completed the two-year practicum under the leadership of Pastor Byggdin, serving as his assistant pastor and also as the director of Christian education. For my thesis or special project, I wrote a two-hundred-fifty-page camp manual. Illustrated by Karen Reilly (who also illustrated this book), this manual covers every aspect of camping. I was flattered to have my professor write the following note:

> *"You have done a tremendous job and if I'm not mistaken, your book will keep on growing. When you have it published, the songbook part probably should be separate from the manual. If you have the opportunity, show this to Bishop Bastian. A plus for M.J. and a plus for K.R."*

Due to all the copyrights involved, I never published the manual. But it has been invaluable to me personally and for training camp staff.

On October 30, 1977, Bishop Donald Bastian ordained me as a minister in the Free Methodist Church. This was a combined ordination and dedication service, "unique in the annals of St. Joseph Island church history," as Ada Tranter wrote in the *The Sault Star.* In addition to my ordination, the newly renovated Island Free Methodist Church was also dedicated. This church had its roots in the latter part of the 1800's. The first church was built at a cost of $729.98 ($36.73 of this was the cost of hand-cut and sawn logs) and dedicated in the fall of 1897. More recently Sunday attendance had increased to the point that renovation of the old part and a new addition were required. This was accomplished under the leadership of Pastor Byggdin.

No Small Thing

To change countries and to change churches is no small thing. As I put down permanent roots on St. Joseph Island, I realized that I needed to transfer my membership to the Island Free Methodist Church. My time, energy, and finances must be given where I worshiped regularly—and I had been involved with this Island church in one capacity or other for many years. I knew all of this in my heart, but it was still a difficult step. I was converted in The Wesleyan Church, nurtured in her Sunday schools, youth activities, and worship services, educated in one of her institutions of higher learning, and had given several years in service to that institution, Marion College.

It was during my third year in college that my heart and life were opened to the blessed Holy Spirit. The divine yes to His will and way became very clear to me. I have found His grace more than sufficient during every trial I have experienced, in every disappointment and through every change. Suffering from a physical and near mental breakdown, resigning from a very satisfying position working with young people, finding a new way of life and now changing my church membership had all been very different from what I had anticipated.

But I had heard the calling: "This is the way, walk ye in it." The safest and most satisfying place to be in the whole world is in the center of His will. I wanted nothing more, nothing less—then and now. I counted it a privilege to become a part of the Island Free Methodist Church fellowship—both as a member and a minister.

Chapter Fifteen

Stretching Beyond Our Expectations

"I can do all things through Christ which strengtheneth me."
Phil. 4:13

The following article, "Age Couldn't Stop Her," was written by Dr. Allen Bowman. It later appeared in the September 17, 1978 issue of VISTA, a Sunday school publication of The Wesleyan Church.

Listening to the director's introductory words that evening at Camp Honey Rock, my friend Millie Jacobs began to wonder. To the gathering of hopefuls in the wilds of northern Wisconsin Bud Williams was saying, "You doubtless have high expectations for this course, but I must warn you—there will be many frustrations and some disappointments."

Later on, Miss Jacobs wrote: "I glanced about at the group of 60-some campers and leaders. It was evident that the oldest person there was standing in my hiking boots!" Was she in the wrong place?

Always eager for out-of-doors activity, Millie had been attracted by ads of Wheaton College's Wilderness Learning Seminar. Clearly the setup was geared to younger folk. But she had registered anyway back in November 1976, with the understanding that exceptions were made for persons over 50 if they were physically fit and had a physician's OK.

Fifty-three years old but lean and active, Millie lives by herself in a rural cabin on St. Joseph Island in Ontario. On the acres she owns there she was in the process of developing a camp of her own with the needs of youth especially in mind. For her two-week wilderness venture in Wisconsin, she says, "I had trained by doing the suggested jogging and pushups and hard physical work around the cabin." But now she realized that the demands would be stiffer than she had expected. "Will this old bag of bones be able to keep up with the others, most of them much younger?" she asked herself.

But she is a determined soul, "The command to love the Lord with all one's strength as well as with heart, soul, and mind," she observes, "had become real to me many years before. As a new convert I couldn't reconcile overeating and obesity with Christianity. Hard work has been a way of life with me. Love for and participation in action team sports still excites me." Besides, as a former Girl Scout director she had become an expert camper.

No, she wasn't about to back out now! "Where else," she thought, "would I have the opportunity to do white-water canoeing, backpacking, rappelling, etc. under supervision?" Afterwards her group leader, Penny Nickel, told her, "I wanted you in my unit to

Millie with tent

see what the result would be for one of your age."

Presently Millie found herself one of a group of ten, the youngest of whom was 24. Penny was a dedicated Christian who commanded confidence from the outset. "We were an eager, willing lot," Millie recalls, "and followed her like sheep." But she adds, "I was disturbed by her frequent references to stress. A nervous break in the fall of 1971 had left me scarred, and I had gone to my home in Ontario to recoup. Iron shots were still necessary. Doubts began to plague me." Fighting off her forebodings, she took refuge in Philippians 4:13: "I can do all things through Christ which strengtheneth me."

"Each of us was given a backpack, duffels for our sleeping bag and liner, a mosquito-net hat, a plastic ground sheet, a rain poncho, a canteen, cup and spoon. The group received five mosquito-net tents, five large sheets of plastic which were to serve as tents in case of rain, binder twine, a heavy rope, portable shovel, four billycans, a skillet and lid, dehydrated food, and a first-aid kit.

"We soon realized that a light pack would be our salvation. My back had never had a backpack on it. Helpful hints were given—but it took some actual hiking before I was comfortable with it. Backpacking over hill and dale, bushwhacking through deep wilderness, slipping through stands of virgin hemlock, crossing streams, spying tumbling waterfalls, reveling in pristine beauty about us, and smelling the pungent odors of nature made the pack seem lighter and my arms, legs and back stronger.

"As we bounced in and out of our canoes when we hit low water on the river, or had the joy of developing a new stroke and finally doing it properly, when we hit white water without filling the canoe or tipping over, the muscles responded without a murmur, and my heart sang."

Swarming insects were but a minor annoyance. Presently the going really got tough. "The long, hot hike up the escarpment for rappelling and climbing was not an easy one. We huffed and we puffed. Hot spots in my boots had turned to blisters—but this was not the time to quit. We were merely getting started and there was the mountain to climb."

Millie was learning a valuable lesson. "At one point along the trail it seemed wise to relinquish my pack and carry a double portion of the food instead . . . and the pain lessened in my feet as the weight was removed. I drove another stake that day in being willing to admit my limitations. I had stumbled and fallen too many times in the past because I had taken on too much and buckled under the pressure."

"Nevertheless," she explains, "I was anxious for the reality of rappelling and climbing." (Rappel is descent of a steep slope by use of a rope passed under one thigh, across the body, and over the opposite shoulder.) "We were at the edge of a cliff. Was it only 100 feet down there? It looked more like 1,000! I felt a surge of excitement and adventure. However, as I was tied in I had some misgivings. They said it was simple: all I had to do was back over the side and walk down the face of the rock." But —

"Hesitatingly I took the first step and then the second." With that, the hesitation vanished. "Shortly I was off and away like a bird in the air. The descent was over before I really realized it."

But the climb back up, even with the aid of the rope, was a different story. "A fingerhold here, a toehold there, a reach, some more stretching, discipline of mind over matter, self-control, determination, generous help and direction from above, a bit of tension, a little slack, and finally over the top! Who said this course was only for college age through 50? I felt akin to a mountain goat."

Plenty of other activity followed. "The ropes course was fun. Previous experience in engineering a jungle bridge across a similar canyon was a help. But I shuddered as I reflected back and realized how few safety precautions I had taken. The emphasis on safety throughout our seminar was evident and very much appreciated. It made me more aware of my responsibilities to future campers."

Millie, I have learned, is used to simple food. But she had wondered: "Would that pile of plastic envelopes containing freeze-dried food actually sustain us through the rugged activities? Could we get by that long without any fresh vegetables and fruit and meat?" She need not have wondered. "We did have full tummies, and it was fun creating meals out of the unknown. We had nutritious and sufficient food. And surprisingly enough we managed those meals on the few simple utensils we had been issued."

The supreme test came at the very end. "As the final days approached, we heard more and more about a marathon. We all knew that the final push and climax would be then. Perseverance and stamina would be a must. I admit it was a stressful situation for me. My feet were covered with blisters, and a toe was infected. Several commented, "Surely you aren't going to attempt that!"

Millie with blistered feet

"The hour came and we were dumped out of a truck 8.6 miles from camp. A few knew they couldn't make it and had accepted the fact. But my mind was made up.

"I jogged along at my own speed, wincing when I stepped on a stone or a branch. Once I got started I never looked back. As I crossed the finish line, the grin which wreathed my face didn't begin to compare with the smile of my soul. Sweet is the taste of victory!"

Some people, learning of Millie's adventure, were appalled. "My conservative friends," she says, "have asked me over and over, 'Why in the world would you put yourself through that?'" Having known Miss Jacobs for most of her life, I can smile along with her over the puzzlement of these cautious souls. But I must say that her undertaking, when I learned all that it involved, raised my admiration for her another notch or two.

The experience yielded definite spiritual values. Association "with ten others for most of 15 days," she says, "enlarged my circle of friends, and new discoveries were made about the true meaning of fellowship with the body of Christ. We shared so much." She is convinced that it will be easier now to keep her own camping program "Christ-centered and primitive . . . I developed a greater appreciation for physical fitness," she observes. "It was good to deny myself. My life is richer."

Out of it all grew a bit of philosophizing with which I heartily agree. "In our present affluent society we are pampered and overfed and under-exercised on every hand. We take the easy way out and grow old too soon, and in so doing we miss so much. How delightful to stretch ourselves beyond our expectations and to discover new perspectives and capabilities."

Millie voices this simple but meaningful prayer: "Don't let me miss out on all that You have for me, Lord!"

Chapter Sixteen

The Ill-fated Moose Hunt

The Ill-Fated... Moose Hunt

"Who are these sad hunters?"
M.J.T.

My nephew John Jacobs came up for my ordination in October 1977. He had more than the ordination on his agenda, of course. An avid hunter, he suggested staying over so we could go moose hunting up in the Wawa area.

The idea of spending time with a favorite nephew out in the bush sounded great to me. I used to tease him about growing up in Wisconsin teething on a gunstock. The proposed hunting trip was even more appealing after the whirl of activities surrounding my ordination. That had been a very busy weekend and I had entertained many guests from Ontario and the States.

John and I both had our own guns. The Charles Arnold family had given me one of Chuck's upon his death. John's Savage 24 S-E had belonged to his grandfather and he prized it highly.

We had enough camping gear between us to make us comfortable under any circumstances. Since I had acquired a real taste for moose meat, I convinced myself that I really could take a shot at a big, bulky moose. (A soft-eyed deer? No!) We were ready. We put my red canvas canoe on top of his truck and we were off.

A Taste for Moose

I had talked to several local hunters who knew the Wawa area well. They marked a site on the map for me, assuring me that we would find lots of moose. We headed up Highway 17 north toward Wawa in high spirits, making several stops along Lake Superior's shore. To me there is no finer scenery between here and the Rockies. We took pictures of the big goose that overlooks the highway and Lake Superior. The huge statue is a real tourist attraction and seems to beckon travelers away from the highway and into Wawa. After looking around the town, we headed off to find our site and to set up camp.

According to the map, we thought we had found the suggested site. There were no signs indicating it to be a privately owned property or a provincial park. And the site included ample parking for the truck and easy docking for the canoe. We made several laborious trips over to our spot. Yes, we were more than a little excited. John set up the tent while I prepared dinner over an open fire. After a long, leisurely meal we sat gazing at our surroundings. We agreed that it was as close to heaven as one could get.

John decided to scout out the land while I did up the dishes. He came back as excited as a kid at the circus. "Aunt Mildred, Aunt Mildred, there are droppings everywhere! We should both be able to bag our moose!" I fell into my sleeping bag early. It had been a long day and I was still trying to psyche myself up. Could I really shoot a moose? Would I embarrass myself and get buck fever? Soon I was fast asleep.

Not a Dream

Suddenly I heard voices. Was I dreaming? Who was talking to John? He stuck his head into the tent and I could tell by his voice and countenance that something was seriously wrong. A conservation officer wanted to talk to me. I slipped into some warm clothes and came out of the tent mumbling to John, "What's up? What do we have to talk about?"

It was not quite as simple as "talking." You can imagine my shock to find that John was under arrest because he was a U.S. citizen hunting in Ontario. The officer was taking him back to Wawa right then and there!

"What?" I asked. "What in the world is happening here?"

"Lady, you are in Lake Superior Provincial Park," the officer announced. "This is a no hunting zone."

I went to my pack and pulled out the map. "Aren't we here?" I asked, pointing to the spot on the map.

"I'm afraid not," he said.

"But how can we be in a provincial park? We never saw any park signs."

"Well, you should be west of here."

This was getting to me and I was more than a little annoyed. "Do you mean to tell me you are taking this fellow with you and leaving me here with all of this gear to pack out?"

The officer coolly replied, "That's right."

A thought came to me and I decided to pull rank. "Sir, as a minister of the gospel, I promise you I will have this young man wherever and whenever you want him, but I am going to have to have his help in getting out of here." (He did not know that I had just become a member of the cloth and that this was my first official declaration.)

He stammered and hemmed and hawed. After what seemed an eternity he said, "I am doing this against my better judgment. How do I know he won't head for the border, never to be seen around here again?"

"Sir, on my word and the Word of God we will meet your terms!" I assured him.

He gave us directions to the town hall and said, "I will be expecting you." Then he slipped off into the darkness with our guns.

The cry of the loon was especially mournful that night. Talk about a crestfallen young lad—I had one on my hands. That nasty officer had his beloved gun. At that moment I am positive John thought more of that gun than he did of me. Neither one of us slept much that night. John had a zillion questions I could not answer. I had enough questions of my own. How in the world did we end up in a provincial park? How would I explain this to my brother Jack? Would his son John actually be jailed? How much was all this going to cost us? Would we get our guns back? What would people think of a newly ordained minister being charged with an offense like this? To say the least, I was upset and embarrassed.

Facing the Music

You can be sure we were up bright and early. We were in Wawa even before the sun was up. I went to a pay phone to call my good friend Erminie who lived in Richards Landing. She always had a shoulder available to cry on and she heard me out. Of course she understood, and yes she would go to the bank and wire whatever money we would need. What else could she do, she asked?

We made our way over to the municipal office without breakfast—we were not hungry. The taste of moose meat was the furthest thing from my mind. We waited a long time for the doors to open. Finally we were ushered into an office. The Provincial Police had to be involved, as well as the young officer who had apprehended us.

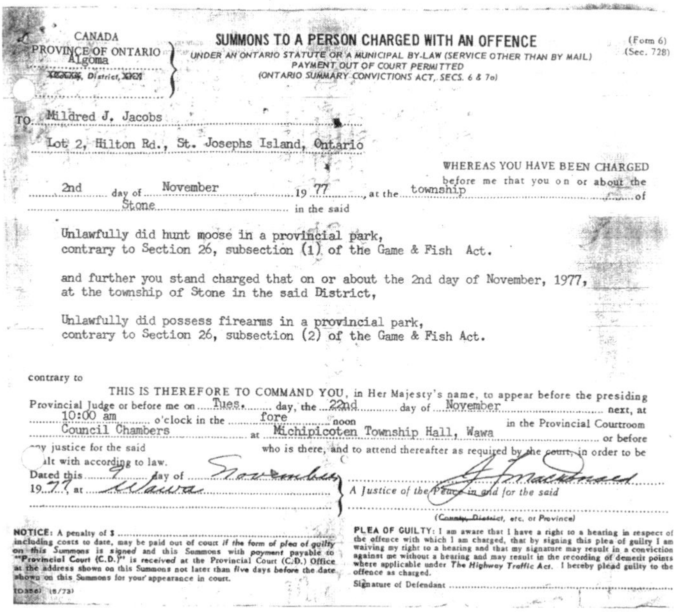
CANADA
PROVINCE OF ONTARIO
Algoma, District

SUMMONS TO A PERSON CHARGED WITH AN OFFENCE
UNDER AN ONTARIO STATUTE OR A MUNICIPAL BY-LAW (SERVICE OTHER THAN BY MAIL)
PAYMENT OUT OF COURT PERMITTED
(ONTARIO SUMMARY CONVICTIONS ACT, SECS. 6 & 7a)

(Form 6)
(Sec. 728)

TO: Mildred J. Jacobs
Lot 2, Hilton Rd., St. Josephs Island, Ontario

WHEREAS YOU HAVE BEEN CHARGED before me that you on or about the 2nd day of November 1977, at the township of Stone in the said

Unlawfully did hunt moose in a provincial park,
contrary to Section 26, subsection (1) of the Game & Fish Act.

and further you stand charged that on or about the 2nd day of November, 1977, at the township of Stone in the said District,

Unlawfully did possess firearms in a provincial park,
contrary to Section 26, subsection (2) of the Game & Fish Act.

contrary to

THIS IS THEREFORE TO COMMAND YOU, in Her Majesty's name, to appear before the presiding Provincial Judge or before me on Tues. day, the 22nd day of November next, at 10:00 am o'clock in the fore noon Council Chambers at Michipicoten Township Hall, Wawa in the Provincial Courtroom or before any justice for the said who is there, and to attend thereafter as required by the court, in order to be dealt with according to law.

Dated this 9 day of November 1977, at Wawa

J. Macdonald
A Justice of the Peace in and for the said
(County, District, etc. or Province)

NOTICE: A penalty of $ .... including costs to date, may be paid out of court *if the form of plea of guilty on this Summons is signed* and this Summons with *payment* payable to "Provincial Court (C.D.)" is *received* at the Provincial Court (C.D.) Office at the address shown on this Summons not later than *five* days *before* the date shown on this Summons for your appearance in court.

PLEA OF GUILTY: I am aware that I have a right to a hearing in respect of the offence with which I am charged, that by signing this plea of guilty I am waiving my right to a hearing and that my signature may result in a conviction against me without a hearing and may result in the recording of demerit points where applicable under *The Highway Traffic Act.* I hereby plead guilty to the offence as charged.

Signature of Defendant ....

(D356) (8/73)

The Summons

I had to talk like a lawyer to persuade them that I would bring John back to court if necessary. Could I post bond? I would do anything they asked. We had unwittingly made a sad mistake and we were sorry. About that time a levelheaded officer spoke up and said, "You have the guns. She is willing to post bond. Why not get this settled so they can be on their way. You know Judge Greco won't be here for a week or so." I could have hugged him.

True to her word, Erminie did her part. It did not take long to arrange the bond transaction. We left Wawa—sans guns—but with an official summons in my hands.

It was not a joyous ride back to the Island. However, when the Gilbertsons invited John to join them on their deer hunt, his spirits flickered back to life. They even loaned him a gun and ammunition. It wasn't long before they spotted a deer. In his excitement John raised his gun to shoot. "Don't shoot, John," came the cry. "Don't shoot. We don't have a doe license!" Poor John. He was just not meant to hunt that time.

Erminie, bless her memory, drove up to Wawa with me at the appointed time. Judge Greco was to hear seventy cases that day. I was case Number 31, sandwiched in with all sorts of criminal activities. When they finally got to me, I could not believe my ears as they read off the wide variety of charges. Although we had not actually hunted in the park, I pled guilty anyway. As I stood and listened to the Judge, a male voice came from the back of the room.

"Your honor, may I speak on behalf of this woman?" There to represent another client, he must have felt sorry for me. Before the Judge could respond, the attorney continued, "It is quite evident that this individual did not intentionally enter the park."

The Judge rapped his gavel and said, "Out of order!" My defender sat down quietly. The Judge proceeded to cross-examine me. After a period of time that seemed like hours, he made a few more comments and said, "Obviously there was no deliberate attempt made to flaunt the law. It was a misunderstanding of the regulations. The fine will be $150 each." I thanked him, breathed a sigh of relief, and sat down.

I later signed another paper, and shelled out a surprisingly small sum of $10 to regain possession of the two guns. My check for the $300 in fines was accepted and I was excused. I could hardly wait to call John. He was overjoyed to know his gun was safely back in my hands. Erminie and I had a much more relaxed drive back to the Island than the drive up to Wawa.

The Grapevine

Meanwhile the Island grapevine had been working overtime. Many had heard about the newly ordained minister who had been in court up in Wawa for illegally hunting moose in a provincial park. I knew I could handle the gossip with good humor, but imagine my chagrin the next day to see a three-column, four-inch-high article in *The Sault Star.* The bold headlines shouted: "Pair draws $150 fines for Superior Park Hunt."

I was more than a little annoyed with that reporter. We had not actually hunted, and of all the charges brought before the Judge that day, Case Number 31 seemed—to me, anyway—the least serious. To this day some of my "kind" friends enjoy refreshing my memory about the "moose that got away." And just in case you're wondering, no, I have not hunted since.

Chapter Seventeen

Saying "I Do"

(1977-1999)

It was the apples..... AND SEEDS!

"Whither thou goest, I will go; and where thou lodgest, I will lodge: thy people shall be my people, and thy God my God."
Ruth 1:16

God works in mysterious ways. As I have indicated, my path and Dick's had crossed in the past. His wife-to-be, May Hollopeter, was my good friend when I was a girl and had been instrumental in bringing me to the Lord. Dick and I even double-dated in high school. After high school, Dick joined the Air Force and served his country while I later made my way to Marion College. When Dick and May were married while he was still in the service, I was very much involved on the campus.

Three boys and a girl blessed their union. These young Troyers all followed in their father's footsteps and attended Marion College. When he enrolled as a student in the mid-30's, he didn't realize he was starting a Troyer tradition. Since then, at least thirty Troyers (including spouses) are now alums. Every time a new alumni directory was issued, Dick would check the Troyer list. Arranged alphabetically, he would often chuckle about being the first Troyer to attend, but the last to be listed.

As I have also noted earlier, his children were students during the time I was the Alumni Director. I often noticed Dick at Homecoming and other events. He always attended the Fort Wayne Chapter meetings. A time or two I was more than a little vexed with him due to the many questions he asked regarding the new Indiana Tax Credit Law. The State Senate had passed a bill whereby a single person could give $200 or a couple could give $400 and get half of it back on their income taxes. (I must include this information for no one, including staff, was as enthusiastic as he was about this program.) After researching the issue, he boldly stated that if every alum in the state of Indiana would take advantage of this offer, the school would not have any money problems. Of course, that was before Dr. Jim Barnes and the Board decided to rebuild the entire campus!

The tax credit deal was like a gold mine to Dick and he wanted the school to dig deep for its riches. He and Everett Sloan ('53) had done their homework and understood the program far better than I or any of the other staff members did. These two kept insisting that we were only scratching the surface. I was more into friend-raising than fund-raising, and he bothered me more than a little with all the questions I could not answer.

Imagine my surprise after his death, to find a card of thanks I had written to him following one of these meetings. He had tucked it into the bundle of letters I had written him while we were dating.

I must confess, however, that it was written not so much to thank him, but to get this man off my case! One of his goals after retiring from All Tribes Christian Camp was to return to the campus to promote the Tax Credit and Matching Gift programs. These programs are still available. You Hoosiers would honor his memory, and help your Alma Mater, by taking advantage of them.

Acorns and Apple Stems

I also recall chatting with him at a college baseball game in Fort Wayne. As the Alumni Director, I attended as many school functions as possible. I wanted to know the students and I wanted them to remember their Alma Mater after they left the campus.

When Dick finished his cup of coffee at that game, he picked up a few acorns and tossed them around in his Styrofoam cup. One day after we were married we were visiting his farm. He took me to "our" oak tree and reminded me of our pleasant encounter at that ball game. I had forgotten all about it. That tree always reminds me of his solid character. Like an oak, he was strong and sturdy in so many ways.

He planted several acres of trees on his farm. One day when we were pruning them, he remarked, "We won't benefit monetarily from these, but I trust they will help with Steph's and Amy's (our grandchildren) college educations." Steph has already been accepted at Indiana Wesleyan University and we hope that Amy will attend there as well. They say the mark of a mature person is one who plants a tree under which he will never sit. Dick was the epitome of maturity.

May died of cancer while their daughter Becky was still in school. Dick later married Tina Palmer. She too died of that dreaded disease. After that I often saw May's sister, Virginia, at my home church. She mentioned several times that I ought to get in touch with Richard. He was lonely and had always admired me. I told her flat out that I was not about to look him or any man up. He had my sympathy, but I was far too busy developing the camp and I was most content with my single status.

I cannot recall what actually brought us together. Perhaps it was the 1976 Homecoming. I do remember that it wasn't long after that he asked me out on a date. He took me to see his farm on a sunny fall day. The drive up to Knapp Lake, where I had lived while we double-dated, was a sentimental journey and I found myself enjoying it more than I had anticipated. We munched on a couple of apples for an afternoon snack and, at the same time, turned to each other and handed over the stems! We had both eaten the entire apple, including the core and seeds. (They say it takes a cupful of seeds to harm you.) His eyes lit up and he complimented me for being one of the few people he had ever met who did not waste a portion of an apple. I thought, "This is unreal." My father had been the only other person I knew who would eat an entire apple.

Guarding the Secret

I returned to the Island with a song in my heart. Dick was much more handsome and fun than I remembered, and he did not mention the tax credit program even once! My cabin did not have a phone then, but he asked for the church phone number. He knew I attended church every Wednesday and Sunday evening. Would I mind if he called once in a while? Pastor Ralph and Joyce Byggdin guarded our secret well, bless their hearts. He called frequently. Two bundles of love letters, his and mine, attest to the fact that we also kept the postal service in business.

There was so much catching up to do, so many questions to be answered, so much praying to do to really know God's will for us. My ordination was scheduled for the end of October. He was most sorry that he had a previous family commitment. Actually, I was relieved, for I was not ready to tell the whole world that there was a man in my life! However, he was there in spirit and his love was manifested in a beautiful rose corsage for my gown. No one knew who had sent it, and I did not reveal the source.

He wanted to come up for the American Thanksgiving holiday to visit me and to check out this camp he had heard so much about. I agreed, but with two conditions: that he bring along some friends and that he not be introduced as a "special" friend. As usual we had a camp project going on. Jerry and Adele Hawdon and others were working there at the time, but no one was the wiser. A delicious turkey dinner with all the trimmings made for a wonderful Thanksgiving Day. And hiking all around the trails made for a memorable weekend. We attended church, as well, but decided on the church in the Sault—just in case. After dinner at the old Purple Lantern, Dick and his friends headed back to Indiana. I returned to the Island to pray. Something was going on in my heart and I was not sure I was ready for it.

The Key to His Heart

Shortly after that weekend, he proposed on the phone. *What?* I thought I might love him, but I wanted to be sure I was not merely in love with love. I had seen too much of that. Would I give him an answer by Christmas? Would I come down for the holidays? I consented to fly down for Christmas, but could not make any further commitment. Yes, I would pray about it. I shared my prayer request with several close friends. Did I love him enough to share the rest of my life with him? That was the question!

After I finally made up my mind that he was the man for me, I wanted to respond to his proposal in a unique way. Aileen Hadden, a former Wakonda camper and a good friend, suggested that I make a heart out of red felt and insert my house key as the arrow.

When he met my plane that Christmas, I wanted to fall into his arms and proclaim to the high heavens that, yes, I would be his wife! Instead, I spoiled our dinner by giving him all the reasons why I would *not* make a good wife. I loved to cook, but could not sew, knit, or crochet—and did not intend to learn until I was ninety-two. I preferred working outdoors to keeping house.

None of that mattered, he said. We loved each other and everything else would take care of itself. We would work it out. He wanted to come up north to mow grass, cut wood, and help me pursue my dream for developing the camp. (We all know he did that and more during his twenty-one years of hard work.)

Even after dinner I stonewalled the decision. But on the way home, as we passed a well-lighted school parking lot, I asked him to pull over, for I wanted him to see something. When he opened the wee box and saw the key, tears rolled down his cheeks. It was one of the few times I ever saw him cry. (He was never guilty of wearing his feelings on his sleeve.) At this point I was sure I loved him deeply and wanted to share the rest of my life with him. He wiped away his tears and said that we would visit his jeweler friend the next day.

I got him to chuckle finally by quoting a wee poem I kept in one of my favorite cookbooks

Any Girl

A little home with a breakfast nook
And a snowy cloth and a cookery book.
A parlor lamp in rose and blue,
An overstuffed lounge and a baby shoe,
These are things I want, don't you?
But whenever a soul's around to hear,
I assert that I long for a career!   Anon

My single days would soon be over and we would share in the dream of building All Tribes Christian Camp together.

Enough for a Basketball Team . . . and Then Some!

As I contemplated our future life as a couple, I realized that another of my childhood dreams would soon come true: that of having six boys, enough for a basketball team. With Dick's children that dream would become reality. There would be David ('69), George, Jim ('73), son-in-law Alvin Wooters ('74), and grandsons Jon ('94), Aaron ('98), and Dan ('99)—making six with one to spare. There was also Becky ('74) and daughters-in-law Patricia Walters Troyer ('67) and Beverly Walker Troyer ('71), plus granddaughters Rachel and Sharyn. Along with me that made enough for a girls' basketball team! Now I would have the family of my dreams—with no morning sickness or labor pains involved. How many women can say that? (At the present time, thirteen grandchildren grace my life!)

Over the years, many have inquired if I ever felt cheated by never having any children of my own. I can honestly say that has never been an issue with me. I have often thought I would much rather deal with a hundred youngsters in camp, than with two or three children around the clock. And the many, many campers who have become like my own have enriched my life. I treasure their friendship and feel blessed rather than cheated. Beth and Brad and their children remain very special to me and seem like my very own.

When it came time to discuss an engagement token, I decided on a necklace watch instead of a diamond ring. Honestly, with all the wood chopping, hammering, digging, and other chores that I was used to doing around the camp, how long would a diamond last on my finger? I have never been a jewelry person and it seemed impractical to have a ring. When jewelry comes to mind, I am reminded of a ditty our friend Howard Noggle used to quote:

Consistency, consistency
Thou art a jewel
But Methodists do not
Believe in jewelry!

Anonymous

The jeweler's watch suited us perfectly. As he was engraving "To Millie from Dick 12-77" on the inside cover, Dick called me aside and said, "Why don't we get fitted for rings now? We could elope and have Christmas together. Why wait for spring?"

That added a whole new dimension to the shopping trip, but I resisted. We needed more time to discuss many things. Besides, after waiting all these years, I wanted to share my wedding day with family and friends. I was not about to settle for a ladder and a justice of the peace!

More Than a Ceremony

I knew making the arrangements for the wedding and executing the plan would be difficult but worthwhile work. While the wedding was important to me, I had seen far too many who had all but killed themselves planning for the big day, without giving any thought to working on the marriage after the ceremony.

A Bright Future

Marriage is hard work. I never worked harder on anything in my life. We do not prepare our young people properly for one of the most important decisions they will ever make. The church and society both put pressure on young people to marry and to live happily ever after, without providing sufficient guidance for the "ever after" part. The present divorce rate tells us that marriage just does not last unless the individuals work at it after the vows are made. When counseling young couples, I tell them that saying "I do" will not make them one. It takes years of hard work, understanding, and patience.

One of the best things Dick ever said to me was, "If we agree on everything, one of us is going to be unnecessary." Married couples have to learn to disagree agreeably. Ephesians 5:20-21 is a big part of the equation: "Giving thanks always for all things unto God and the Father in the name of our Lord Jesus Christ; submitting yourselves one to another in the fear of God."

We announced our engagement at our son George's home that Christmas. In this joyous setting, I already felt a part of the Troyer family. George spread the word quickly. I am not sure how much their phone bill was that month! Dick and I had the pleasure of spreading our good news with many in our own way. Needless to say, there were many surprised and shocked people. How had one Richard Troyer convinced Millie Jacobs to forsake the single life to marry him? It was simple. I knew he was the man for me. "Dan Cupid" had sent a warm arrow deep into my heart.

Our May 19 wedding date coincided with his retirement from the postal service. (Years after his retirement, I told people he still knew how to deliver the mail!) We chose the College Wesleyan Church as our wedding site. When I checked with the young assistant pastor about the date and arrangements, he asked, "And what is your daughter's name?"

"What daughter?" I answered, chuckling. "This is *my* wedding!" Our paths cross now and again and I still think I see a twinkle in his eyes.

After the holidays I returned to the Island. Fortunately, the time between the end of December and the beginning of May flew by. Ma Bell, Uncle Sam, and Her Majesty's Postal Services shortened the miles between and made the separation a bit more bearable. I am so glad our courting and letter writing took place before E-mail. Dick rarely ever wrote a letter without rewriting it. He always expressed himself so beautifully. E-mail may be much cheaper and faster, but it will never take the place of a handwritten letter for me.

Then we began the detailed wedding plans in earnest.

I don't much like showers and I especially don't like the silly games they often play. I had always said that "if and when" I got married and had children I never wanted any showers. I wanted to furnish my own kitchen and dress my own children. Consequently, I have attended very few showers, opting instead to give the bride-to-be or the mother-to-be a check, so she can do her own shopping.

We had two furnished homes between us and had requested no gifts. However, we did consent to two showers. The women of my home church, Spring Street Wesleyan, wanted to get together for a personal shower. I had an enjoyable time (sans games) and am still enjoying many of those gifts. Dick's home church, Laotto Wesleyan, gave us a linen shower. In fine indelible ink, someone wrote the names of the donors on the sheets and towels. It warms my heart to this day to read those names when I use the linens. We were showered with many other gifts at the wedding receptions also. People are kind.

Richard's Landing?

We also decided to have the wedding reception before the wedding. No late getaways for us! I have always felt sorry for couples who cannot seem to find a gracious way to make their exit until late—very late. By having our reception first, we thought we could solve that problem. More on that later. Lucille Phillips ('34), an active alumna and reporter for the *Marion Alumni Journal*, captured our plans in this article:

"How's Millie?
Richards Landing

"There is more to that headline than meets the eye.

"Millie Jacobs of Richards Landing, Ontario, Canada, will become the bride of Richard Troyer, Churubusco, Ind., at 2:30 p.m. on May 19 in the Marion College Church on campus. They are college alumni. Miss Jacobs formerly was president of the college Alumni Association and later was its executive director. The couple has invited all alumni and friends to attend the wedding. There are to be no gifts. At 12:45 p.m. there will be an honor luncheon for the couple at Baldwin Center. The event will be given under the sponsorship of the alumni association with Michael Roorbach ('73), alumni director in charge.

"Since leaving her position at the college, Miss Jacobs has developed a camp and retreat center where many Girl Scouts, church groups, and other organizations have held activities. Only a few months ago she was ordained as a minister in the Free Methodist Church. For many years Mr. Troyer was a postmaster at Churubusco, and more recently he has been a rural carrier. He plans to take an early retirement. Tentative plans call for Miss Jacobs and Mr. Troyer to live at Richards Landing after their marriage — Thus Richard is landing there."

I could not believe how everything fell into place. Family and friends were most helpful. Who said planning a wedding had to be hectic? Stepdaughter Peggy Palmer Johnson ('78), daughter of Tina, loaned me her wedding dress. It was a perfect fit. Julia Hobson Medows ('54) and her alumni Activities Committee did an outstanding job in organizing the wedding luncheon. The room was picture perfect with many spring flowers. Handsome glass kerosene lamps and lilacs made delightful centerpieces for the tables. My former office secretary, Jean Strawser, made all of the flowers for the wedding party and decorated the church. The bridesmaids were able to find suitable pastel dresses.

Dick thought it to be a perfect waste of money to rent a tuxedo for one occasion, so he and the other men in the wedding party all wore light suits with bow ties. Dick wore his "wedding" suit for years and it was always one of my favorites. (He did not think a wedding should be a show. He never put on any show of pretense at any time. He was what he was. He was practical. He was a man after my own heart.)

Mrs. Alex Cain (Marie, daughter of Ralph, my fireplace builder), made the wedding cake. She sent it down with my good friends Dora and Ellice Hunter from the Sault. Marie and I had several chuckles over that cake. Earlier in the winter, I had visited their home on the Island. She had just made a wedding cake for a friend. In addition to the bride and groom on the top of the cake, her decorations included a church with a handsome red velvet carpet coming down the various steps.

Quite casually I said, "If I ever get married I would like a cake like that." Of course I had not yet let on that Dick was in the picture.

She responded, "Millie, if you ever get married, I will make a cake like that for you."

During that same visit, her daughter Coleen Paat had been playing the piano. I suggested she play some wedding songs. It was quite an evening and it still makes me smile. I apologized later to Marie for withholding the truth, but she said she meant what she had said—that she would make a cake for me. And she did.

A Picture-Perfect Day

Our wedding day couldn't have been more beautiful. And yes, the sun did shine on the bride and groom. Indiana on that day in May was one large bouquet of flowering trees, lilacs, and a variety of other spring flowers. The day began with an early morning breakfast in the President's Room in the Baldwin Food Center. I had invited my Canadian friends who had traveled from the Island, the Sault, North Bay, Ottawa, and Toronto to be my guests at that time. John Harsha, the Food Manager, did an outstanding job with the breakfast, as well as the luncheon. He said this was his wedding gift to us.

Right after the repast, we slipped over to the nearby College Church for the rehearsal. All went well and we were soon entering the dining area at Baldwin. We could not believer our eyes—Julia and her committee had transformed the place. Then we could not believe our ears when we were given a standing ovation as we made our way to the head table. It was a very humbling experience. How very priceless are friends.

I cannot recall what was on the menu, but I can still hear the words of our friend, Dr. Allen Bowman. He had been asked to give the toast. In his own unique way he said, "For years I have admonished my students never to jump to conclusions, but I am afraid I have done just that. Years ago I concluded that our dear Millie would never marry." He all but brought the house down.

Our wedding invitations included a "no gifts" request, but many ignored that suggestion. On behalf of the Alumni Association, Mike Roorbach ('73) presented us with a handsome engraved pewter serving tray. Our most unusual gift came from Hy Goldenburg, a former board member for the Girl Scouts. He collected outhouses and displayed them along the lane leading up to his home. For our facility on the Island, he made up a vent using galvanized drain pipe with a copper top, and the words "Manufactured in Passwater, Conn." on the label.

All too soon that lovely event was but a memory. We rushed back to the College Church and dressed for the most sacred part of the day. I must confess, I was beginning to feel like a quick-change artist. I had already worn two different outfits, and would wear two more before the day was over. I had just slipped into my gown when I was summoned to the phone for a call. (Had the groom changed his mind?) No, the call was from former Island camper Jim Dennison, who was in California serving as a youth pastor. He had just heard the news and thought "best wishes" were in order.

For the couple with everything: a galvanized outhouse vent

I was proud to go down the aisle on the arm of my brother, Jack. Sister Ruth had preceded us as the matron of honor. Eight other family members made up the wedding party. I remember smiling at our guests as we proceeded up the aisle, but I had more than a smile for one of the men standing at the front. Handsome Sir Richard looked like the victor he was.

Daughter Becky played the organ. My friend Hilda Clarke who had sung at my ordination, sang during the wedding ceremony. I still remember her reaction when I called her to ask her to sing at our wedding. It was 10:00 p.m. and I inadvertently awakened her from a deep sleep.

"What are you doing on May 19th?" I asked.

"How would I know, Chicken? (her pet name for me) It's the middle of the night!"

"We would like you to sing at our wedding," I announced.

"What? Who you gonna marry?"

"Dick Troyer."

"POPS? Of course I will."

She had gone to school with some of the Troyers and knew and loved Dick.

Cheer, Cheer!

Howard Noggle and son George heard our vows and tied the knot. We were pronounced man and wife, and presented as Mr. and Mrs. Richard Troyer. The congregation exploded with applause and cheers. Hand in hand, we started down the long aisle, accompanied by lovely recessional music. Halfway down the aisle, however,

Mr. and Mrs. Richard Troyer

Becky, Hilda, and many others broke forth with "Cheer, Cheer for Marion College," our school song. Dick squeezed my hand even tighter and we both grinned from ear to ear. Our love for one another and our Alma Mater was no secret.

The receiving line was long. Hundreds had come to witness an event they had been sure would never happen. We were hugged and kissed by many but did not get to greet them all. The Senior Class of '78 was waiting in another line to enter the church for their Baccalaureate service, so we had to dismiss the reception line early. Sadly we missed many of those who had come to honor us with their presence. It was not until we saw the wedding pictures with various views of the guests and read the guest book that we realized how many of our friends had actually been present.

Dick thought the pre-wedding reception a good idea, but we did not get away as early as expected. When we set our date, we were unaware that Beth would be graduating from high school that evening. She was one of our bridesmaids and we definitely had to see her receive her diploma. In our euphoria, though, the drive up to Fort Wayne and back was a short one.

The Long Way Home

We spent our first night in the same log cabin where I had earlier begun my recuperation. Located just outside Marion, owners Sam and Ethel Good had offered it to us. I had spent many pleasant times there with the Goods and faculty members. [Professor Rod Crossman ('76) now owns that property.]

We were soon on our way North. Sir Richard had to get acquainted with the Province of Ontario and some of my camping friends, including the Steve Tracy family in Wisconsin. Patti is one of our favorite campers. From there we went on to the Lakehead and out to Kakabecka Falls for our second reception. The drive across the northern route gave Dick a taste of the true North. He loved it. We also enjoyed receptions in North Bay and Ottawa. We then had a few quiet days at Camp Kalalla in Quebec. It was there that Dick met the infamous black flies for the first time, and he was not impressed. They were so vicious we could not sleep in our small tent. Instead, we ended up sleeping in the infirmary.

We returned to the Island to yet another reception, hosted by the Byggdins and Rose and Bernt Gilbertson. Poor Dick was on his feet greeting and meeting people for about three hours that night. One former camper who attended the reception looked me in the eyes and said, "Now you have everything, Millie!" She was one of the many who never understood why I had never married. It does pay to wait for Mr. Right!

We soon settled into the cabin and the camp routine, proud to be co-managers of All Tribes Christian Camp, but most especially proud to be Mr. and Mrs. Richard Troyer.

Chapter Eighteen

A Classroom of 100 Acres

The Crown Jewel

"All things were created by Him and for Him."
Colossians 1:16 NIV

Trying to write a chronological history of All Tribes Christian Camp is a bit like trying to walk a straight path through a forest! Along the way, there are too many interesting tangent trails to investigate in order to get the most from the experience. However, when the Edna Lee Lodge was dedicated in 1992, everything seemed to come together. This "crown jewel" of the camp symbolized the solidity of All Tribes Christian Camp and paid tribute to the countless people involved in realizing the camp's purpose and mission.

What's In a Name?

As a child, I had been sensitive to racial discrimination—before we even began to call it that. I have mentioned my childhood concern for the black people who always seemed to be serving white people in downtown Ft. Wayne. I also was influenced by my Cherokee heritage. Of all my siblings, the physical traits of high cheekbones, dark eyes, and dark hair came out in my brother Chick and my sister Betty. At an early age, I remember reading about how badly the first inhabitants of North America were treated. The Trail of Tears is a blot on the North American governments and humanity as a whole.

The name, All Tribes Christian Camp, was my way of recognizing and incorporating these early influences into the camp I envisioned for the future. All Tribes refers, of course, to my own Cherokee Indian blood, but also to the biblical tribes of Israel. This camp was always meant to be and has remained interdenominational and open to all seeking to deepen their relationship with God.

From Then to Now

From that first group of a dozen campers in 1963, we now have over 1000 campers annually from May to November. Our first VBS started with twenty-five or thirty campers and has grown to 120 or more. A wonderful aspect of this is to see twenty or more seventh and eighth graders still coming to VBS. Youth and adult retreat groups average from twenty-five to fifty people. Indiana Wesleyan University classes have made use of the site since 1985. "Writing in the Woods" seminars allow budding Thoreaus and Wordsworths to indulge in uninterrupted hours of reflection and writing amidst pines and ponds. We envision other classes (arts and various science classes) making use of this site. The cross-country track team has been challenged by our hiking and cross-country ski trails.

In 1986 Dick and I deeded the property to the school. We dubbed it "The Canadian Campus." A full-color picture of us graced the cover of the 1987 winter issue of *The Triangle* (a magazine published three times a year for IWU's alumni and friends). The lead article was entitled "Our 100-Acre Classroom."

We applied to the Canadian government for a charitable or nonprofit status. Our application was rejected because the property was owned by an American institution. We then formed a board of directors and drew up a set of by-laws, renaming the camp "All Tribes Christian Camp (Algoma) Inc." The school sold the camp to the board for one dollar. After these changes our application for nonprofit status was accepted and we are free of burdensome property taxes. We can also apply for a refund on the Government Services Taxes. This money is invested in the camp to serve the community as well as the school.

Although we continue to call it the Canadian Campus, the university does not receive any monetary benefit from the camp. In fact, we are the beneficiaries in many ways. Faculty and student groups have traveled north to work on numerous projects. One winter an outdoor recreation class built igloos and slept in them in -27°F temperatures. They also cut down pine trees for logs, which were later used to build a shelter on Pisgah's Peak. Each spring the outdoor recreation majors have classes here. They get the camp ready for the season and in doing so learn what is involved in operating a camp. Faculty and students were also instrumental in helping to construct the Edna Lee Lodge and the new shower house.

Time Well Spent

A large variety of groups come to All Tribes Christian Camp. Many are youth and adult groups from local area churches. I am available to assist them with their programs. For youth and adult retreats, our camp activities include personal devotions (morning

Inside the Lodge

watch, or time alone with God), flag ceremonies, Bible studies, speakers, seminars, vespers, worship services, crafts, swimming, sports, hiking, treasure or natural scavenger hunts, campfires, singing, cooking meals, and clean-up duties. Campers come for a weekend or a week. Various groups also come to do service projects, which have resulted in upgrading our facilities or building new ones. The camp is also used for family reunions, weddings and receptions, anniversary and birthday celebrations, outdoor church services, concerts, and other events.

We have sponsored an annual, weeklong Vacation Bible School for the past twenty years. The mornings are filled with Bible stories, music, and crafts. The afternoons are devoted to outdoor activities. Volunteer staff members from local churches serve as leaders for the groups, which comprise senior kindergartners to eighth graders. In recent years we have ministered to over 100 campers per year in VBS. It is especially gratifying to see former campers return to serve as staff. Directing this annual VBS camp remains a great privilege for me.

It is a well-known fact that small private camps or retreat centers are not moneymakers. Our fees would have to be prohibitive for the camp to break even. Dick and I lived on our retirement and invested more than a little time, effort, and money into the camp.

We are indebted to the many generous donors who also support the camp on a regular basis.

Our facilities are winterized. The next camp directors, Shaun and Marlene Spence, plan to continue the present programs, as well as offer year-round camping, setting up established camps for youngsters to stay overnight for extended periods.

The Edna Lee Lodge

In the early days of the camp, we slept out in tents, a covered wagon, and five huge teepees. Boy Scouts and Girl Guides brought their tents for summer and winter camping. When Dick and I returned from our wedding trip, we found that a two-car garage had been built for us by Jerry Hawdon. This soon became a gathering place or overnight sleeping quarters for some groups. In the early seventies, Jerry Hawdon, Russell Adcock and his son Clifford helped me build a cook shack, which is still great for outdoor cooking. These two facilities served as our primary "gathering" sites.

We knew a big lodge would add much to the camp, but we weren't in a financial position to build it. When the Beards expressed an interest in the camp, we became serious about adding a lodge.

Edna and Lee Beard came into my life when I was working with the Girl Scouts in Fort Wayne, Indiana. While Edna served on our camp committee, Lee was quite involved with the physical aspects of our campsites.

I remember Edna best for her friendship and concern for others. She was a beautiful, dignified, and gracious lady in every sense of the word. While she contributed much to our meetings, her service went beyond the walls of the committee room. She was a hands-on person, well versed in camping and nature. I appreciated her support of my leadership and her contribution to our entire Girl Scout Council program.

My first real encounter with Lee came when he called the office and all but commanded me to bring the Girl Scout truck and meet him at a cement block company in Fort Wayne. He had persuaded the owner to donate blocks to build steps at Camp Ella J. Logan on Dewart Lake near Syracuse, Indiana. My job was to take the load in the truck from the cement block company to the camp. Lee was an engineer and a superintendent at The Taylor Street General Electric Company. He informed me that he would meet me at the camp the next day with some students from the local engineering school.

The truck was loaded—overloaded! The bed was so heavy in back that the front wheels barely touched the road. This made steering precarious. Added to that little problem was the fact that the truck was a standard shift. However, I safely made it to the camp and the engineering students installed the steps.

Weaving a Legacy

After I left scouting, I kept in touch with the Beards. They made numerous trips to the Island. Edna transplanted several trillium plants that still bloom each year. Some of them can be seen from the cabin's kitchen window. Each spring they remind me of my friend with the lovely white hair and sweet disposition. Lee was a fixer and made many repairs about the camp. He was also creative and built a wooden horse named Homer, complete with saddle and braided ropes for a mane and tail. Young and old enjoyed riding on Homer before he finally passed from our midst.

Some years later when Dick and I were conducting Triangle Tours at the college, we invited the Beards and some of their friends to acquaint them with the campus. Triangle Tours came about because of Dick's concern in the early eighties that too many Wesleyan youth were studying in state schools instead of their own school, Marion College. He thought the school should set up a program to invite youth and adult groups to the campus for a tour, free meal, slide presentation, and a word of welcome from a member of the faculty or administration. With then president Dr. James P. Hill's blessing and good friend Howard Noggle's advice, we initiated the program between camping sessions. We sent letters to Wesleyan pastors in several nearby states and were gratified with the response.

The Beards first came to the campus because they were interested in knowing what we were doing at the school they had heard so much about when we were Scouting together. They were so impressed with what they saw that Lee wanted to get involved with the school. His first contribution was a pair of speakers for the music department. A master craftsman in wood and metal, he soon crafted utility cabinets for the Eastburn and Phillippe student apartments. Next, Terry Porter and the Athletic Department were the recipients of an oak trophy case that matched the other trophy cases perfectly.

On our Triangle Tours, we preached the gospel of Indiana Tax Credit and matching contributions by the donor's employer. Dick pointed out to Lee that while General Electric was a matching company, Lee had to be an alumnus to qualify. Because he was already involved in weaving, we suggested he see Ardelia Williams ('51), the head of the Art Department, and that he sign up for a course in weaving.

He enjoyed working with Ardelia in her weaving studio, the beginning of a close and far-reaching friendship. I helped him register for the course and paid his fee as a way of saying thanks for all he had done for us. I didn't know then that he was a millionaire, but it proved to be a good investment. He was soon making shuttles and repairing looms in the classroom.

Edna was suffering with terminal cancer during this time period. Before one of his weaving sessions, Lee stopped by to see us. In tears he informed us that Edna wanted the camp to be included in their estate planning. We prayed with him and comforted him the best we could. We then suggested that we build a lodge at the camp in honor of Edna. She sent us the following note from the nursing home:

> *June '86*
> *Dear Millie and Dick:*
> *I can't think what to say. This is the greatest honor we have ever known. This may be the last thing I*

write. (It was.)
I love you,
Edna

She died shortly after that. Although the Beards were good people, they did not take time for church or believe in a personal relationship with Christ. Edna had requested that her ashes be scattered at the camp. Lee did not want a religious ceremony, but I insisted on a memorial service for her—including prayer, Scripture, poetry, and hymns. Lee seemed pleased with my efforts.

Their neighbor, Delmer Weaver, flew Lee, Sandy (their adopted daughter), and her husband, Don Irwin, up to the Island, where they landed at Francis Nelson's airfield. After the service, Lee and Sandy scattered Edna's ashes on the present site of the Edna Lee Lodge.

I am happy to report that before Lee died, he made his peace with God. Ardelia Williams and other faculty members helped him see his need for a Saviour. When he died a few months later, Dr. J. Barnes, Ardelia and her husband, Wilbur ('51), assisted with the memorial service here at the camp. Sandy and Don scattered his ashes over the site of our proposed guesthouse.

But that is not the end of the story.

The Beard Art Center Building on the Marion Campus was made possible due to his largess. In addition, his will stipulated $3,000,000 more to the university. At the time it was the largest gift in the history of the school.

Building the Lodge

Lee and his friends had made a contribution of $30,000 toward the building of the lodge. We hired an architect who drew up plans for a 30 ft. x 50 ft. two-story building with a 10 ft. x 50 ft. screened-in front porch. We then accepted tenders for the construction of the basement and septic system. Don Gilbertson excavated the site, George Hadden put in the septic system, and Tom Young completed the basement. Tom and his crew were also responsible for the

The Crown Jewel

handsome "blue pine" ceiling in the upper part of the Lodge. Alex Cain cut and delivered cedar logs that were straight as an arrow. Many, many people spent hours peeling those logs. (Some of the logs did not want to part with their bark, so it was tough work.)

Al Matthews, a Wesleyan friend from Mio, Michigan agreed to oversee the log work. He and his wife Wilma moved their small camping trailer to the location. Our neighbor and good friend, Jim Snider, volunteered to assist Al. Dick and I were very willing helpers.

One by one the logs went up until soon it was time for the trusses. Charley Nelson brought the Lion's Club members for a day to take care of that job.

It quickly became evident that we needed additional help. Jim suggested I call Ron Beaupre. He came for the lodge project and he is still volunteering today. Our "Number One Volunteer," Ron now serves on our board of directors. The Lodge and other camp facilities exist largely because of him. Gifted beyond measure, he is a quiet, modest kind of guy who seems to be able to turn his hand to anything.

At the dedication of the Edna Lee Lodge in 1992, he was presented with a beautiful plaque, on which these words appear:

"Indiana Wesleyan University, Presidential Citation, presented to Ron Beaupre. Words and wood, walnut and paper attempt to recognize the quality of work you have done over a period of five years. From kitchen sink to ceiling fans you have labored toward the completion of the Edna Lee Lodge. Cupboards and countertops, drop ceilings, rest rooms, windows and lighting reflect the efforts of a versatile volunteer. May God bless you and those who enjoy the fruits of your labor. This citation is hereby awarded this 10th day of July, 1992.

James Barnes, President of the University."

Special Thanks

A score or more volunteers gave of their time and talents to bring the lodge to completion. It would be impossible to name all of the volunteers and contributors. I trust everyone who helped in any way will have the satisfaction of knowing that she or he had a part in providing a remarkable facility for young and old to enjoy.

However, the following people went beyond the call of duty as volunteers.

My brother Jack Jacobs in Wisconsin made arrangements for us to pick up a semi load of free insulation from a company in Milwaukee, Wisconsin. Brian Bringleson hauled it for us.

Dane Whonsetler ('77) cooking breakfast at an alumni camp.

Two couples from Pinconning, Michigan—Eldon and Virginia Foor and Otis and Evelyn Whittum—framed the base for the 10 ft. x 50 ft. porch on the front of the lodge. Their local Wesleyan Church has regularly sent campers and workers to the Island.

Dean Allen of Thessalon, Ontario was the master craftsman who created the magnificent and massive pudding stone fireplace.

Trapper Jim Reed gave a generous contribution towards the beautiful hardwood floor made from maple trees cut on the camp property. Jim's sister Pearl Court contributed to the shower and restrooms.

The Edna Lee Lodge has been beautifully furnished through the generosity of many friends. Herman Medema of Michigan persuaded his friend Dale Schaap to give us one hundred and twenty-three solid, handsome chairs. These grace the main area and the dining room. Don and Ruth Gilbertson outbid several others to obtain a large propane gas range from an old restaurant in Richards Landing, then gave it to the camp.

Maxine McDougal, a Girl Scout friend, gave us a valuable rock collection in an attractive twelve-foot-long lighted case. Dr. Donald ('40) and Osea Boone ('43), Wisconsin, enlivened the lodge with an array of stuffed and mounted birds. Don Gilbertson, Gord Hawdon, Jim Reed, Brad Bollinger, Ada Tranter, Naomi Taylor, Charlie Stevenson, Leslie Samu, and others have also contributed animal and bird mounts, as well as furs.

My brother Jack's Boy Scout Troop from Wisconsin donated authentic Indian headgear. Bea Sturgeon donated two fine Indian prints by famous Russian artist, Nicholas de Grandmaison. Leo Hubel made the frames.

Ron Beaupre did all the wiring and plumbing. He also built the bookcases that house the *National Geographic* magazines that date from 1915 to 1987. The magazines were a gift from his mother, Laura.

Several Indiana Wesleyan University faculty members and students put in many hours of "sweat equity" by cleaning logs, staining wood, installing insulation, and creating The Edna Lee Lodge sign.

The Dedication

In a formal dedication service, the Edna Lee Lodge was dedi-

Dr. Howard Noggle and Millie

cated to the glory of God on July 10, 1992 to a capacity crowd. Nancy Turbin, on behalf of the All Tribes Board of Directors, presented the camp and lodge to Dr. Barnes to be "dedicated to God as a place of education and fellowship to the glory of God and for the extension of His kingdom." Dr. James Barnes ('65), President of Indiana Wesleyan University led the litany of dedication, gave special presentations, and received the camp keys from Randy Gill, member of All Tribes Board of Directors. Dr. Howard Noggle, special assistant to Dr. Barnes, led the prayer of thanksgiving. Bernt Gilbertson, former owner of the property, offered "A Look Back." Tony Martin, M.P.P., Sault Ste. Marie, responded with "A Look Forward." I gave the welcome and announcements and recognized the many volunteers listed in the Order of Service. Rev. Dale Kessler, Pastor, Soo Michigan Wesleyan Church, offered the Benediction. Pauline Jagger, pianist for the dedication service reflected on the dedication:

> *"I felt privileged to have been asked to be a part of the special day. Even though ceremonies were held inside (due to uncertainties of weather), nobody seemed concerned. There was a low buzz of excitement and some anxious moments, hoping everything would go as planned.*
>
> *"It was a special moment in time when everyone could celebrate the God-given talents and gifts that helped to complete the Lodge and bring it to dedication. The camp itself is a haven of serenity, thought, prayer, and the gift of children, for which now the Lodge is a very integral part."*
>
> *"Dick and Millie had worked very hard to organ-*

ize everything for the dedication of the Lodge. Dick in his quiet manner did what needed to be done and then would check with Millie. I noticed him at different times watching Millie as she continued to put finishing touches on everything. What drew this to my attention was the look of pride on his face. It was so very obvious that he admired his wife and was extremely pleased with how the plans of the day unfolded. Just another special moment that made the day so great!"

The Crown Jewel

Michael Heintzman of *The North Shore Sentinel* described The Edna Lee Lodge in these words:

> *"Complete with full service kitchen and grand hall, The Lodge was constructed in 1987 and is the 'crown jewel' of All Tribes Christian Camp.*
>
> *"Every nook and cranny is filled with some donated item of interest, highlighted by a gleaming rock and mineral collection, a full range of mounted wild life and pelts, including pheasants, a bobcat, lynx and a Remus monkey from Kenya. Moose antlers, a beautifully mounted deer head, and two sets of deer antlers, believed to be from the same deer, were given by Don Gilbertson. A timber wolf head was donated by the Gord Hawdon family. There are animal hide lap robes for winter sleighing and a large black bear pelt—one of Trapper Jim's own—stretching out across the handsome maple hardwood floor made from trees from the camp property."*

The basement of the Lodge contains the kitchen and dining areas, plus a shower and two restrooms. Many different groups for a variety of special occasions and events use the Lodge. It has to be seen to be fully appreciated! In my sixty-five years of camping, the Edna Lee Lodge has the best features of all the lodges I have ever seen.

Interesting donated items continue to come to the Lodge. That's one of the best things about this "living museum." From the basement to the roof, every square inch of this masterpiece has a story to tell.

Chapter Nineteen

Reduce—Reuse—Recyle

"Everything from picking up litter to planting trees can be an act of worship."

MJT

Several signs around the camp pretty well sum up my feelings about litter and recycling. The sign that seems to get the most attention is an old Persian Proverb:

If you with litter will spoil this place
May indigestion rack your chest
And ants invade your pants and vest!

Another reminder is clearly visible in one of the play areas:

> *Leaves that fall from the trees and shrubs during autumn form a natural beauty. Cigarette butts, aluminum cans, candy and gum wrappers all form a carpet of ugliness. Please pick up litter wherever you see it. Thanks*

Our buildings are all smoke free. However, those who still insist on ruining their health and wasting their money can find one-gallon cans filled with sand here and there. These are marked with the message: *"Butt Out Here."*

In the kitchen and dining area, these words above several recycling containers encourage campers to join the effort:

> *Just as nature recycles, so can we. Much of what we throw away contains renewable resources. We encourage you to recycle here and at home.*

We discourage the use of plastic utensils and paper or Styrofoam plates and cups. Washed glass, aluminum cans, tin, plastic, and Styrofoam containers are all taken to recycling centers. All food waste is either composted or fed to the birds and squirrels. Some think we should install a dishwasher but there is a wonderful fellowship in doing dishes with fellow campers. A small sign over the sink chides reluctant souls with this verse:

Thank God for dirty dishes.
They have a tale to tell.
While folks are going hungry,
We are eating very well.

Waste Not, Want Not

"Waste not, want not!" was on the lips of many when I was a child. This saying does not seem to influence most people today. Many of us are familiar with the Superdome in New Orleans. I have been there and was most impressed. But I am less than impressed with the fact that Americans produce enough garbage each year to fill that mammoth stadium from top to bottom twice each day, every day of the year! Worse yet, 50% of all that garbage is recyclable. Does that bother you? It should.

Mock grave of mankind's trash, 1994

High on my list of concerns in this area is the way we dispose of aluminum cans. Too many of them are never recycled. Do you know that before each soda can reaches your lips it has been part of the earth? There is still aluminum in the ground. We mine it and use it for cars, bicycles, airplanes, and many household items, as well as over eighty billion pop cans yearly. I have heard that we can save one cup of gasoline by recycling one pop can. I have also heard that the energy saved by recycling one aluminum can will keep a TV set running for three hours. It is a known fact that there is no limit to the number of times a can may be melted down and reused. Picking up those cans does more than merely make our roadsides look better. Give it some thought.

I am also bothered by the amount of glass we toss out. Did you know that we throw out enough jars and bottles to fill up a giant skyscraper every month? The energy saved from recycling one glass bottle will keep a 100-watt light bulb burning for four hours.

Our indiscriminate use of paper products troubles me as well. Millions of feet of paper toweling and napkins (or serviettes) are used annually. Nobody knows for sure how many trees are cut down for just those two items alone. I always use linen or cloth serviettes in my home.

When you add this to the amount of printed paper we use, the waste is astounding. Consider how much is wasted on junk mail alone, let alone all the other trillions of pages printed out on one side only. Much of this manuscript has been first created on the reverse sides of discarded paper.

Old News Is Good News

Newspapers and magazines consume vast quantities of paper, too. I confess to being a news junkie. Dr. Bowman got me hooked on *Time* when I was a student. The professor declared that we could not pray intelligently for the world about us if we did not know what was going on. I agree wholeheartedly.

While traveling I make it a practice to pick up *USA Today* to keep abreast of the news. When I am home I listen to the TV news on a daily basis. Thanks to Margaret McKay, I keep up with the news by reading her copy of *The Sault Star* (after another neighbor reads it first). I also receive the regional paper, *The North Shore Sentinel*, after Pastor Tom and Jan Gurnick read their copy. Finally, I use the papers for starting fires or make them available for camper's needs. Most of my magazines are passed on to friends, who in turn pass them on to nursing homes or the Sault jail.

These disposables are all part of our natural resources. We use them once and out they go for garbage. My good friend Erminie Smedley taught me a great deal about the expression "Waste not, want not!" Her friends teased her about being so frugal, but she was a good steward and years ahead of our present-day environmentalists. She used paper towels sparingly, opting instead for the clean rag she kept nearby for wiping up spills. I had never seen anyone wash and reuse aluminum foil and plastic food wrap until I met Erminie. She even recycled her dishwater by using it to water her beautiful flowerbeds. She wasted very little of anything. (I was pleased to share with her the way to extend the life of toothpaste and hand cream tubes. You would be surprised how much remains inside after you can no longer squeeze out any of the contents. Just cut them open and use what adheres to the inside. To keep the tubes from drying out, wrap them in a bit of aluminum foil—used, of course).

Some Startling Facts

Are you aware that if you leave the water running to rinse off your dishes you can waste thirty gallons of water? That's enough to wash a car. If you leave the water running while you brush your teeth, you can waste up to five gallons of water. It is reported that 20% of all toilets in American homes leak. In one year a leaky toilet can waste over 3,000 gallons of water. Even a wee faucet leak can waste gallons of water.

Our landfill sites involve more than using up acres and acres of ground. Many of them are leaking hazardous chemicals into our water supplies. How long will it take us to wake up before our home planet becomes one large dump?

Some Alternatives

I think we are also overly dependent on our cars. During World War II people frequently asked this question: "Is This Trip Necessary?" In light of our present energy crisis, we would do well to revive that slogan. In many cases we can walk rather than drive. The exercise is good for us. We can also share rides. I frequently phone friends who drive past my lane and ask for a lift to church. It not only saves gas and fuel emissions, it gives me an opportunity to chat—something we do all too infrequently with our very busy schedules.

Several alternative energy systems that are very environmentally friendly are now available. As you know, I was quite firm about refusing to install "hydro" electricity. I had designed the cabin for a simple lifestyle. Further, I could not stand the thought of spoiling the lovely spruce logs by chiseling into them to insert light switches. And I certainly did not want electrical outlets every four feet in the bottom log near the floor.

However, we needed more light for Dick, who was an avid reader. Dick had poor eyesight and could not read very well by the kerosene and propane lights. He had been following the development of solar energy and he wanted to investigate the possibilities. Eventually we opted for solar, a system that comprised four panels and a pack of batteries. Local solar businesses operated by Stan Mole, John Kent, and Laurence and Diena McKay installed our system and have maintained it. At the time of installation, we could run the main cable across the attic floor and drop the lines down to the fixtures. The switches were on the fixtures instead of the walls.

Many comment on the uniqueness of these fixtures. Jerry Hawdon, a former camper, is a clever fellow. I gave him two copper teakettles, one small wooden pail, a large seashell, an antique kerosene lamp, and a wagon wheel hub. He transformed them into lovely lamps.

The village blacksmith, Jimmy Harten, who at one time had a shop in Richards Landing, gave me the wheel hub. It was in his junk pile with its jagged spokes still protruding. When John McMaster spotted it at my place, he knew where I had been. He claims that in his younger days he had wrecked one of his father's wagons and that was the one wheel that he had been unable to repair. I took it down to the campus with me and spent several of my lunch hours in the old maintenance shop removing the spokes with a wood chisel.

While on an alumni trip, I explored an antique shop in Columbus, Ohio and discovered the old kerosene lamp I would hang above my dining room table. It has a milk glass base and shade held together with black lightweight chains. Surrounding the base is a trio of Englishmen wearing top hats and riding on horses.

Twin propane lamps in the living room and kitchen produce both bright light and heat. I also use several old kerosene lamps and candles here and there throughout the cabin.

My favorite lamp is a hanging oil lamp in the living room. The fourteen-inch shade and base are adorned with hummingbirds and pastel morning glories. The chains and holder are brass, from which hang the fifty crystal prisms. I prize it highly because it was given to me by Winnie Hadden. Originally a wedding gift to her mother, Emma Gennings, it is a true antique.

An extra benefit gained from all of these beautiful and unique alternative energy appliances is that I never have to worry about the electrical power going off, as it does periodically in the country. Due to the size and needs of the Edna Lee Lodge, I agreed to have electricity installed in that area of the camp.

I am reminded of the challenge Marion College's business manager, Russell Baldwin, tossed out to us in the late 1940's. We were complaining about the scarcity of phones on campus and were involved in a campaign to get a phone on each floor of the dorms. (No, we did not have them on every floor, let alone in every room!) One day in chapel he announced that if we would turn out the lights when we left our dorm or classrooms, cutting down on the school's utility bills, he would see that we had our phones. We did, and he did!

An Awesome Trust

I could go on and on about the two E's—Ecology and Environment—and the three R's—Reduce-Reuse-Recycle—but my book would be twice as long if I did! By the way, have you heard the term "precycle"? It simply means to refrain from buying the things that cannot be reused, like plastic wrapping and other packaging. In light of all we know, I trust we shall become better stewards of all He has given us.

The following two passages of Scripture have intrigued me over the years. I have tried to take them to heart. Will you do the same? In Genesis 1:28 we read: "And God blessed them, and God said unto them, Be fruitful, and multiply, and replenish the earth, and subdue it: and have dominion over the fish of the sea, and over the fowl of the air, and over every living thing that moveth upon the earth."

A former Wesleyan missionary, Barry Ross, says that dominion over all creation is the functional result of bearing God's image. Humans are to be God's visible representatives, ruling creation as God would rule it.

Psalm 8 is a song of praise that centers on the wonder of God Himself, particularly as seen in His creation and treatment of humanity. In verses 6-8 we read: "Thou madest him to have dominion over the works of thy hands; thou hast put all things under his feet: all sheep and oxen . . . and the beasts of the field; the fowl of the air, and the fish of the sea, and whatsoever passeth through the paths of the seas."

Regarding this portion of Scripture, Barry comments: "What daring faith in humanity by God! What an awesome trust committed to humankind. Whatever honor belongs to humanity is only a reflection of the greater glory of God."

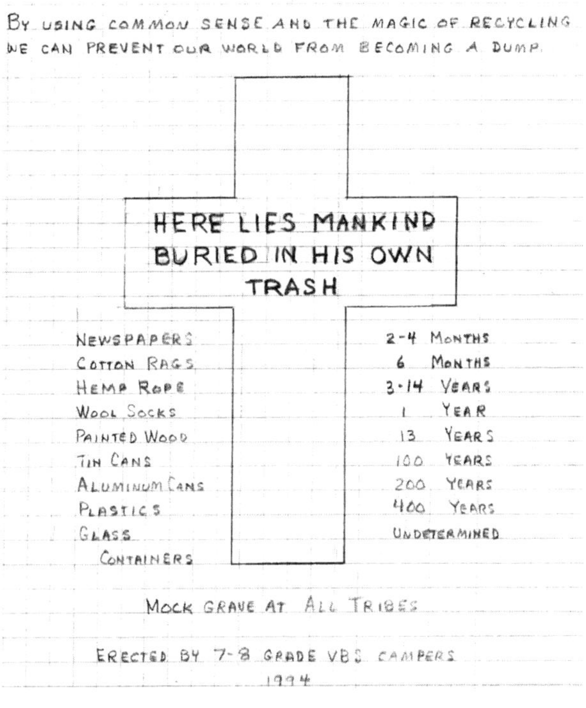

Sketch of mock grave

Chapter Twenty

Fire's Burning, Fire's Burning

CAMPFIRES

"Fire's burning, fire's burning, draw nearer, draw nearer
In the gloaming, in the gloaming, come sing and be merry."
Camp Song

Poor indeed is the individual who has never sat around a campfire, singing that ageless old camp song. However in over fifty years of camping, only one child has ever asked me what the words meant—five-year-old Sarah Elizabeth Kidd, Beth's daughter and one of my favorite great-godchildren. Singing softly, we were sitting on a log at the All Tribes campfire. Out of the blue she asked, "What does gloaming mean?"

"Early evening, almost nighttime," I replied.

"Why don't you just say so then?" she asked. "And what about 'draw nearer, draw nearer'?"

"Come closer, come closer," I explained.

"I like that better," she said. "And one more thing, what is merry?"

"Be happy, be cheerful."

"Well, why don't we sing it like that, then?"

Out of the mouth of babes!

Stored Sunlight

Campfire. The very sound of that word sends a warm, fuzzy feeling through my very being. The numberless campfires I have enjoyed with campers for over half a century have enriched my life. Even now as I sit alone watching the flames in my cabin's impressive pudding stone fireplace, I can see former campers huddled around a fire. All of them know, as I do, that not only is it the fire but also the singing, sharing, fun, and laughter that contribute to the memories.

However, few of us ever think about the wood that fuels our campfires and fireplaces. It is stored sunlight, releasing warmth and comfort when we need it most—at camp when we seek fellowship or alone at home on a cold winter day. In managing the harvest, transporting, and storing the wood, we control our lives from a temperature perspective, just as we do from renewable resources that generate our electricity.

As I have already described, among my best memories was the huge fire that resulted from burning the old barn during my Sabbatical. And I can still taste the special breakfast I cooked on the first fire in my cabin's brand new fireplace.

I have relived numerous campfires, and the feeling of comradeship they generated, but one evening has been etched in my memory forever. Near the end of our program, a storm arose suddenly on the shores of Lake McCarroll at Camp Wakonda near Echo Bay, Ontario. Bolts of lightning flashed across the lake and thunder pealed forth above the nearby hills. I knew we had to get to our cabins quickly, but I also wanted to preserve the mood of the evening. And I did not want the campers to go back to our rustic cabins fearful or afraid. To circumvent a hasty, disorganized retreat, I suggested that we sing "Safe Am I," and that we leave the site in single file. As the children slipped away, their words echoed back to me where I had stayed to douse the fire just in case the rain did not materialize. "Safe am I in the hollow of His hand." A deep appreciation for His care, the camp, and the campers swept over me. Safe we were. And are.

Smoky Bear Sez . . .

Another campfire in Quebec at Camp Kalalla was altogether different. We had been on an overnight some distance from the main camp. As good campers do, we had put out the fire before snuggling down in our sleeping bags. After a good night's sleep, we didn't bother with a fire and instead ate a cold breakfast, then hiked back to camp. In the middle of the morning, a fire ranger drove in requesting help from some of the staff. The nearby cottagers had already been recruited. Unbeknownst to us, our fire had gone underground and cropped up some distance from where we had camped. It seemed so incredible I could hardly believe it!

As the camp director, I felt responsible for the whole smoky mess. How could I explain it or justify my actions? When the fire was finally out, I identified myself to the ranger and offered my apologies. He took my word that we had, to the best of our knowledge, doused our campfire properly. He also said he was familiar with fires traveling underground, for it had happened before in this area. We went back to camp dirty and weary. A swim in Long Lake washed away the dirt and a portion of our weariness, but the memory of the fire lingered.

Imagine our surprise when later in the summer we each received a check in the mail for our part in helping to put out the fire—for which we were indirectly responsible! I am not sure how the Quebec government balanced their books that year, for I never cashed my check. I kept it as a souvenir and as a reminder to do as Smoky Bear sez, "Make double sure that your fire is out!"

Organized camps use this verse in one of the many beautiful ceremonies at campfires:

"Kneel always when you light a fire.
Kneel reverently and thankful be
For God's unfailing charity.
And on the ascending flame inspire
A little prayer that shall upbear
The incense of your thankfulness
For this sweet grace of warmth and light,
For here again is sacrifice for your delight
Kneel always when you light a fire
Kneel reverently and thankful be
For God's unfailing charity."

Anonymous

Close Calls

In 1963 I would have been out of house and home had my neighbor Elgin Eddy not been driving by. He saw smoke and came to my rescue. A grass fire had gotten out of hand. In a later grass fire, Dick and I lost an old outhouse where the amphitheater now stands. Those two fires made me realize I could no longer depend on an old, hand-operated weed whip to keep the grass away from the buildings. Although the whip was good for my golf swing, I decided a mower was a must. (During my first year on the Island, I had told Cal Kent, the owner of Kentvale Merchants Ltd. that if and when I ever needed a mower I would leave.) A few years later I reluctantly purchased an International Cub Cadet with a mower, but I used it sparingly. I did not want the place to look manicured.

Millie Mobile (golf cart) going up in flames

It now takes almost three days to mow the grass and at least a day to use a gas weed whip to keep the grass in check around the buildings and play areas. And sad to say, it does look more manicured than I prefer.

Two fires in the year 2000 really put the fear of God in me. Spring and summer had been unusually dry. Even the petunias I had planted needed to be watered daily. We were in the process of finishing the shower house and there seemed to be endless piles of trash to burn. Late one day I walked away from the burn barrel, thinking the fire was under control. I was too weary that night to think about preparing the evening meal, let alone water those pesky petunias! However, my sense of "duty to beauty" got the better of me, so after a short rest I went out to give the petunias a drink. As I opened the back door, I saw a thick cloud of smoke and heard a horrible crackling noise. A grass fire had taken part of the rail fence and flames were approaching the base of a spruce tree. I dashed back into the cabin and called the volunteer fire department.

By the time the men arrived, I had used a rake to put the fire out at the tree. I also had pulled the fence apart, but not before the compost box and eleven sections of the century-old cedar rails had been destroyed. The fire department soaked down the area and commended me for my quick thinking and action. I thanked them and the Good Lord for a group of volunteers in our community who work so hard to keep us safe. (The driver of the fire truck was Ian Murdock, one of my favorite former campers.) I was also grateful that the wind was blowing in the right direction. Had the fire been blown the other way, the old barn and the Lodge could have gone up in smoke. I shudder to think of that loss!

The second fire of that year involved my grandson Dan and the "Millie Mobile." The Millie Mobile was an electric golf cart that we used as a general grounds vehicle. Quiet and quick, it could carry all the tools and people we might need for a job. Most of all it was versatile, for it could take us over the humps and hollows of the camp trails without complaint. Dan and I had gone up to the bush on the Millie Mobile to clear the trails of fallen trees. We left the cart and most of the tools in an open space and went off to work. After a while we looked back to see a wall of smoke. We dashed back in time for Dan to save the chain saw, but everything else went up in smoke. The six batteries that provided the vehicle's power went off like small cannons. Fortunately, we were able to contain the fire and neither of us was injured. The Lord is good!

A Vital Sense

In recent years I have lost my "smeller." I am not sure exactly when this happened or why, but it is gone. The good side, of course, is that I cannot smell skunks or any other foul-smelling thing. On the other hand, I cannot enjoy the smell of cooking food, which is a real loss. They say our sense of smell adds so much to our enjoyment of a meal. I still eat like most people and I enjoy eating, but perhaps I am not tempted to eat as much. That works in my favor, for it is easier to keep my weight in check.

The worst part is that I cannot smell smoke, and that is not good. Often at night Dick would smell smoke and get up and check the fireplace or stove. Before he died, he told me over and over again that it would not be safe for me to live in the cabin alone. I thank the Lord for whoever invented the smoke alarm. Recently I was rudely awakened by my smoke alarm at four in the morning. The cabin was full of smoke. A log had come too far forward in the fireplace and the smoke was building in the cabin. I pushed the log back, opened both doors, and cleared the smoke by fanning two tea towels. I recall my mother doing the same thing on occasion.

After giving the problem much thought, I determined that the horseshoe andirons I had been using were much too short. I asked

Joe Hendershott and Laurence Misener, employees of Gilbertson Enterprises, to cut an old grader blade into two twenty-three-inch pieces. Four inches wide, they are perfect to prop up against a log to prevent it from rolling forward. I feel much safer now.

A Shocking Discovery

Dick and I were off on one of our longer jaunts during the early 1980's. Our good friend, Erminie Smedley, took care of our mail and banking and checked out the cabin on a regular basis. We phoned her weekly for a report. Often Dick would thank her for being there so we could be here (wherever that was). She always asked if we wanted the good news or the Island "griefs." As a true Islander and former telephone operator, she seemed to know everyone and she kept us posted on Island happenings.

However, on this one day she was unusually quiet. When we pressed her she said, "You don't really want this news." She reluctantly told us about stopping by the cabin to find everything inside covered with a thick, black greasy film. The propane heater had malfunctioned. Although technically there had not been a fire, the place was a mess. Nothing had burned, but what should she do? We advised her to call the insurance company and we would take care of it upon returning. We could not imagine the extent of the damage. Since nothing had been charred, we did not think it necessary to cut the trip short. Philosophical Dick told her not to worry about it. We continued on our journey, totally unprepared for what we saw when we opened the cabin door upon on our return.

To describe it as a mess was an understatement. The lovely, soft, satiny log walls were black. All of the contents of the cabin were covered with a horrible, greasy film. The insurance adjuster met us and advised us to check into a motel. The company would cover all of our expenses. They would also hire a cleaning crew of Merry Maids and we could return home when the job was completed.

Erminie insisted that we stay with her. I maintained I would be part of the cleaning process. I was not about to abdicate my responsibility. There were too many delicate antiques, and I could not let just anybody handle them. And what about sorting through all of our clothes and personal belongings? Unfortunately, the closets and dresser drawers did not keep out the soot. Everything, and I mean everything, was covered in it.

The Merry Maids brought in a gas generator and used vacuum cleaners to remove much of the film. Everything was washed at least twice. I sorted our clothes. What could be washed went to the local Laundromat. Coats, suits, cushions, rugs, and those kinds of things went to the dry cleaners. The bill was staggering, but true to their word the insurance company paid it all. They even paid me for the hours I spent cleaning. (Wisely, Dick removed himself from the scene and did important things like mow the grass.) The only thing that kept me going was the thought that we had, at least, something to clean. The cabin could have burned to the ground.

That fire, or explosion, is now just a memory. Life went on, teaching us another lesson about our reactions being more important than our actions. As Dick said, it could have been worse.

The Price of Burning Wood

The cabin is still heated by wood. I do have a propane back-up heater, but you will understand why I rarely use it. I love the challenge of keeping the place warm and toasty, and a crackling fire is great company. An old saying explains that burning wood warms you three times: the first time when you cut the wood, a second time when you split and haul it, and a third time when you sit in front of the fire. That is the benefit and the price of burning wood. There are ashes to carry out as well.

Cooking chicken under a bucket

In many buildings today, open fireplaces have given way to fireplace inserts. Granted, these are more efficient. Wood-burning cook stoves have been replaced with gas or electric models. Perish the thought! When I can no longer meet these challenges, I will know it is time to move on. In the meantime, come and enjoy a meal with me cooked the old-fashioned way. Later, we will settle down for a cup of hot chocolate in front of a blazing fire.

"Fire's burning, fire's burning, draw nearer, draw nearer..."

Chapter Twenty-One

Thanksgiving Days to Remember

"It is the attitude of our gratitude which really counts in life!"

For years on Thanksgiving Day I have made it a practice to thank God for all those who have touched my life in one way or another. I start as soon as I wake up in the morning, going back in memory as far as I can. This is a wonderful exercise and leaves me feeling blessed beyond measure. I am amazed that I can still recall so many people from my earliest childhood. It takes me all day and often on into the night to visualize them, but what a blessing. I recommend the habit to all.

Early Roots

My parents are the first who come to mind. Although my mother was not at all well for most of my childhood, she loved us all dearly and manifested it in so many ways. She was a wonderful cook. If and when I find myself getting a bit homesick, I resort to cooking up some of the meals she used to make. The Depression did not allow meat to be a part of our daily diet, but my mother's Swiss steak, mashed potatoes, and red (tomato) gravy was something to look forward to on a Sunday. Other creations—her "tater" soup with wee dumplings, macaroni in stewed tomatoes, corn bread and beans, kidney beans with a bit of bacon mixed with scrambled eggs—all filled our tummies. I do bless her memory.

Dad's enthusiasm for life, his love for his family and the out-of-doors was contagious. I bless him often for so many things that he taught me. For Thanksgiving we could not always afford turkey, but Dad made sure we had meat of some kind, even if it was pheasant, rabbit, or squirrel. Since we preserved our garden produce in a variety of ways, we were sure to have a bountiful holiday meal. This special family day was made even more enjoyable because Dad was home from work and had the day with us.

Dad's mother, Grandmother Hill, also comes to mind. Her large lap was made for grandchildren. She had a windmill in her back yard covered with grapevines, a perfect hideout for her grandkids. It was that memory that inspired me to erect a windmill at the camp.

My four siblings made me feel special. Ruth would read the funnies to Chick and me every Sunday morning. When Mother was too ill to cook and attend school functions, Ruth took over. She nursed our cuts and scrapes and made them better with her kisses.

Betty was the first in our family to follow Christ. She and her friends and their steady witness later convinced me. As her maid of honor, I wore a formal for the first time at her wedding.

In younger days: in back row: Jack, Betty and Ruth. Millie and Chick in front

Strong and handsome, Jack was my hero. Even at an early age, first in the Civilian Conservation Corps and then later in the Navy, Jack helped provide for our needs. His monthly check was a lifesaver for the entire family.

Chick did much more than cause me to fight his battles whenever the kids teased him. We were close in age and interests, so we were coconspirators in many activities. Most of these were amusing, but when we had to suffer the consequences of our mischief, we found that they were not always fun.

Of course, there were aunts, uncles, cousins, and neighbors who played an important part in my life. The latter made us feel loved

Millie's brothers and sisters in 1955. L to r. Betty, Charles, Ruth, Jack, and Millie.

and safe in our neighborhood. They helped to teach us how to work and gave us the opportunity to do so. My teachers in grade school instilled in me a love of learning. The pastors and Sunday school teachers, the "Mothers in Israel," and others in the church encouraged me in The Way.

The list of campers, counselors, college friends, professors, coworkers, and others who inspired me is very long. My life has been enriched by so many and continues to testify that all those who touch us become a part of us and remain in our hearts.

Different Day, Same Idea

When I started to work at the Y in the Sault, I learned that Canadians observe Thanksgiving in October. My boss, R. J. Smith, and his family invited me to spend the day with them. While they served a very delicious meal, the thing I remember most came later. Mrs. Smith took it upon herself to teach me to knit. (She thought I had been neglected. Every young woman should know how to produce something with two needles and some wool, she thought.) With her help and that of her daughter Mary, we came up with two maroon mitts sans thumbs—we could do those another day. We put the mitts with the needles into an old Tinker Toy container. Years later I found them among my things, still without thumbs. They never did get finished.

R. J. thought I should have the American Thanksgiving off as well, so I celebrated two times that year. I had an apartment on the corner of Bruce and Wellington streets and I invited several friends who had some Yankee blood in their veins. They were unaware that I was dating a local fellow at the time. He came earlier for lunch. The evening guests thought it strange that a wing and drumstick were missing, but they were none the wiser until much later.

For that celebration I had decorated the apartment with a huge American flag. I also had many small ones all over the place. The next year when I invited these same people for Thanksgiving dinner, they came draped in Canadian flags. The meal was interrupted by a phone call from the husband of one of my guests. When I picked up the phone, not a word was spoken. Instead, I was serenaded by his bagpipe version of "Yankee Doodle," his way of saying Happy Thanksgiving.

Losing Track of Time

As I have already described, Thanksgiving 1977 was made so very special by Sir Richard's first visit to the camp. He seemed to be impressed with both my cooking and me. I certainly was impressed with him. We enjoyed Thanksgiving together every year thereafter until 1999. That year Dick was in the hospital following his heart attack. He was feeling quite well that day, so I decided to slip across the river to post some letters. I had forgotten completely that it was Thanksgiving! Much to my surprise, everything was locked up as tight as a drum. I could not even buy stamps, and only McDonald's and the Ramada Inn seemed to be open.

Once I realized it was Thanksgiving, I knew I did not want to settle for a hamburger and French fries, so I opted for the Ramada Inn, which was serving a buffet meal. Since there were few diners that day, the waitress was not busy, so she spent quite a bit of time at my table. A student at Lake State University in Sault, Michigan, she had decided she needed the money more than she needed a trip home. She helped to make my lonely meal a little more pleasant.

Since the Post Office was closed and some of my letters had to be weighed, I decided to look up some friends to see if they would post them the next day. I stopped by the Ron Edgerly home. They were just sitting down to their turkey dinner. Would I join them? I was already stuffed with turkey, but found room for my second piece of pumpkin pie that day. I then returned to the hospital and played several hands of Skip Bo with Dick. I drove back to the Island that night thinking what a strange way to celebrate Thanksgiving. But seeing Dick so much improved made me forget my rather lonesome meal. However, I decided I would never eat a holiday meal alone again.

Never Really Alone

Thanksgiving Day in the year 2000 fell on November 23, the anniversary of Dick's first heart attack. Although I was now alone, I remembered my vow not to eat alone on a holiday. I contacted eleven friends who the previous year had come immediately after Dick's heart attack to see if they could help in any way. I shall never forget their kindness. I chose these friends as my guests for that Thanksgiving meal.

Several days before the holiday, we had had a good snowfall—ideal for scaring up rabbits. But I chose turkey instead. I put five boards in the old oak table that Eva Gilger and I had brought up from her home in Kansas. The turkey was done to a turn. The guests came with all the trimmings. Good friends to both of us, they made Dick's memory a very important part of that meal. We shared some photos and talked freely about him. (This is an important facet of the grieving process. Grief is not a matter of bottling it up. It is a matter of giving it up.) We thanked God for him. We remembered his humor and talked about how he had touched our lives. Thank God for memory.

Between the main course and pumpkin pie, we went out, lighted the huge nativity scene, and broke forth with "Joy to the World." I purchased the nativity scene that year in Dick's memory and it is to be left at the camp for the years to come. We then proceeded to Dick's Place, the new storage shed purchased with funds from his memorials. Cami Gurnick, one of his favorite campers, cut the ribbon. Pastor Tom, Cami's father, dedicated the building. It all seemed so very appropriate to sing that old hymn "We Gather Together" before going back to the cabin for our dessert and an evening of reflection.

I have so very, very much to be thankful for and I pray that the attitude of my gratitude will be acceptable to Him for whatever years I have left.

Chapter Twenty-Two

Christmas on the Island

Celebrating Christmas from Creation

"A time of wonder and sweet delight,
Of glowing stars that fill the night,
Of glistening snow and firelight . . ."

Anonymous

Anticipating my first Christmas in my adopted country could be likened to a small child awaiting her first visit from Santa. As soon as I settled into the cabin after a summer of camping, I began to visualize what the place would look like at Christmas. I knew exactly where I was going to put the tree and how I would decorate it. Since this was 1963, I was occupying the old cabin, not the beautiful log cabin of today. Still, I knew exactly how I was going to decorate it for Christmas.

Who Needs Electricity?

I spotted the perfect tree on one of my daily hikes. (Cutting my own tree has been a tradition for years, a tradition that began in the early fifties when I worked in the Sault. Of course, the search for the ideal tree always begins early in the spring.) I knew the tree I had selected for my first Christmas on the Island was going to be too big. Even before cutting it down, I figured it would touch the ceiling and take up too much space in the small room. But it was Christmas after all, and that was the tree I had to have.

Heightening my excitement was my good friend Meg's visit from Massachusetts for the holidays. That meant lobster for our Christmas Eve meal, followed by a sleep in the snow, and lots of skiing for the week.

The summer and fall slipped by all too quickly and soon it was time to cut my tree. I hauled it in right after American Thanksgiving. I had brought my ornaments up from Indiana and had already made garlands out of popcorn and cranberries, so it did not take me long to decorate the tree. I was quite proud of my efforts—until darkness settled in. And it was dark. Because I had no electric lights, I lit the kerosene lamps and a few candles, hoping for a transformation. But my Christmas tree was dull and plain. The only things that glittered were a few gold-colored ornaments that picked up the soft light of the lamps and candles.

Then an idea struck me. Why not bring my tree to life with gold-sprayed natural items like cones and seedpods? Electric lights were not a necessary component to a beautiful Christmas tree. And electricity was not a necessary component for my happiness. I fully intended to live the simple life. But that didn't mean it had to be dull and plain.

I hiked the three miles over to Kent's, our Island general store. Kent's boasts that it has everything you need or they'll get it for you. And true to their claim, they had gold spray paint. I was amazed at the variety of seedpods I found while hiking to and from the store. Milkweed pods make delightful wee cradles. Pin five of them together and you have a perfect star for the top of the tree. (Recently my friend Bill Hibbard shared an idea for the use of the actual fluffy seeds in the pods. When they are dry they can be blown onto the tree to imitate snow.)

That year I entertained a few of my friends from the Sault and they were impressed with my tree. A tradition was born. Since then, in my travels around the globe, I have acquired a wide variety of seedpods. My favorites are the round gourds and cotton seedpods found in the southwestern states. The latter look like stars. I now have an abundance of such ornaments, sharing the extras with guests each Christmas.

That first Christmas I also set out a small basket of green pine cones. As they ripened they opened with a quiet popping sound, much like popcorn. As well, I cut a piece from the tip of a spruce tree. It was loaded with cones that gave off a wonderful aroma. I enhanced this swag with a jaunty red bough. To complete the scene, I placed candles in the windows and hung a wreath on the door.

With a good stash of firewood, I was ready for Christmas and the snow. I also knew how to use the shovel just outside the door. (Today, except for the cabin doors, storage shed, and Lodge, I do very little shoveling. Long ago I learned to pack the paths down with my snowshoes. This makes for a very serviceable and easily kept path during the entire winter.) I also had a good supply of food on hand, so I would not need a last-minute rush to the store for anything. When you have a three-mile hike to the store and back, you learn quickly to plan ahead.

Life was good. It was going to be a perfect Christmas. And it was!

Are We Ever Rich?

I follow an old French custom and set up several small decorated trees in the house as well as the main tree. These small trees are easy to find along our road allowances. If not removed, the snowplow or brush hog eventually destroy them anyway.

We set the large tree in a pail of water, after gashing the bottom of the trunk with the chain saw to allow the tree to drink more water. It absorbs at least a quart of liquid a day. With the steady heat from the nearby fireplace, the tree usually has fresh tips growing from the ends of the branches before the end of the season. One year the tree rated an article in *The Sault Star*. While we also set the small trees in water, they have never shown any new growth.

An all-natural tree, decorated with seed pods and cones sprayed gold

Transforming the cabin for the holidays is easy work. All the pictures, plaques, and decorative plates on the walls are stored away. The mantle corner cupboard and two coffee tables are also cleared. Boxes and boxes of decorations come down from the attic. Soon the whole house takes on the spirit of Christmas. Work? I never think of it in those terms. I enjoy every minute of it and revel in the finished product.

Five nativity sets find their way to the two coffee tables and the large windowsill nearby. Any visiting children are permitted to play with four of the sets. It is interesting to see how they rearrange them. One small tyke put all of the figures, including the animals, as close to Jesus as she could get them. A practical lesson for all of us.

Assorted Christmas mice find their way to the mantle, which is covered with red pine boughs. The guns resting on the moose antler gun rack, as well as the antlers themselves, make perfect resting-places for the colorful creatures.

The master bedroom is known as the angel room. A large collection of angel cards and wee angels sit on the mantle around the Ben Franklin stove. Angels hang from the ceiling and log walls. One of the small trees houses dozens of very luminous angels. They absorb the light from the overhead fixture and glow in the dark for a long period after the light has been turned off.

The "throne room" tree is heavily loaded with miniature wooden ornaments. Even the toilet is not left out of the festivities. A Santa Claus face of felt covers the toilet seat lid. When you lift the lid, you see a blushing Santa covering his eyes with his mittens.

For years I have made it a practice to mail out my annual Christmas epistle early in October. That way I am never overwhelmed with the task during the actual Christmas season. But what does one do with the hundreds of cards and letters that arrive in return? They are much too beautiful to be crowded into a basket where they cannot be seen. A few years ago I solved that problem by looking at the log beams overhead. I realized I could hang the cards on strings and add to the colorful decoration of the room at the same time.

An old cartoon on the refrigerator door best describes my feeling about Christmas cards. A mother has just glanced through the day's mail. A small child asks, "Are those Christmas cards? Are they from our friends? Are all these ours?" When answered in the affirmative, the child exclaims, "WOW! Are we ever rich!" I am indeed wealthy and blessed beyond measure by my friends.

Christmas Spilling Out and Over

I also decorate the porch entrance to the cabin for the season. Huge wooden butter bowls contain gold-sprayed pinecones of various sizes. The small tree on the table is adorned with small bells. I also hang a number of larger bells here and there. The prize brass

Nativity scene in Dick's memory

bell with a red bow comes from the Queen Mary Passenger Ship. I found this bell in Taiwan at a shipyard where ships from around the world are repaired or outfitted.

The cabin's outside door always features a pretty wreath. The glass windows on either side of the door frame two posters: "Wise Men Still Seek Him" and "Jesus Is the Reason for the Season." A small snowman banner flutters in the breeze near the door. Around the corner on another shutter a large banner also proclaims that "Jesus Is the Reason for the Season." And He is.

You cannot miss the old red and black antique sleigh at the corner of the cabin. It is filled with pine boughs and colorful packages wrapped in green, red, and yellow plastic, as well as a variety of toys for the children. The sleigh comes complete with a whip that is topped with a red bow. A "Reindeer Crossing" sign sits nearby.

The major outdoor display is found in front of the woodshed entrance, which is draped in a blue tarp. This provides a lovely backdrop for a large, white, wrought iron Nativity set. The Angel and Joseph are over eight feet tall. While much smaller, Mary and Jesus are covered with white lights. The flashing lights piercing the darkness illustrate the true meaning of the Season.

Not Just Once a Year . . .

I have made it a practice to invite friends in for an afternoon or evening between December 1 and January 10. For many years I baked up a storm and was proud of the wide variety of goodies I served. Not only is this time consuming, but most of us indulge in too many sweets at this time of year. I now serve warm popcorn in wooden bowls and hot or cold cider in Santa mugs. While the adults enjoy an evening of conversation, the younger set can play board games or entertain themselves in the bunkroom with a host of stuffed animals.

Before I was married, I always invited my single friends in for a turkey dinner and day of fellowship. After Dick and I were married, we continued the tradition of inviting those who might be spending Christmas day alone. One year we decided to invite five friends for dinner from The Algoma Manor, a nursing home near Thessalon, Ontario. Since this is thirty miles away, I stayed home to keep the fires burning and to put the finishing touches on the meal. Dick and Erminie Smedley drove down to get them. During the meal Patience Crossley, who was over 100 years old, clapped her hands and exclaimed, "What a wonderful gift!" Dick and I looked at each other in surprise. There were no gifts to be seen. She went on to say, "To be invited to your lovely home for such a delicious meal!"

There are so many different ways to observe Christmas—to decorate, to entertain, to bring cheer to others. But Christmas isn't just something we celebrate once a year. May we ever keep Christmas in our hearts and share it generously with others.

Chapter Twenty-Three

Tributes to Sir Richard

"Remember all the best of our past moments
and forget the rest."

Ellen Terry

After Dick's passing, I sent the following letter to our friends. I needed to share the news of his promotion and the beauty of our last days together. That time was so special, almost unreal. The

Lord was and is good. Here is the letter in its entirety:

Home for Christmas

"'He is not here. He is risen!' Sir Richard lived well and he died well. He has gone to be with our Christ whom he loved and served. Although I miss him more than my feeble tongue can express, I can not mourn as one who mourns without hope.

"A heart attack at home on November 23rd took him to our local emergency station and on to a Sault hospital through December 2nd. He was sent home feeling fine. We had another beautiful day together sharing, resting, and enjoying a fire in the fireplace. Another attack early on December 4th put him back in the hospital. There was talk about a pacemaker. At one point his heart rate had plummeted to 31. During an angiogram on December 8th his noble heart could not handle the blood clot on one side of his heart. I felt so sorry for Dr. Matthews who had to give me the sad news.

"Except for the first day, he did not suffer very much. Nitroglycerin, oxygen, morphine and a massive dose of streptokinase brought him back to good color, great spirits, and his usual sense of dry humor. He was alert, loving, jovial, and ready for a game of Skip Bo. The nurses appreciated him.

"The days were long and the nights short (for me), but we had rich times of sharing, reading the Word, praying, and planning. From the beginning of our marriage we made it a practice to read the Bible and pray together daily. I shall miss his prayer, 'Lord, bless Dick and Millie today.'

"Although he was not morbid he seemed to have his feet in both worlds. He made up 'what to do' lists regarding his farm in Indiana, his retirement benefits, insurance policies, social security, our investments, and other concerns. When I chided him he cheerfully quoted an insurance salesman saying, 'Well, you know good men are dying who have never died before!'

"From his hospital bed he bought us a 1992 All Wheel Drive GMC Van. He had dreamed about a vehicle like that for months. He also wrote a check for an All Terrain Vehicle with an electric start.

After his passing, I cancelled the latter. The Sloan electric cart which we already had would be sufficient for me.

"We had worked hard together and prepared well for fall, winter, and spring. The camp looked great. But in an attempt to have everything well in hand before he came home to recuperate and be tempted to go back to stressful work, I hurt his feelings. I had a friend help me tow Dick's aging tractor to a garage for repairs and then we hauled extra firewood down to the cabin. Never have we had so much wood on hand. There is more than enough for this year, and the next.

One day he exclaimed, "I don't really know why I am in this bed, but I know you soon will be if you don't slow down." Well, it all got done including the transformation of the cabin for Christmas. We were all set for his return home for the second time, but he did not make it. Bless his memory, he went **home** *for Christmas.*

"The Lord was good in giving us twenty-one years together. His father and three brothers preceded him in death due to heart problems. Since our wedding in 1978 I had lived in holy fear of finding him up in the bush far from help. That would have been most difficult to handle. In light of that fact, we had made several plans years ago. If and when the Lord came for him, Don Gilbertson and I would take him back home to Indiana in a Gilbertson Company van. However, they did not own a van at that time, so Dick took his second and final ride in the van he had so recently purchased. I could not stand the thought of sending him home alone in a hearse.

"The trip to Indiana was uneventful except for crossing the border. A young, cocky, self-assured customs officer asked all the usual questions—citizens of what country, where are you going, how long are you staying, are you leaving anything in the States, and so on. To the question about leaving anything in the States, Don calmly responded, 'Just a body.' Then he handed him the official papers that had been prepared by the funeral home. After a hurried phone call to his superior, he sent us on our way without another word. Don remarked later that instead of the officer being in charge, we were. Can you not imagine the miles Dick would have gotten out of

that story? Methinks he may be still chuckling.

"A very meaningful funeral service was held in his home church in Laotto, Indiana on December 13th. The pastor, Lois Watkins, spoke so well on his being a wise man and developed her points with **W** *for wise,* ***I*** *for investing wisely,* **S** *for a servant's heart, and* **E** *for his eternal viewpoint.*

"Grandson Dan Troyer played his trumpet and later played taps. Grandson Aaron Troyer, in uniform, presented me with the American flag. Nephew Dale Whonsetler ('77) gave a very moving and appropriate eulogy. Our good friend Hilda Clarke, who had sung at my ordination and at our wedding, sang "Because He Lives" and "I Will Rise Again" for his coronation. A memorial service was held at the Free Methodist Church on the Island on January 15th. Memorials were designated for the camp.

"During the hot days of July and August of Dick's last year and the cold days of October and November, Ron and Dick and I worked entirely too hard on the shower house. Perhaps too hard. Dick kept insisting that this was going to be our last project. For him it was. (I still have three or four more projects in mind that I would like to see completed before turning the camp over.)

"Our proposed trip to Costa Rica was cancelled. We had arranged to travel during the winter so that Dick would not be tempted to remove every snowflake which hit our roofs. Even at 81 he was still clambering around knee deep on snowy roofs clearing them with his shovel, for he was afraid they would cave in. We had also planned to go to Kenya, Madagascar and South Africa to visit missionary friends. It was a difficult time, but I completed that trip by myself.

"So for Sir Richard and me it was not the end, but the beginning. And with His help I do not intend to become a weeping widow. He is Lord. Thanks so very much for your prayers and the many expressions of your love and concern. 'He is not here, He is risen!'"

Dick's Place

The cards, letters, and checks that came in great numbers overwhelmed me. Over $8,000 in memorials was designated for a much-needed storage shed for the camp. Additional memorials were given to other worthy causes. I am sure the Lord is pleased with our stewardship—not wasting money on flowers, which fade away all too soon.

Gilbertson Enterprises picked up a 10 ft. X 40 ft. metal shipping container in North Bay and delivered it to the site. They then installed a metal door on the side to compliment the heavy metal doors at one end of the container. After sandblasting and painting it, they moved it with a heavy front-end loader to its place among the pine trees. By Thanksgiving Day 2000 it was finished and dedicated as "Dick's Place." Our thanks go to Don, Ruth, Calvin, and Brent Gilbertson, Scott Eddy, David Campbell, Joe Hendershott, Lawrence Miesener, and Jacob Kent for going way beyond the call of duty. Brian Bringleson also donated time to this project. Board members Randy Gill and Ron Beaupre leveled the new facility and put shelves in the building. Items from seven different sheds are now in storage there. Needless to say, as a result of all this effort, the camp is better organized and much neater. Dick would certainly be pleased.

An Echo of Wisdom

Of all the tributes that came for Dick, the following one from Steve Graham said it best. Pastor Tom used a portion of it at the memorial service:

"I don't really know how to write this letter but I know I can't put it off another day. I feel like there is nothing that I can say which would help to ease the pain that you must feel. Every word I think to write sounds like a cliché. There is no doubt that you know all the words of comfort at a time like this because you have comforted so many. My wish is that you can take comfort from the echo

of your own wisdom.

"Dick was a big influence on me as a young man of sixteen when I spent the summer at your camp. He always had the right thing to say, and knew when to say it and he knew when to say nothing at all. He knew how to work hard with his hands but he also knew how to work with his brain. I think his quiet wisdom impressed me the most. He knew the ways of the world but he was set apart from them. He was his own man.

"He inspired me then, and his memory inspires me still. You know and I know that Dick has gone on to a better place, but it isn't much better, because I could see in his eyes that he had found heaven on earth right there on St. Joseph Island with you and the camp. That was obvious though I was only sixteen. I saw a man who was content with his life and with what God had called him to do. He had what so many people today are searching for, a meaningful life.

Millie, Dick and grandson Danny

"When Mother called to tell me she had bad news I didn't know what to expect. I didn't expect this. Dick was always so steady it seemed like he would live forever. He taught me to live in the present and enjoy life every day and enjoy every little thing.

"Millie, I want you to know that, even though we live far away from each other, you are always in my thoughts. You and Dick have really been a big influence on my life. And for that I will always be grateful. I wish I could be where you are right now so I could hug you and tell you that everything will be all right. I know that you have comforted many people in their hour of need; please draw on the strength of those around you and know that we all care. My thoughts and prayers go out to you. Let God be your strength."

S.G.

Christians never say good-bye for the last time

A Jagged Journey

Several months have gone by since Dick left us. People still inquire as to how I am doing. My honest answer has been, "With His help and that of family and friends, fine." Their responses vary:

"I know how you feel. I have been through it."

That really is not true for we all react differently.

"You must be very lonely."

I must confess I am at times but not unduly so, for He is ever present.

"So you are now a widow and all alone."

My response? "No sir, I am not a widow and I am not alone. I am the daughter of the King and He is very much with me."

The most touching tribute came from five-year-old Leanna Kidd. *"Mern, Dick was my buddy and he didn't even tell me good-bye."*

My response? *"But one of these days you will be saying, 'Good morning, Dick!'"*

The words and actions that have meant the most to me have been, "I love you" or "I am praying for you," followed by a hug and a peck on the cheek.

For years I have been disturbed by the way many Christians react to the passing of a loved one. Some mourn as those without hope. I have finally concluded that sentimentality plays a far greater role than it should. Too many think of heaven as a physical place rather than a spiritual reality.

We are not going to heaven to see our loved ones. We are going to meet Christ and to worship Him forever. Jesus said, "You are in error because you do not know the Scriptures or the power of God. At the resurrection people will neither marry nor be given in marriage; they will be like the angels in heaven" (Matthew 22: 29-30, NIV).

I will agree that grief is a jagged journey. It does take time to travel that road. And I have read that Jesus wept at the tomb of His friend. But He moved on and so must we. Grief must not consume us nor render us helpless. To be sad for very long is to be selfish.

He is able to meet every need. I would suggest we spend more time in His Word, more time with Him in prayer, keep busy with others, and give ourselves to those who need a word of cheer or a helping hand. Get out of yourselves and into the lives of others. No amount of grieving will bring our loved ones back. Life must go on, and for me it is. It is a brand-new ball game for me, but it is far from the last inning.

I am most grateful for all Dick and I shared, for all he taught me, for all he gave to me, to the camp and others. He was a unique individual, a man of deep insights and integrity. My life is richer for our time together. "I do thank my God upon every remembrance of him" (Philippians 1:3, adapted).

Chapter Twenty-Four

Camp Comedy

THE LIGHT in the DARK

"Happiness is a running stream, not a stagnant pool."
J. M. Good

Much to our delight over the years, people like Art Linkletter and Bill Cosby have shared the humorous phrasings and antics of children. The following are some of the more memorable moments I have enjoyed over the years. And, as you will see, you don't have to be a child to have fun.

If You Want Something Bad Enough

Of all my frog hunting expeditions, Long Lake at Kalalla was the best. I could barely hang on to them. They were so large, you could eat the front legs and the backs, as well as the chunky hind legs. The hind legs, by the way, taste very much like chicken. Catching a frog on a lake is quite simple. Merely slip up to them in a spot of lily pads, shine a light in their eyes and then grab them. I usually put them in a damp gunnysack and kill them later.

One summer I was having difficulty recruiting a staff member to join me. It takes someone else to paddle and ease the canoe up to the lily pads where the frogs are usually resting (just waiting to be caught, as it were). Finally former camper Bev Hill offered to go with me. It would take a few days before she would be free, she hedged, but she would be my paddler. When we got out into the water on our frog hunt, she did a wonderful job of easing the canoe right up to the frogs. Several times I complimented her on her expertise. After I had bagged our catch, I asked her where and when she had learned to canoe.

"Here. A few days ago," she said.

Talk about determination. She remembered that when she was a camper, she had always envied those who accompanied me on the frog hunts. And she decided that this time would be her turn! She just had to learn how to paddle a canoe first.

It's Not Always the Animals that Keep You Awake

During my Girl Scouting tenure, I shared a tent with Evelyn in a unit rightly called "The Ledges." Our platform was perched in a precarious position on a rocky ledge. Evelyn snored louder and longer than anyone I have ever heard, and I have been kept awake by the best of them. (I could write a book on this subject alone. One chapter would include sleeping in a bathtub in a Chicago hotel, thanks to another snoring Girl Scout friend. And there would be pages about the night I spent on a wicker chaise lounge in the famous Banff Hotel ladies room. The attendant surmised I was inebriated.)

Evelyn and I were total strangers. Although our walking sticks were intended for use during the day, I ended up using mine at night as well. She kept me awake all through our first night together, and by the second night I was getting desperate. I finally picked up my stick and thumped the floor several times. She bolted upright as if she had been shot out of a cannon. I feigned sleep. She soon settled down, only to resume snoring. We played our little game on through the night.

In the morning, she asked our neighbors and me if we had heard any strange noises during the night. We had not. This game went on for two more nights, until I finally had the courage to tell her I was moving to another tent. She understood. We kept in touch until her passing some years later.

Serious About Baseball

Elizabeth Kerr Pearson, former Girl's Work Secretary of the Ontario Religious Education Council, sent me a letter enclosing some of her memories of our work together. The following paragraph describes camp fellowship better than anything I can say:

> *"Millie became the sports leader because she was very good at organizing sports. It was with great wisdom that she divided girls and leaders into baseball teams. All went well until the final game when Millie, who was pitching, laughed so hard at my efforts to hit the ball, that she could hardly pitch, and so the whole team in the field dissolved in laughter."*

Committed

I shall never forget an experience I had with Marty Thomas, a fellow Girl Scout and Kalalla counselor, while we were traveling. We drove off the ferry at Port aux Basques, a rugged rocky port. Marty and I saw much of the Maritimes by car and canoe on that trip in the 50's. After leaving the ferry, we decided to eat out rather than cook over a campfire. The only place open was a rundown, weather-beaten hotel. It looked like something out of an old movie. We were welcomed warmly by a wee elf of a man who apologized that his wife and daughter could not be there to help him. They were in the hospital, he said. (He did not tell us it was a mental institution.)

We were hungry and asked what he had to offer.

"Girls, the place is yours," he said. "Go to the kitchen and help yourselves. It's on the house."

Amused but naïve, we took him up on his offer. Reality set in when I looked into a double sink and found, instead of pots and pans, his dirty underwear. His long johns were soaking. We should have had the good sense to back out gracefully right then. Instead, I whispered to Marty that the only thing I was going to eat in that place was lobster from a can and hot tea made with boiling water. Of course, the cups would have to be rinsed well. Some toast from a fresh loaf of bread looked safe enough. We prepared our meal and marched out to a table (which we also had scrubbed). Our benefactor made small talk about his hotel and Port aux Basques. We ate our food, took our dishes to the kitchen, thanked the wee man profusely, and left.

We learned later from the horrified United Church minister and the not-too-pleased village clerk that we had taken our lives into our hands by going into this man's hotel. Steps were being taken to commit him to the same institution that held his family.

Future Camp Director?

A precocious young camper spiced things up for us in Wisconsin when I directed the Evanston, Illinois area Scouts. As she assisted me with the Saturday evening service, she was annoyed that many of her fellow campers were not responding to the readings.

Topsy-Turvy Day: Co Directors

"You're supposed to be answering me!" she hollered in a booming voice.

Every paper went up and from that moment on she had their full attention. Later, as we were about to partake of the grape juice and cookies, a few small fingers reached out for cookies too soon. This time we heard, in the same no-nonsense, door-rattling voice, "It ain't even been blessed yet!"

I often wonder how many people are being put in place today by that former Scout.

Mighty Blue

During my time as executive director with the Girl Scouts, I was often invited to attend troop meetings. At one particular session, I sat next to a small girl named Jennie. Her leader was an elderly woman whose beautician had tinted her hair a little too generously, so that it appeared to be more blue than gray or white.

Jennie scooted over close to me and in a loud whisper asked, "Miss Japets, what color is that woman's hair?"

In a much quieter voice I said, "I think it's gray, don't you?"

"It looks mighty blue to me," came the very audible reply.

Night Wanderings

A camp counselor was concerned about a certain girl's night wanderings. She asked if I could come over and check out the situation. I slipped up quietly behind the offender and in my not-too-quiet voice asked, "And what are you doing out here at this hour of the night?"

Without missing a beat, she stopped dead in her tracks. Imitating a bird dog, she stood on one foot while raising the other and pointing with both arms. She said, "I am a bird dog. Why?"

In a louder voice I said, "Young lady, point to your tent and stay there!" She did.

My strangest experience at McMillan involved a child from my home church. My tent was across two ravines and two narrow log bridges from where her troop was encamped. Around midnight I heard this plaintive voice crying out, "Millie, Millie!"

When I answered, she asked, "Will you take me home?"

My heart sank. Was she homesick? Home was in Fort Wayne quite a few miles away. "Home where?" I answered.

"You know, over there," came the reply. She had walked in her sleep across the log bridges and the ravines. No one had missed her. I walked her back and tucked her into her sleeping bag. We had knowing smiles and winks for each other the next day, but we never shared our secret with anyone.

Homesick

I was used to dealing with homesick campers. But one incident at Camp Pauwating stands out from the rest. A driver in a beat-up truck came into camp. He explained he had come to take his daughter home. When I asked him why, he said he just knew she would be homesick. Well, how did he know, I pressed? He just knew. That daughter happened to be happily sweeping the porch of a nearby cabin. When she saw him she yelled, "Dad, what are you doing here?" With tears in his eyes he said, "Her mother and I have missed her so." Then he turned and left in his truck.

Creepy Critters

At the beginning of one camp session at Camp Pauwating, a child asked if I would check their heads. I absentmindedly agreed. A day or two passed and she asked again. I asked her, "What are we checking for?" She answered, "I think we have head lice. Everyone is scratching their heads." That got my attention fast, and the nurse confirmed her suspicions.

I immediately phoned R. J. and insisted that the next group of campers be checked before they boarded the bus. He complied and one child in that group had to stay home. Later I received a plaintive letter from her mother that read: "I ask you, Miss Jacobs, how would you feel if you looked forward to camp for months, only to be sent home because you had head lice. Now I ask you again, Miss Jacobs, how would you feel?"

I was touched, but unmoved.

On the water with Joel and David Bollinger

Gone But Not Forgotten

At Camp Logan I well remember a crestfallen young camper sitting next to me at breakfast one morning. She was the daughter of my physician, Dr. Leslie, so I suspected homesickness. I inquired about her unhappiness.

She broke into tears and said, “I dropped my flashlight down the greenie hole (latrine).”

“Well, we can fix that,” I soothed. “You can get a new one at the Trading Post (campstore).”

“But it’s still burning,” came the mournful reply.

The Sound of Rain

On a very rainy day another small camper burst into my office in the Lodge, crying out, “Millie, Millie! Do you know what the rain sounds like in our tent?”

“No, what?” I replied.

“Just like a lot of little people clapping their hands!”

That just about says it all, doesn’t it? You can’t work with kids and remain unaffected by their joy, their sense of wonder, their bright idealism and openness, their innocence and simplicity. And since the bulk of my life has involved working with children, I am blessed beyond measure. They continue to amaze and surprise me even today.

I Am Camp

I am camp.
I am sunlight, a sheen on the water, mist on the hills, and stars.
I am a doorway out of the commonplace into a new adventuring experience.
I am a place where youth learns the joy of play without a sting, of fellowship without regrets, of creative effort that wearies not, of a good time that leaves no headache, or heartache, behind.
I am a new purpose of life that will make the years different.
I am noise – and silence with a thrill to it.
I am laughter – and quiet resolution that seeks the comfort of the hills.
I am energy – and the touch of loving service.
I am youth – and the slowly emerging habits that make matured experience worthy.
I am today, and also the tomorrow that is being shaped.
I am a giver of gifts that pass not away, that time will not chill, that poverty will not quench, that riches will not deceive.
I am habits, ideals, ways of living, confirmed attitudes in the soul of youth.
Because I am all these, and more, and because I demand of youth its best,
I invite youth into fellowship with me.
I am camp.

—*Anonymous*

Chapter Twenty-Five

Passing of the Torch

"So be my passing!
My task accomplished and the long day done,
My wages taken, and in my heart
Some late lark singing."

Wm. E. Henley

Dick and I had always known that the time would come for us to turn the camp over to another couple. It was inevitable. Nothing is forever. After observing his 80th birthday, we informed the Board that it was time to advertise for our replacements.

An Island Connection

Seven couples responded to the announcement. Several were outstanding and the final decision was not an easy one to make. However, Shaun and Marlene Gill Spence seemed to be the answer to our prayers. Marlene was an Islander and had grown up in the camp. This should make it much easier to relate to the community. And that is a big factor, for we have depended on the people here in so many ways. Shaun has served as a youth pastor in a Free Methodist Church and has had excellent camping experiences. Best of all, they and the Board felt that they were the couple for All Tribes Christian Camp.

Shaun and Marlene Spence

Some quotes of a portion of the publicity release say it well:

> *"Marlene, who grew up on the Island and attended the camp as a camper, is a talented individual. She completed her teaching requirements at Lakehead University. She also took a Special Education Behavior elective from Nipissing University. Shaun was a youth director in the Toronto area. He has had a lot of experience working with young people in areas such as camping skills, sports programs, drama and counseling."*

The Spences have expressed a desire to continue the programs that are currently in place at the camp, including the Alumni Camp, VBS, youth and adult retreats, family reunions, wedding receptions, and other gatherings. Some of their plans for the future include new basketball and tennis courts, beach volleyball, mountain bike and cross-country ski trails, an ice-skating rink, high ropes course, and a climbing wall.

They are due to arrive at All Tribes Camp in the spring of 2002. I plan to work with them until late in the fall. In the meantime, letters and E-mails have been going back and forth. I recently spent some quality time with them in Australia where we were able to discuss my unfinished hopes and dreams, as well as share some mutual concerns. I am excited about their coming. The Spences have accepted the challenge of raising their own funds on faith. Contact me if you wish to assist them.

Leaving the Island

Will it be difficult to leave the Island, my log home, the camp, and campers? Yes and No! Humanly speaking, it will not be easy. My roots go deep here and I have had the pleasure of watching a generation or two grow up, as well as the fun of having their children and grandchildren as campers. To say I love all of this is really an understatement.

But ever since accepting Christ, I have been conscious of His leadership in my life. I firmly believe He does guide our steps if we are committed to Him. I have considered all of my past work assignments or careers as chapters in my life. It is like reading a good book. We turn the page and find another new, exciting chapter waiting for us.

The satisfying aspect of all of this has been the inner and outer consciousness that at each particular stage of my life, or chapter, I was convinced that I had the best job in the world. Each step has gotten better. That has to come from Him. His ways are past finding out.

Each assignment has been nothing less than exhilarating. However, that is not to say there have not been moments or periods of frustration and disappointment. We do not live in a perfect world. We are human and have to deal with other humans. That means we have a tendency to slip up and disappoint each other from time to time. I have lived by the following two Scriptures: "As thy days, so shall thy strength be" (Deuteronomy 33:25) and "The joy of the Lord is your strength" (Nehemiah 8:10).

I do have life-use of my home and could stay here, but I do not feel it would be fair to Shaun and Marlene. When they come as the new managers, they have every right to chart their own course under His direction. I do not want to stand in the way or hinder them in pursuing their dreams. I have had my day. The Lord willing, I will visit from time to time, but it will not be at peak seasons with campers here.

One aspect of our retirement plan has been to turn the cabin into a museum that will be open to the public. My dilemma at this point is what do I take with me? I treasure so many books and various mementos. But those things as well as the future are in His hands. Where He leads me I will follow.

The Next Chapter

Many have asked what I plan to do. At this point I can honestly say I do not know. My inner inclination would be to return to Marion. My years there as a student were some of the best years of my life. I shall forever be indebted to those dedicated faculty members who gave me so much. I would like to start paying the interest on that debt. My work as the president of the Alumni Association and as the Alumni Director did much for me. I now have friends all over the world and cherish their friendships. How rich I am. Marion seems like home to me.

If I return I should like to work with the students in some way. I hope to do more than lick stamps or stuff envelopes, as important as that is! I repeat—my future is in His hands.

He doeth all things well.

Chapter Twenty-Six

A Walk-About through the Camp

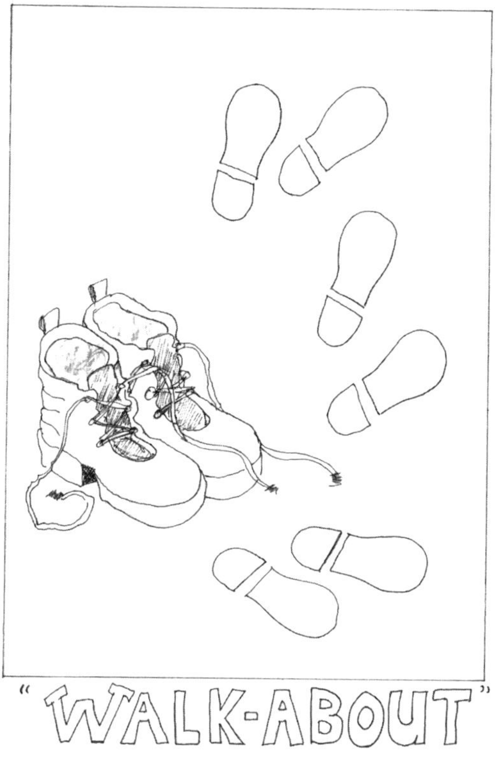

"If you are weary of city streets and busy people, come join us for an hour, a day, a week..."

M.J.T.

I trust the following description of the buildings and facilities will give you a picture of the camp. So lace up your hiking boots and prepare to tramp around—or hop on the Millie Mobile—on a tour of All Tribes Christian Camp.

5TH SIDEROAD
M&N
CANVAS TEPEES
INDIANA WINDMILL
TIRE WORM
COOK HOUSE
SPRING
PLACID POOL
NATURE CABIN
TIRE TREE
FLAGS
EDNA LE
DINING
FRIENDSHI
CIRCLE
HAIGHT'S DAM
AQU
HU
POND WALK
TRAPPER JIM'S MUSEUM
TIRE TRIO
MEG'S PLACE
SPORT SHED
WOOD SHED
COMPOST BIN
TROYER'S Log Cabin
BADMINTON
TETHER BALL
MINI GOLF
HORSE SHOES
CRAFT HUT
GARAGE
ARROWS
ALL TRIBES
FUTUR
MOTE
HILTON ROAD
P.R.Troyer

PISGAH PEAK
HILLSIDE SHELTER
OTTER LOG CABIN
ERMINE LOG CABIN
CREE TEEPEE
HIKING & CROSS COUNTRY SKI TRAILS
BEAVER LOG CABIN
BAWATING SHELTER
CHEROKEE TEEPEE
SHOWER HOUSE
CACHE TREE HOUSE
OJIBWA TEEPEE
BASSWOOD MANSION
FITNESS COURSE
REG HAWDON PLAYING FIELD
DICK'S PLACE
ALL TRIBES CHRISTIAN CAMP
St. JOSEPH ISLAND · ONTARIO · CANADA
INDIANA WESLEYAN UNIVERSITY
CANADIAN CAMPUS
2000

Placid Pool

Approaching the camp from the north on Hilton Road, Placid Pool is visible through the trees. As you proceed you will pass two huge arrows that Brent Gilbertson and Jim Reid made from telephone poles. The rustic All Tribes Camp sign at the camp entrance was made by the Troyer Clan. Do not overlook the Indian maiden which Dawn Tweedle painted on a nearby large stone.

The first driveway takes you to my log cabin. Just beyond the cabin, the small body of water comes into view. It was not always a pond or pool. It began as a cedar swamp, fed by numerous springs. As I mentioned earlier, the property was once known as Crystal Springs Farm.

Beth Bollinger Kidd and her daughters, Sarah Elizabeth and Michelle on Placid Pool. Aqua Hut in background.

Speckled trout, descendants of those Del Haight introduced so many years ago, still flourish in the pond today. It is fun to watch young and old alike catch fish from Placid Pool. The fish are always released afterwards to resume their life of freedom and maintain their numbers.

In 1992 the Cheboygan Wesleyan Men put in a new pond walk. In 1993 Don Gilbertson, Scott Eddy, and other men from Gilbertson Enterprises removed 130 dump truck loads of muck and debris from the pond. The trucks dumped their loads at the edge of The Reg Hawdon Playing Field, expanding the field considerably. Accomplished during the winter, this project was no small feat of engineering

Wesleyan Men from Sault Ste. Marie, Michigan built a small screened-in cabin, The Aqua Hut, which rests on stilts in the middle of the pond. It is a favorite of campers both by day and by night. Built-in bunks have made it possible for many of us to enjoy overnights there. Bob and Doris Fraser and The Church of Jesus Christ of Latter Day Saints in Sault, Ontario, gave the door to the camp. Dr. Maurice Burns carved the canoe paddle that serves as a door handle. A chorus of frogs and the hoots of Great Horned Owls enhance spring evenings in the Aqua Hut.

More recently, Andy Clark, owner of Clark's Cove Marina, gave us a 7 ft. x 28 ft. fiberglass boat, which serves as a fun sleeping quarters for six campers. Named the Good Ship Hope, Ron Beaupre and Bill Hibbard have closed it in to make it "rain and skeeter proof." This is one acquisition I've wanted for years!

Beth and Brad's Wee Tree House

As I mentioned earlier, my godchildren Beth and Brad spent two weeks with me in 1967 while we were building the cabin. George and John took time out to make them a wee tree house in a very old apple tree. It is located just in front of the Trapper's Museum. Some thirty years later, my godchildren's children enjoy the tree house. It is so popular with the younger campers that some days we need a timekeeper to make sure everyone has a turn up among the apple leaves.

The Craft Lodge

While Dick and I were on our wedding trip in 1978, Jerry Hawdon and others built us a two-car garage. Dick was not planning to dig his car out of a snowbank every time he needed it during the winter. During the camping season, we set up tables inside and outside the garage for our craft sessions. Prior to building the Edna Lee Lodge, the garage was our mini-lodge. We installed a Ben Franklin stove, kept our library there, and used the garage for opening sessions of Vacation Bible School (VBS). It was also available to use as sleeping quarters for the girls, while the boys usually slept in tents and the covered wagon.

Wee Wee Teepees

Two Wee Wee teepees were added in 1980. The number of campers had increased and the "three-holer" with the picture window was no longer adequate.

The Cabin Woodshed

In 1982 a large three-sided woodshed was set up behind the cabin. Roy Trump, our son George's father-in-law, designed it and supervised its construction. Some of the International Harvester crew also assisted. We keep the two sides and one end filled with firewood for the fireplace and the cookstove, rotating the wood regularly. The Senior Kindergarten VBS campers meet there and have the sole use of the nearby picture window outhouse. The four solar panels on the roof of the woodshed supply the cabin's electricity.

Pisgah's Peak Shelter

In the fall of 1963 I hiked alone to the highest point on the property to absorb the beauty of the fall foliage. The mixture of the flaming maple leaves with the dark green of the pines was spectacular. All of a sudden I felt like Moses standing on Mount Horeb when God spoke to him and said, "Take off your sandals, for the place where you are standing is holy ground" (Exodus 3:1-5 NIV).

I also thought of God's word to Moses when he was surveying the Promised Land from Pisgah's Peak. God said to him, "Lift up thine eyes westward, and northward, and southward, and eastward . . . for thou shalt not go over this Jordan. But charge Joshua, and encourage him, and strengthen him: for he shall go over . . ." (Deuteronomy 3:27-28).

In my mind's eye, I could see the future camp. I felt like Joshua and took God's promise to heart: "Be strong and of a good courage; be not afraid, neither be thou dismayed: for the Lord thy God is with thee whithersoever thou goest" (Joshua 1:9). But of course He has used many others to keep me encouraged to pursue my dream.

In the winter of 1984, Professor Tony Moreillon ('77) brought an outdoor recreation class to the camp for a Winter Survival Course. That course eventually became the Wise Owl course under the direction of Dr. Mike Fratzke. These recreation management majors open the camp each spring under Pisgah's Peak shelter. The winter of '84 brought over two feet of snow, with temperatures at times plunging to -27°F. The group cut down some large red pines and carried them to the top of the hill, staggering through the deep snow. (In the past, Beth and Brad and I have called it "The Top of the World.") The next summer Al Matthews and campers from the Mio, Michigan area constructed the three-sided shelter from the logs. Professor Wanda Heater Clement ('61) and her husband, David ('64), put in a door and screens.

We named the shelter Pisgah's Peak. From there we can see ships in St. Mary's River several miles away. It is also a great place for a ski or toboggan run. Many have helped to make it a safe trail by keeping the hill clear of trees.

The Windmill

A sturdy 90-foot windmill looms over the camp. On sunny days it casts its shadow on happy campers. The squeaking of the moving head or fan when the breezes blow is like music to my ears. Manufactured many years ago at the now defunct Flint Walling Factory in Indiana, it is the only traditional windmill on the Island. The few windmills that remain are like ghosts of the past. I hauled it up from Indiana on a trailer that was much too small for the job, and getting it through customs at 2:30 in the morning is a story in itself. Jim and Faye Newman Voyles '74 helped me over that hurdle.

A group of employees from the International Harvester Plant in Fort Wayne put up the structure. Gord Hawdon brought in a boom truck to install the head. We set it over a 40-foot well dug by Louie Knoll, the brother of a former Free Methodist pastor, John Knoll, and christened it with a bottle of Pepsi. We used the water that the windmill pumped from the well until Cal Kent and Brent Gilbertson piped in spring water to the Lodge. Grapevines now cover the lower part of the windmill, providing a quiet getaway spot for campers. Further enhancing the windmill is a sign painted by Gord Hawdon that quotes Psalm 147:18. "He causeth His wind to blow, and the waters to flow."

The Cook Shack

Our first camping structure built just for camping was a cook shack put up in 1974. It is an open-sided building, 14 ft. x 24 ft., constructed of cedar poles with a metal roof. In one corner we set up an altar fireplace with a six-lidded iron top. The staff of Fort St. Joseph donated the heavy metal top for the stove. Willis and Eleanor Wass, parents of Mrs. Harold (Lynn) Campbell, made two large storage cupboards with doors along one side. With all that, there is still plenty of room for four picnic tables and a serving table to fit quite nicely. Before the construction of the Edna Lee Lodge, all the camp cooking was done in the Cook Shack or over open fires. During VBS, it remains the special meeting site of the fifth- and sixth-grade campers.

The Nature Center

Jim Snider headed up a group of men in the community to put up the Nature Center in 1986. This is the second largest structure in All Tribes Christian Camp. Cedar poles support the large roof. A low railing which can be used for seating extends around three sides. Many shelves have been added to house scores of nature specimens. The Nature Center can also hold six or eight picnic tables, extending its usefulness for large gatherings, as well as for our music sessions during VBS camp. During construction, Dick and I were amazed to see Lawrence Reid helping to shingle the steeply pitched roof on his seventy-fifth birthday! Later, however, we thought nothing of Dick being on the roof of the shower house at age eighty-two. Do we get younger as we get older?

The Edna Lee Lodge

Most of the information on the Edna Lee Lodge can be found in Chapter 18. Sometime later, Dick decided he would like to have a workshop and storage area under that sizeable porch. This necessitated carrying out many buckets of sand by hand. Dick took out enough sand to come up with a small room, but in recent years, others have enlarged it further. It is now a 10 ft. x 50 ft. room with a workbench, shelves, and wood racks.

The Fitness Course

In 1990 Coach John Foss ('83) and his cross-country track team set up a fitness course. In designing the various events of the course, they found a great use for many old tires. They also set up a small climbing wall and a belly crawl.

Trappers Museum

Trapper Jim Reed came into my life unexpectedly. Kent's General Store asked him to drop off some groceries at my place while I was sick with the flu. After delivering my groceries, he insisted on taking me to our local hospital.

Later, he requested permission to trap nuisance beavers and pesky coons on the property. He had trapped since he was seven years old and knew the Island wildlife well. I had heard he was an expert trapper, so I gladly consented. More than a trapper, he was clever in other ways. Over the years, many admired and enjoyed his flower and vegetable gardens.

He lived with his sister, Pearl Court, but it was several years

Trapper Jim Reed

before I realized he was a bachelor. They were brother and sister, not man and wife! One winter day, he found me tramping on snowshoes, carrying a pail of water from the spring barrel. He said, "You shouldn't be doing this. I am going to put drinking water in the cabin for you next spring."

I thought, "Yea, yea." Besides, I already had a small hand pump in the kitchen that brought water up from the cistern.

True to his word, however, he was back the next spring and he did indeed put drinking water in the cabin. Running a plastic pipe from the cabin to the spring barrel, he weighed it down with half cement blocks. Then he brought a brass foot valve from the farm, connected the pipe, and put it in the spring barrel. In the thirty years since, it has never frozen up.

Although small in stature, he was bigger than life itself. A regular around the camp, rare was the group that didn't get acquainted with and love Trapper Jim. When he was ready to leave his farm and move to a senior's apartment in Richards Landing, he announced that he would like to donate much of his trapping equipment and many of his photographs to the camp. A group of Indiana Christian Camping men came to our rescue and built a small museum to house his artifacts. Older VBS youngsters under the leadership of Lyle Rowat and other campers completed the task. Trapper Jim was a vital part of the camp until he left us on New Year's Eve of 1999 at the age of ninety-three. It was my privilege to conduct his memorial service in 2000. He is greatly missed.

The Reg Hawdon Playing Field

Reg Hawdon's large monetary donation made it the playing field possible. Many old rotten apple trees were removed, after which Brent Gilbertson and Reg's son, John, leveled the field. John and his brother Harold and others built the backstop. As mentioned earlier, the field was expanded when the muck from the pond was dumped there in 1993. Many, many campers spent hours picking up stones, branches, and other items over the years so that the area can now be mowed with the riding mower.

The Village

An area known as The Village is located just east of the Edna Lee Lodge. Our sleeping quarters, three shelters, and the shower house can be found there. The three log cabins can house eight campers each, while the three teepees have room for a total of nineteen campers. Cabins and teepees now have lights, outlets, and electric heaters, compliments of Brent Gilbertson and Ron Beaupre. (So much for my ideals of rustic camping in tents when I first started on this enterprise!)

Assisted by Lyle Rowat, the Indiana Christian Campers group put up the Ermine Cabin in 1989. Graham and Dick Kent, Tolbert Stinson, and the Wesleyan Men from Cheboygan, Michigan built the Otter and Beaver Cabins in 1994.

The idea for the unique teepees came from Arizona. Nephew Phil Troyer ('93) made up a prototype from a picture I had taken. Ron Beaupre took it from there, using several groups of campers to assist. Raising the tall two by four frames was no small feat and required many hands. The "Cherokee" teepee built in 1993 houses five, and the "Cree" and the "Ojibway" teepees, built in 1997, each house seven. The Wesleyan Youth from Greentown, Indiana, paid for the Ojibway teepee.

Shelters

In 1991 we purchased two open-air shelters (24 ft. x 32 ft. each) from the St. Joseph Township Centennial Grounds. Don Oliver, Keith Armstrong, Bob Fraser, and Jim Snider cut the structures in half with a chain saw and hauled them to the camp on a hay wagon. They then reinforced and trimmed them, converting half of one into a storage area and woodshed at the end of the Lodge.

The other parts were reconfigured into three open-air shelters called Sharing Spot, Hillside, and Little Bawating. Used for smaller group sessions, each shelter houses three picnic tables. A large pictorial map of the camp painted by Gord Hawdon fills one end of the Sharing Spot. Seventh- and eighth-grade campers use the Hillside Shelter during VBS. Clotheslines on all four corners of the Little Bawating permit it to double as our "solar dryer."

The Shower House

Ron Beaupre designed, engineered, and served as construction manager for the much-needed 20 ft. x 36 ft. concrete block Shower House. Dick and I, with the help of Ron's wife, Bonnie, mixed the mortar and handled the blocks. Several camper groups assisted by

The Shower House

cleaning and painting the blocks. Ralph Nelson donated the cedar for the gable ends. Brent Gilbertson leveled the site, hauled in fill, and dug the trenches for the water and electrical lines. Zora Jean Tomlinson, former Wakonda camper, and Vi Dobbs painted all of the shelves. The mirrors, towel racks, coat racks, shower floor racks, wooden benches, shower curtains, and wastebaskets were all donated. This new facility includes a utility room with a washer and dryer. And once again Gord Hawdon lent his talent by painting the signs.

The new restrooms have put the Wee Wee Teepees out of business, although they will be kept on standby in the event of a power outage. The new showers are certainly a cut or two above the original solar showers we had near the windmill! Again, we were indebted to many volunteers who helped with this project. They say that the labor is more than double the cost of building materials, but the comfort and convenience provided by this facility make it priceless. We dedicated the facility on July 30, 2000.

The Cache

The idea for the Cache originated from our three trips to Alaska. Many trappers keep a cache near their cabins, a place to store their meat and other supplies. They are built on high stilts so the animals cannot reach the meat. They can also be used in case the main cabin burns down. Our Cache was built by Reg, John, and Harold Hawdon and the Wesleyan Men from Cheboygan, Michigan in 1992. All Tribes campers use it for a tree house.

Basswood Mansion

The Basswood Mansion is a large tree house nestled up high in a mammoth old basswood tree. It is located some distance from the camp and is another favorite spot for overnighters. The Cheboygan Wesleyan Men, Ron Beaupre, Christian Campers, and our grandson Danny all had a hand in producing this enjoyable place, which was completed in 1998.

The Amphitheater

All of our outdoor sessions for VBS, church services, reunions, and other large gatherings take place in the Amphitheater. Brent Gilbertson built it on the site of the old original bank barn. The Bruce Mines, Ontario Wesleyan Men put in the cedar slab seats. Wally and Bev Anderson, summer residents from Des Moines,

Amphitheater, Cabins, Teepee

installed a cross and two flagpoles. The Gilbertsons hauled in the large granite boulder from a gravel pit nearby, the perfect choice for a podium. Dick had had his eye on that rock for several years. Randy and Donna Gill, Brad, Joel, and David Bollinger made the five flagpoles from small cedar trees. This site was named The Rose and Bernt Gilbertson Amphitheater in 1992.

The RV Sites

They say necessity is the mother of invention. In 1994 the local Kent Reunion Committee booked All Tribes Camp as the site for its annual reunion. They expected about 200 people from all over the country, many of whom would be traveling in RVs. Harold and Lynn Kent stepped forward and accepted the project, hooking up the electrical wiring and water outlets, as well as installing a large tank donated by Ron Kent to use as a waste disposal system. Many have used the RV sites since then. There's room for your rig, by the way.

Dick's Place (see Chapter 23)

The Circular Drive

Several years ago Don Gilbertson got stuck in our drive. I recall his words, "You need some gravel there, Millie." Before I knew it, a Gilbertson truck was in and out of the camp leaving in its wake a solid road. No one has gotten stuck since. The drive completely encircles the camping area. Many drive through just to see what is going on. We don't mind—visitors are always welcome.

The Friendship Circle

On a sunny day one can usually find a group of campers in front of the Lodge, relaxing on an array of lawn chairs and a picnic table or two. The focal point of this spot is a sundial, my gift to Dick on his seventieth birthday. Inscribed are these words from Robert Browning: "Grow old along with me. The best is yet to be." The area tempts one to "come and sit a spell," to just relax and be quiet.

The Bush Trails

True to his word, Dick did mow the grass and cut the wood. (And a lot more!) However, there was purpose in his cutting. He removed the old trees to clear the woods of debris and to provide us with firewood. As a result we have always had a good supply of fuel for the cabin and the Lodge. His other motive for cutting wood was to mark out a number of trails for hikers and skiers. Clever signs are sprinkled throughout the camp, but two of my favorites are along these trails. One says, "Step softly along these trails, for they are the record of dreams" (Anonymous). How very true, and I always think of Dick when I pass the other sign: "In the woods, too, a man casts off his years just as the snake his skin, that whatever period or age of life, he is always a child. In the woods is perpetual youth" (Emerson). Tony Turbin painted these and the other smaller signs. Of the many tasks Dick was involved in at the camp, he seemed always to be happiest working in the bush.

Our Fences

As you come up the drive to the cabin, you will see a rail fence on your right and a stone wall on the left. When I first came in 1963, there were only broken-down wire fences here and there. I loathed them, for one should be free of such things when hiking about. Now only a few remain within the property lines. The ones along the boundary serve as markers. Someday I hope we can find a different way to denote the property lines.

When I first rented the place, Bernt gave me permission to remove the old fence along the Hilton Road. I had found remnants of rail fences, some seven rails high, all around the orchard. Most of those old rails were well over one hundred years old and in remarkable shape. The teenage boys who worked with me in 1963 carried the rails down from the edge of the bush. Jerry and Gord Hawdon, and Jim and Bob Dennison carried many of these by hand but quite a few came down in the trunk of my old '59 Chevy. We were quite proud of the new rail fence we built along the road. As time went on, we carried even more rails down, extending the fences.

The old stone fence was another matter altogether. Bill Ross planned to bulldoze down his old milk house on the Smedley Homestead near Richards Landing. Erminie Smedley asked if we could have the stones. Although they were soon on their way to the camp, I can assure you they were not as easy to move as the light cedar rails. Heavy, bulky, and awkward, we had trouble getting them in and out of the trunk of the car. When we resorted to a small trailer, we could not get the hitch to stay in place. We finally persuaded Dunc Brown, Harold's father, to haul them in his pickup truck. Time and time again, he backed up to the stones so that we could load them. On our arrival at camp, he backed up to the site, allowing us to unload the stones and put them in place before we returned for the next load. It was wonderful. The fence stands as a memorial to Erminie. Bless her memory!

Meg's Place

Meg's Place is named after my long-time friend Meg, who has figured periodically in this book. The building is a storage shed which houses our canvas teepees and the canvas cover for the covered wagon. We also store our glass jars, tin and aluminum cans, and plastic containers for recycling in this storage shed.

The Athletic Equipment Barn

The only building left from the Gilroy era, the Athletic Equipment Barn once protected the Gilroys' cutter and buggy (or "democrat" as a buggy was sometimes called) from the weather. We now store all of our athletic equipment and bikes in that building. The building also contains a workbench for making minor repairs on the equipment.

To Complete the Dream

All Tribes Christian Camp is the culmination of a dream. While I am delighted with the progress we have made, I am not quite satisfied—yet. Before I feel that I have done what I started out to do, I would like to finish three more projects. My list includes a small cabin at the edge of the bush, away from the mainstream of activity. Self-contained, this cabin could be used as a hideaway for honeymooning couples or a "Balm of Gilead" for those in need of recharging their batteries.

A sundeck for the Lodge would make another place available for groups to meet. Charles Egglesfield from Desbarats has drawn up the plans. The Pinconning Wesleyan men have promised to build it. (As this book goes to print, the beautiful new sundeck has been completed.)

The third project, and the most ambitious, is to build a two- or three-bedroom home for Shaun and Marlene Spence, the new camp directors. In the meantime, a 14 ft. x 70 ft. mobile home has been set up at the camp for the Spences until a home can be built. I would like to see motel-like units attached to the far end of the proposed house. The entire building as well as the Lodge would be heated with an outdoor furnace. We have been assured that the Lodge can be heated with the same unit. These furnaces are much safer, cleaner, and cheaper than gas, oil, or electricity. With our one hundred acres and good tree management, the camp should never run out of fuel. Units with showers would make it possible to serve those who do not enjoy rustic camping—the Holiday Inn set. More conferences, retreats, and camping experiences could be made available to seniors and the camp could offer year-round programs much more easily.

Volunteers

The preceding pages have given only a partial list of the volunteers who have been involved in this wonderful undertaking over the years. Among them is one group I do not wish to overlook — IWU's maintenance department. These employees have been most generous with their time and talents over the years. The camp has lock sets from old Teter Hall, a drinking fountain from Williams, and too many other items to mention! Now you must realize why I cannot say enough about them and the hundreds of other volunteers who have made All Tribes Christian Camp what it is today. I bless them all and honor them for giving so freely of their time, talents, and energy.

My friend, Gerry Crowder, expressed it so well in her recent Christmas card: "You have so many, many friends in your life to affirm you and you will see your dream finished." The end is in sight.

Epilogue

Age is An Attitude

"Age is an opportunity no less than youth itself."
H.W. Longfellow

Above my head in the window bed of the cabin is the poster "How to Stay Young." I read it frequently and wish to share it with you:

"Youth is not a time of life . . . it is a state of mind. Nobody grows old by merely living a number of years; people grow old only by deserting their ideals. Years wrinkle the skin, but to give up enthusiasm wrinkles the soul. Worry, doubt, self-distrust, fear and despair . . . these are the long, long years that bow the head and turn the grieving spirit back to dust. Whether 60 or 16 there is in every being's heart the love of wonder, the sweet amazement of the appetite of what's next, and the joy and the game of life. You are as young as your faith, as old as your doubt, as young as your self-confidence, as old as your fear, as young as your hope, as old as your despair."

Anonymous

What's Inside the Package?

A small card in my office reads "Age is an Attitude." If we took these thoughts to heart we would be much happier and more productive.

It is so very true that fear sees the obstacles, faith the opportunities. We are basically children. Age does not make us an adult. One thing that helps to make us old is broken-heartedness. That is something that can be cured by prayer, faith, hope, and trust. We can be renewed day by day.

I have often wondered why some people seemed to be born old. They act old while others are young and bouncy. I heard a speaker talking about the difference in the way a grandchild and a grandmother open a gift. The child rips it apart and wastes no time getting to the present. The older one, on the other hand, takes off the bow and sets it aside, then lifts off each piece of tape, raises each flap of paper very carefully and then folds it neatly. She cannot stand to spoil such a pretty package. The child has to get to the gift. What is inside is what counts. Kids understand that.

What is inside of us? If you think you are old just because you have lived so many years, then you are old. The impact of our attitudes on our lives is more significant than our past, our level of education, our finances, our failures or successes.

I have come to realize that my reactions are much more important than my actions. I am in charge of the former. It has been said that 10% of life is what happens to us and 90% is how we react to situations. Much of the time we have little or no control over what happens, or what people do or do not do to us. But we are very much in charge of how we react. Yes, even to our aging.

Another birthday? So what! Count your blessings instead of your years and thank God for the years He has given you. It is a fact that as soon as we are born we begin to age and our body starts to deteriorate. That is life. But there is an alternative. As the old saying goes, "We could be six feet under, pushing up daisies."

Birthdays are to be celebrated. Why not be grateful for another year to anticipate? Why not enjoy the beauty that surrounds us, and the family and friends who love and support us? Black balloons and birthday parties in funeral homes? Perish the thought.

Taking Responsibility

Many things affect the aging process. Our lifestyle is a major factor. Do we keep active or are we the proverbial couch potato? A recent survey concluded that over 60% of Americans are overweight. Overeating causes much of that. What an indictment when so much of the world goes to bed hungry every night.

Full of promise, full of hope

Public health experts estimate that we can reduce our risk of heart disease as much as 80% by adopting a healthy lifestyle. Losing weight can alleviate pain in the joints or back. Walking relieves the onset of diabetes, coronary heart disease, and strokes.

I have long maintained that taking those extra forks of food to the mouth is one of the best exercises we can do without. What about those second helpings and extra desserts? Who needs them? We women can help prevent that too-early matronly look, and most men do not have to develop that tummy that bulges and overlaps the belt. Do we really love Him with all our being?

Our environment is another factor in the aging process. I think one of the worst things we do in our culture is to isolate ourselves in communities of older people. I love to be around all ages. Have you ever observed what a puppy will do to an old dog? Quite often the old dog becomes rejuvenated, in spite of itself. That teaches us an important lesson.

A ninety-plus alumnus used to hobble into the alumni office to cry on my shoulder. "I didn't know what it was like to be all alone," he would moan. He had outlived most of his small family and all of his friends. I tried to comfort him, but his forlorn state showed me the value of continuing to develop a wide range of friends. Working with kids most of my life has been wonderful. I have heard it said that being with young people will keep us young but trying to keep up with them will kill us. I do question the latter part of that statement.

They also say our genes play an important part in the aging process. A gene is a minute part of a chromosome that influences the inheritance and development of character. According to the *Journal of Longevity*, until recently scientists were firmly convinced that aging was predetermined by our genes. There was little we could do about it to determine our destiny. (Many of our young people beg to differ. They still define themselves by the brand or color of their *jeans*.)

Today, scientists have discovered many more factors play into the aging process than genes. If you live in a polluted environment, eat a large amount of rich food, smoke, or even spend a lot of time in front of a computer or TV, you produce a lot of oxygen waste—something that affects your aging process. But far worse is the waste we hang on to: bad temper ("I was born that way"); pouting, gossiping, backbiting ("It's all in my spiritual genes"). Can we not take responsibility for ourselves?

Merry Heart or Broken Spirit?

I will admit that accepting Christ does not solve all of our problems. As we grow older, there has to be ongoing growth and change. Jesus Himself increased in wisdom, in stature, and in favor with God and man. Do we? The Apostle Paul said, "I have learned . . ." (Philippians 4:11). We should all be learners. We are on a journey through life. One of our better road maps is the Bible. Life habits, attitudes, diet, and associations all influence us.

We cannot control being short or tall, but many things are in our hands—are we happy or sad, serious or lighthearted, fearful or serene, afraid or trusting? Do we have good or bad habits and attitudes? These all help to make us who and what we are. We are created in His image and have access to His Word. I love the verse: "A merry heart doeth good like a medicine: but a broken spirit drieth the bones" (Proverbs 17:22).

I will admit that state of health makes a huge difference in one's outlook on life. In recent years I have been blessed. Rare is the morning that I do not thank Him for good health. However, it has not always been smooth sailing. Along with my breakdown, I have had several operations. (I will spare you the details. There was a lengthy stay in the hospital with cancer and MS scare. A virus in the spinal fluid kept me incapacitated and the doctors puzzled for weeks. A great deal of prayer and a grueling therapy program—under the direction of a trainer for the Fort Wayne Komet Hockey Club—along with Dick and Beth's help, got me back on my feet.)

I have little patience with those who refuse to follow through with a recommended therapy program, just because it is painful (I can tell you about pain), or requires too much of their time and energy. We are all responsible for our own health.

I have also had more than my share of broken bones and cracked ribs. The ski slopes were responsible for several breaks, as well as the famous sleigh ride. One break came as a result of a horrendous fall from a ladder. Yes, I still do climb ladders. And trees.

I can tell you all about the Intensive Care Unit. And "Arthur" does come calling from time to time. My sleep is erratic at best, but I try not to make an issue of it the next day. Several doctors have told me that as long as people are in a horizontal position, then they are at least resting and should not worry about it.

Age is an attitude

Three Score and Ten

I never dreamed I would live to be seventy-seven. My mother died at thirty-seven and my father at fifty-three. I had never been around very many older people until I moved to the Island. I fell in love with Grams Bookman, Hawdon, and Smith. They were delightful ladies. When I first met them they were in their late sixties and early seventies, but they seemed very old to me. I often told them I wanted to be like them "when I got big."

It used to be that when someone I knew reached the ripe old age of seventy, I had a pat message for them. In all seriousness I said, "The Bible promises us three score and ten years. From here on your years will be bonuses. Let's thank God for each one He gives you and make the best of them." It hasn't been that long ago that I shared that particular "wisdom." In my mind they were very, very old. It embarrasses me now to think about it. In fact I am downright ashamed. I must confess that I really meant those words. What a dumb-dumb! Shame, shame on me.

But seventy really did seem old when we were young, did it not? I proclaim to one and all that seventy-seven is not old. I think I am living proof of that. And I do not want some youngster reminding me that I only have bonus years left.

Living Well

For many years Dick and I said we wanted to live until we died. He was granted his wish. He lived well right up to the very end. I also fully intend to, but Dick often warned me that if I did not live more carefully I would never live to be old.

I am encouraged by the statistics that claim the fastest growing age group is 85 years and over. The second fastest is 100 years and over. But what is old? Let us examine that: Old—having existed a long time; of age; not new; ancient; much worn by age or use; having much experience; length of life to a specified time; full or average time of life.

Maturity is defined by some as the effects of growing old—fully developed in mind and body. We say he or she is mature for their age. Aging and maturity possess so many deep, often mysterious meanings. Are we really as young as we feel?

They say life is all downhill after forty. Nonsense! Life really did begin at forty for me. That was the year I put a down payment on my 100 acres of paradise. I have been going strong for most of my time here, and intend to until I retire. Dick and I both flunked out on our first retirement. It will be interesting to see what happens when I leave the camp in 2002.

Aging is the process in a person's life that allows experience, maturity, and wisdom to come to the fore. We are free to approach aging in our own way, but we must remember attitude has much to do with the process. How we define ourselves is what we ultimately desire and become. It is important that we be ourselves in Him.

We cannot let the media and others define our age. Far too much time and money goes into denying the aging process. Instead, we have the privilege of discovering ourselves in Him.

I will close this chapter with the words from the Psalmist:

> *"O God, thou hast taught me from my youth: and hitherto have I declared thy wondrous works. Now also when I am old and grayheaded, O God, forsake me not; until I have shown thy strength unto this generation, and thy power to every one that is to come" (Psalm 71:17-18).*

Regardless of our age we have a job to do. The present generation and the next are counting on us. Let us be ourselves. A greater life lies ahead. Age is an Attitude!

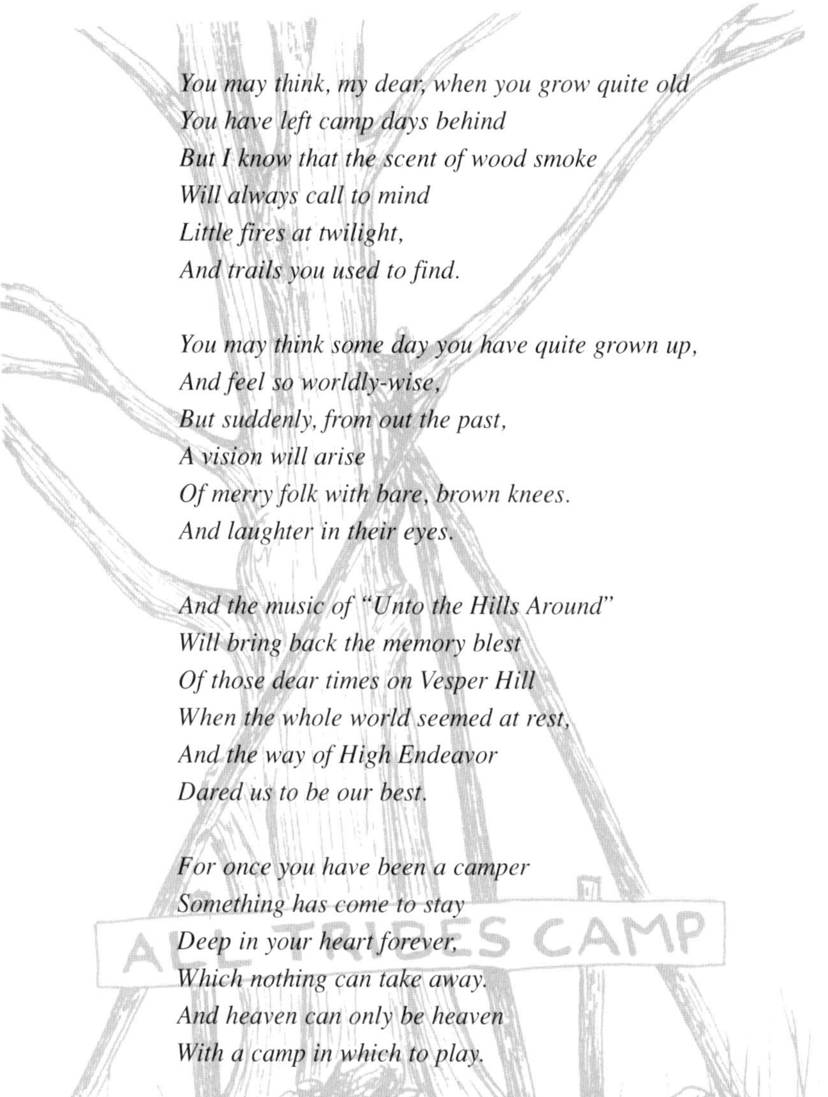

You may think, my dear, when you grow quite old
You have left camp days behind
But I know that the scent of wood smoke
Will always call to mind
Little fires at twilight,
And trails you used to find.

You may think some day you have quite grown up,
And feel so worldly-wise,
But suddenly, from out the past,
A vision will arise
Of merry folk with bare, brown knees.
And laughter in their eyes.

And the music of "Unto the Hills Around"
Will bring back the memory blest
Of those dear times on Vesper Hill
When the whole world seemed at rest,
And the way of High Endeavor
Dared us to be our best.

For once you have been a camper
Something has come to stay
Deep in your heart forever,
Which nothing can take away.
And heaven can only be heaven
With a camp in which to play.

—Anonymous

Praise for *Look to This Day*

Millie Jacobs Troyer is one of those truly rare individuals few of us are privileged to know. Through her positive spirit and contagious enthusiasm, her boundless energy and unbridled zest for living, and her passionate commitment to her life's goals and dreams, Millie changed her world.

Millie's spiritual and vocational pilgrimage reveals her quest to know and serve God. Whether directing the Girl Scouts, serving as the first female Alumni Director of her *alma mater*, Marion College (now Indiana Wesleyan University), or establishing and building All Tribes Christian Camp on St. Joseph's Island in Ontario, Millie has modeled Christlikeness and servant-leadership.

Millie's extraordinary life story is sure to inspire and prompt readers to weigh their lives in terms of what is truly important.

James Barnes
President
Indiana Wesleyan University

Millie Troyer came to faith in Christ in her early youth and, with that, to a commitment to Christ's cause from which she held nothing back. Out of this grew a life of service that she lays before us in her autobiography, telling of a love for youth exercised in years of strenuous service to her Alma Mater, Marion College of Marion, Indiana. And she tells of her love for camping, which came to fulfillment in the development of All Tribes Christian Camp in Ontario. Her account of her autumn romance with "Sir Richard" is really romance at its best—with elements of surprise, realism, and tenderness that may bring tears. Anyone who wants to see how one woman set about to make a difference in the world will find this book a good read.

Donald N. Bastian, Bishop Emeritus
Free Methodist Church

I have known Millie Jacobs Troyer to be a powerful communicator, a person with great vision and boundless energy—devoted to making a difference for Christ in the lives of people. In *Look To This Day For It Is Life*, we get the inside story of her attempt to love God with heart, soul, mind and strength through the unfolding of a ministry that has touched thousands of lives. I loved this book. It made me laugh and cry and pray. It inspired me and challenged me. Sometimes it surprised me. Written in a clear, down-to-earth style, it is inspiring, challenging, and filled with life lessons that work. It is a story of growth, grace and goodwill from someone who genuinely knows what it is to love people, pursue dreams, and follow God.

Tom Gurnick, Pastor
St. Joseph Island Free Methodist Church
Ontario, Canada

"Millie Jacobs Troyer was born to be a trailblazer, both literally and figuratively. Her life story is not only about a woman of self-sufficiency but of a person who knows the value of continued learning through the actions and words of others. With the Bible as her road map, and inspirational passages scattered like seeds, Millie also shares her journey of spirituality. Her calling to write her life story—from her childhood in Fort Wayne, Indiana to a Christian Camp on St. Joseph Island—will leave believers and nonbelievers filled with inspiration and looking towards a new role model."

Cindy Ellen Crawford
Author of *The Island Fairy Godmother: Florence Whaley Orrel*
St. Joseph Island, Ontario